CITIZENS
OF A
STOLEN LAND

THE STEVEN AND JANICE BROSE LECTURES
IN THE CIVIL WAR ERA

Rachel Shelden, editor
William A. Blair, founding editor

The Steven and Janice Brose Lectures in the Civil War Era are published by the University of North Carolina Press in association with the George and Ann Richards Civil War Era Center at Penn State University. The series features books based on public lectures by a distinguished scholar, delivered over a three-day period each fall, as well as edited volumes developed from public symposia. These books chart new directions for research in the field and offer scholars and general readers fresh perspectives on the Civil War era.

A complete list of books published in the Steven and Janice Brose Lectures in the Civil War Era is available at https://uncpress.org/series/steven-janice-brose-lectures-civil-war-era.

CITIZENS OF A STOLEN LAND

*A Ho-Chunk History
of the Nineteenth-Century
United States*

STEPHEN KANTROWITZ

THE UNIVERSITY OF NORTH CAROLINA PRESS

Chapel Hill

This book was published with the assistance of the
George and Ann Richards Civil War Era Center
at Penn State University.

© 2023 Stephen Kantrowitz

All rights reserved

Designed by Jamison Cockerham
Set in Arno, Scala Sans, IM Fell DW Pica, and Archive Antiqua
by Jamie McKee, MacKey Composition

Cover illustrations: Map of Sauk County, Wisconsin, by William H. Canfield, 1859, courtesy of the Library of Congress; photograph of Roaring Thunder (Wakąjaxetega), 1863, courtesy of the Wisconsin History Society, WHI-61426.

Manufactured in the United States of America

LIBRARY OF CONGRESS CATALOGING-IN-PUBLICATION DATA
Names: Kantrowitz, Stephen David, 1965– author.
Title: Citizens of a stolen land : a Ho-Chunk history of the ninteenth-century United States / Stephen Kantrowitz.
Other titles: Steven and Janice Brose lectures in the Civil War era.
Description: Chapel Hill : The University of North Carolina Press, [2023] | Series: The Steven and Janice Brose Lectures in the Civil War Era | Includes bibliographical references and index.
Identifiers: LCCN 2022033430 | ISBN 9781469673592 (cloth ; alk. paper) | ISBN 9781469673608 (paperback ; alk. paper) | ISBN 9781469673615 (ebook)
Subjects: LCSH: Ho-Chunk Indians—History—19th century. | Ho-Chunk Indians—Land tenure—Wisconsin. | Ho-Chunk Indians—Relocation—History—19th century. | Forced migration—United States—History—19th century. | Citizenship—United States—History—19th century. | Settler colonialism—United States—History—19th century. | Government, Resistance to—United States—History—19th century. | United States—Territorial expansion—History—19th century.
Classification: LCC E99.W7 K36 2023 | DDC 977.5004/97526—dc23/eng/20220727
LC record available at https://lccn.loc.gov/2022033430

For Elliot and Sophie

Contents

List of Illustrations   ix

Note on Language and Sources   xi

Introduction   1

1 CONFRONTING INVASION   13

2 ALLOTMENT AND ITS DISCONTENTS   57

3 CITIZENS, WARDS, AND OUTLAWS   93

4 TO REMAIN UPON THE LAND   133

Epilogue   161

Acknowledgments   169

Notes   173

Bibliography   197

Index   213

Illustrations

FIGURES

1.1. Survey of the Four Lakes region, 1835   *36*

1.2. Wisconsin Territorial Seal, 1836   *38*

1.3. Wakąjaxetega (Roaring Thunder), 1840–1841, in a naturalistic rendering   *47*

1.4. Wakąjaxetega (Roaring Thunder), ca. 1841, in a second rendering   *48*

1.5. Land owned by Aahucoga (Blue Wing), 1859   *53*

1.6. Aahucoga (Blue Wing)   *55*

2.1. Wakąjaguga (Coming Thunder Winneshiek), 1863   *58*

2.2. John St. Cyr, 1875   *88*

3.1. Wakąjaxetega (Roaring Thunder), 1863   *95*

3.2. Certificate of Naturalization, 1872   *129*

4.1. Hotokawinga (Mary Crane)   *137*

4.2. Black Hawk, John St. Cyr, and Short Wing Winneshiek, 1875   *152*

4.3. Annie Blowsnake Thundercloud, ca. 1882   *158*

MAPS

0.1. The Ho-Chunk People in the Civil War Era   *6*

1.1. Ho-Chunk Ancestral and Treaty Lands   *16*

1.2. Treaty Boundaries of Native Nations, 1825   *24*

1.3. Ho-Chunk Treaty Lands, 1829–1832   *27*

1.4. Ho-Chunk Treaty Lands, 1832–1837   *31*

2.1. Ho-Chunk Treaty Lands, 1832–1865   *68*

5.1. Ho-Chunk Removals   *160*

Note on Language and Sources

This book focuses on the Ho-Chunk people, whom European and U.S. authorities formerly called by other names, including "Winnebagoes." It shows how a complex nineteenth-century history of exile, diaspora, persistence, and return left the Ho-Chunk people concentrated in two geographically and politically distinct nations. One of these nations, headquartered on tribal lands on the Missouri River, is today known as the Winnebago Tribe of Nebraska. The other group, composed of those Ho-Chunk people who won the right to remain in Wisconsin, were formerly known as the Wisconsin Winnebagoes, but since the 1990s have been formally known as the Ho-Chunk Nation. In the orthography employed by the Ho-Chunk Nation Language Division, the name for themselves is rendered "Hoocąk." Because "Ho-Chunk" is today the most common written version in English, familiar to the most readers, I have used that spelling.

Throughout this work, I present terms as they appear in the sources; otherwise, I strive to call people what they wished or wish to be called. Except where sources dictate otherwise, I use "Native Americans," "Native people" (always with a capital N), or "Indigenous" to describe individuals. I generally use "Native nations" to describe Native political sovereignties and relations; I use the terms "Indian," "tribe," or "tribal" when that was or is part of a self-description (for example, "Indian agents" or "Ho-Chunk Nation tribal members"). When discussing people of mixed Native and settler descent, sources often use now-offensive terms such as "half-breed" and "mixed-blood"; I use these terms only in quotation and only when important meaning would otherwise be lost.

During the era explored here, only a few Ho-Chunk people left written records; the sources upon which this work rests were mainly produced by settlers, officials, travelers, and journalists. However, numerous articulations by Ho-Chunk people reside within settler archives, including speeches, petitions, and other testimonies that made their way through interpreters, officials, and newspaper editors. In interpreting these sources, I have made use of my own very limited understanding of Ho-Chunk culture and language. I have also sought the advice of employees of the Ho-Chunk Nation Language Division and Cultural Resources Department, as well as of other Ho-Chunk people. Errors and omissions are mine alone.

CITIZENS OF A STOLEN LAND

INTRODUCTION

In the spring of 1873, as forces gathered to expel them from their Wisconsin homeland, 224 Ho-Chunk people pledged their allegiance to the United States government's most ambitious projects of national and cultural transformation: the century-old program called "Civilization" and the much newer one called "Reconstruction." Their petition to the federal Office of Indian Affairs first invoked the keywords of the long-standing effort to transform how Native Americans related to one another and to the land: it declared their eagerness to sever their tribal ties, "purchase real estate," and "adopt the habits and customs of civilized life." Along with cultural assimilation, the petitioners sought political incorporation, which they articulated as the desire to obtain "the constitutional and inalienable rights of men." With these words they conjured a place for themselves in the postwar nation, not just among native-born and immigrant whites—the traditional American bearers of those rights—but also alongside the millions of African Americans to whom the laws and amendments of Reconstruction promised equality. The Ho-Chunk petitioners underscored their embrace of "Civilization" and Reconstruction by asking the government to grant them the status that policy makers imagined shimmering at each policy's end: "citizenship."[1]

Nothing about the history of this group of Ho-Chunk people suggests that they actually sought the assimilation and incorporation for which they petitioned and which citizenship implied. To the contrary, for four decades this group had defied federal plans for their deportation, exile, and cultural transformation. Since an 1837 treaty that stripped them of the last of their homeland, they had lived as outlaws in that territory, evading repeated military campaigns to expel them and maintaining Ho-Chunk ways of life amid a growing settler population. Even their name for themselves, "the descendants of what was known in the year 1837, and subsequent, as Dandy's Band," captured the tenacious spirit of what White Earth Ojibwe literary critic Gerald Vizenor would later term "survivance"—not simply "resistance" but "the continuance of stories."[2] "Dandy" was the American moniker for Roaring Thunder (Wakąjaxetega), a leader who for more than three decades had been the face of Ho-Chunk resistance to removal from Wisconsin. "Band," meanwhile, signified the voluntary affiliation of multiple families into a mutually responsible community; within that community, civic obligation revolved around twelve clans, each bearing distinct responsibilities to the community and to the land.[3] The petitioners lived as Ho-Chunk people, which is to say that they had little use for American ideals of private property, individualism, and self-supporting households. The Ho-Chunk term for "citizen"—higi here—does not signify a set of rights but a person's belonging to a group or place.[4]

In fact, when the concept of citizenship had entered the Ho-Chunk world decades before, it was as a tool of conquest: a keyword in the lexicon of invading settlers and their governments and a banner under which Native people were dispossessed and exiled. Many Ho-Chunk people living in exile reservation communities west of the Mississippi came to understand citizenship as a mechanism of "civilization" and a means by which American authorities hoped to break up Native political sovereignties and transform their collectively owned lands into private property. It was one of the forces threatening their destruction as a sovereign people.

But throughout the middle decades of the nineteenth century, as Ho-Chunk people in Wisconsin and the exile diaspora studied the invaders, they learned that American citizenship, however dangerous, was also protean and ill-defined. They were not alone in reaching this conclusion: as late as 1862, the attorney general of the United States wrote that "eighty years of practical enjoyment of citizenship ... have not sufficed to teach us either the exact meaning of the word or the constituent elements of the thing we prize so highly."[5] Even as the laws and amendments of Reconstruction sought to clarify and extend citizenship's implications, this ambiguity persisted for Native people. Throughout the era, U.S. officials puzzled over the definition of "citizenship" and its relationship to various forms of landownership, tribal status, and treaty rights. Policy makers insisted that citizenship should somehow mark the end of Indianness, but they were unable to say with clarity what path led to that destination or what arriving there would mean. The Ho-Chunk people came to understand, through the confusion of American policies and demands, that

Americans did not really understand their own ideal or how it would apply to Indigenous societies. Citizenship's messiness and internal contradictions opened a path for Native people's struggle, resistance, and endurance.

The Ho-Chunk people's nineteenth-century history reveals how citizenship was forged in the colonial encounter. That history shows how a people at the margins of the nation's political life could deduce citizenship's perils and possibilities and use them to achieve their own, quite different goals, including the right to remain in their stolen homeland. When Dandy's Band invoked "citizenship" and "civilization," real estate and rights, they were not appealing to the ideas that had driven the growth of the settler nation. Rather, they were mobilizing histories that they had helped to shape: the history of the settler conquest of their lands; the history of Native resistance and persistence in those lands and beyond; and the history of American citizenship itself. Understood in this light, the 1873 petition for citizenship was not a capitulation to the American conquest but a carefully crafted bid to overcome it.

The Ho-Chunk encounter with citizenship does not map easily onto the ways Americans conventionally think about that status. National citizenship first took clear legal form after the Civil War to establish the equal standing of African Americans and defend their civil rights. In many Americans' imaginations, citizenship remains tightly linked to that momentous Civil War transformation, to its rhyming sequel in the post–World War II civil rights movement, and to narratives of immigrant struggle and incorporation. Taken together, these stories frame the background of much of what has come to be called and celebrated as American history. Beyond its formal meanings, that is, the word "citizenship" connotes aspiration, equality, democracy, and progress.[6]

This book, by contrast, explores the role of citizenship in Americans' efforts to eliminate the Ho-Chunk from their homeland and replace them with a settler society, and in Ho-Chunk survivance in the face of what scholars call "settler colonialism."[7] "Eliminate" is a hard word, reflecting brutal realities that historians have not always adequately conveyed. Settler-colonial elimination in nineteenth-century North America took many forms, including dispossession and exile (euphemistically dubbed "removal"), the seizure and cultural reeducation of children ("boarding schools"), and campaigns of extermination that meet modern definitions of genocide (a word that until recently most scholars of this era have resisted).[8] At the same time, there was more than one form of colonialism at work in the American conquest, including colonial relations of trade and labor that required the presence, not the absence, of Native people.[9] But even those settlers who welcomed the continued presence of some Native people assumed that settler society's needs were paramount, and they relied on their relationship to the state—their actual or prospective citizenship—to defend those interests.

Brandished by invading settlers, the term "citizenship" bespoke a determination to replace Native sovereignty over the land with American forms of authority. It was in the conquest of Native lands that settlers developed a sense of themselves as people engaged in a common project of state making and "civilization." Many of the settlers who invaded the Ho-Chunk homeland in the early nineteenth century were not yet U.S. citizens, but both actual and would-be citizen settlers asserted the same entitlements: to claim Native people's land, to use force against Native people who resisted those claims, to call on American laws and armies to support them, and to collectively govern the conquered territory. State, territorial, and national governments generally agreed and cooperated, treating these settlers and their project of conquest as critical parts of the nation's work.

Pressed on Native societies by federal officials, "citizenship" was a settler-colonial practice. When American policy makers envisioned Native people becoming citizens, it was in order to destroy their societies or transform them so radically that they posed no challenge to U.S. territorial expansion. The term implied the severing of their ties to one another, the end of their collective ownership of land, and the reorganization of their lives around individual landownership and allegiance to the United States. Just as treaties demanded that Native people surrender their sovereignty over territory, U.S. citizenship usually insisted that they renounce their status as an independent, self-determining people. Together, these policies met settlers' demands for land and authority by stripping Native people of their national identities and their collective claim to lands.

National identities and collective claims were at the heart of Native people's assertion of sovereignty—of their status as self-determining political and territorial bodies. To take Native sovereignty seriously is therefore to consider citizenship from a different starting point: not one where individuals and groups sought equality within the United States but one where federal policies aimed to undo Indigenous autonomy and integrity while Native people responded to those pressures. The equal national citizenship proffered during Reconstruction meant something different from the viewpoint of a people who conceived of themselves not in racial but in national terms and whose overriding goal was not to secure equal rights within the United States but to retain their self-determination alongside it. Some Native people, including the 1873 Ho-Chunk petitioners, did claim U.S. citizenship during this era. But they did so as citizens of a stolen land.

This book explores the Ho-Chunk people's long removal era, a history that unfolded simultaneously with and in intimate relation to what historians call the Civil War era. Map 0.1 traces their odyssey during the first half century of their encounter with American power. The story begins with the invasion of the Ho-Chunk homeland by U.S. settlers in the 1820s and then explores the ensuing history of treaties and deportations. Underlying these pivotal events were ongoing colonial pressures on Ho-Chunk people's cultural and political lives and the ever-present threats of settler vigilantism and military removal. By the 1870s, Ho-Chunk responses to these challenges had produced a wide array of outcomes: exile reservation communities west of the Mississippi River; continued (though largely illegal) residence in their homeland; and a range of experiments with landownership and citizenship as bulwarks against dispossession. The Ho-Chunk story of persistence, resilience, and victory over removal challenges many American stories about Indigenous people's inevitable disappearance. It represents the "removal era" as a period of conquest, dispossession, and violence, but also one of resistance, resilience, and return.[10]

Histories of American conquest and Native survivance are often told in isolation from those of the sectional crisis, the Civil War, and Reconstruction. But the U.S. republic in which citizens struggled over the future of African American slavery was at the same time a colonial power, a "settlers' empire" hard at work stealing a continent.[11] Both the Southern cotton kingdom worked by enslaved laborers and the "free soil" Midwest were established in the seizure of Native lands. American settlers' demand for new western lands drove the Ho-Chunk people's dispossession from their ancestral homeland in the 1830s and then from a succession of new homes in western territories that Americans today call Iowa, Minnesota, South Dakota, and Nebraska. The map reminds us that when one people said "Manifest Destiny," "expansion," or "homestead," another experienced invasion, dispossession, or annihilation. Between 1825 and the Civil War, the United States acknowledged the Ho-Chunk claim to a succession of territories in their homeland and beyond. During that same period the United States took every one of those territories, only once with anything that could be construed as actual consent, and turned them over to American settlers. Like the map, then, this book asks us to think about what "free soil" meant from the perspective of people who already laid claim to that soil.

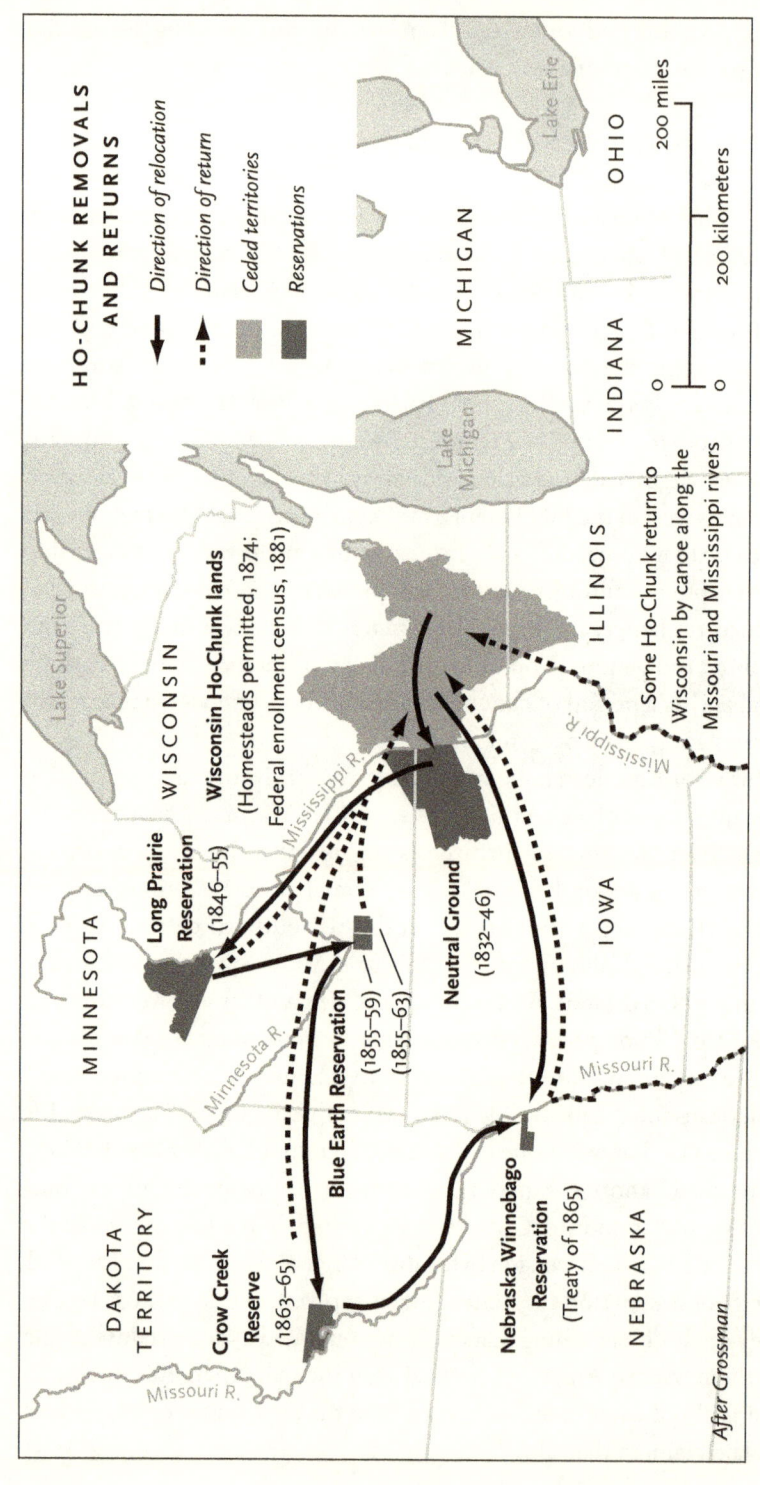

Map 0.1. The Ho-Chunk People in the Civil War Era

The violence of dispossession was intertwined with the violence of the Civil War, and in many ways they were the same war.[12] Those bloody connections played out in national terms in Kansas in the 1850s, where pro- and antislavery settlers struggled for control of territory that was literally still the property of Native nations. During the Civil War itself, the Ho-Chunk whose lands then lay in southern Minnesota found themselves in the middle of another war—the 1862 conflict between the United States and the Dakota people. This U.S.-Dakota War drew large U.S. armies onto the Great Plains for the first time. Its reverberations cast many Ho-Chunks farther into exile in the Dakota Territory, hardened Wisconsin settlers' eyes toward the persistent bands in that state, and set a third group of Ho-Chunk people on a course toward U.S. citizenship in Minnesota.

Finally, the map of Ho-Chunk dispossession, resistance, and return is also a map of Reconstruction's remaking of the nation's civil and political life. Reconstruction is conventionally thought of as a Southern story, and foremost among its imperatives was to transform the status, rights, and social position of formerly enslaved people. But the laws, amendments, and policies of Reconstruction unfolded in a nation that increasingly turned its face toward the West. The Republican politicians who codified national citizenship in 1866 never wavered in their commitment to conquer that region in the name of "free soil, free labor, free men," and as they debated Reconstruction they reflected on its implications for that conquest, and for Native Americans. Throughout the post–Civil War period, U.S. officials simultaneously extended their jurisdiction over the half-restored states of the defeated rebellion and over the Native nations whose land the United States described as its "unorganized territory."[13] The final chapters in the Ho-Chunk people's long removal era, including the moment of crisis engaged by the petitioners of 1873, were profoundly shaped by these forces. And these forces, in turn, would go on to shape the history of U.S. empire beyond the North American mainland.

If this book's account of westward expansion, the Civil War era, and citizenship seems unsettling, it is because Americans have generally learned to tell those stories as though Native people—if they were present at all—played only minor or reactive roles. That is not an accident. Cherished American stories of unification, progress, equality, and shared purpose cannot easily contain the history of the Ho-Chunk people's (or any Native people's) encounter with the United States.[14] Indigenous histories stretching back thousands of years, brutally disrupted by invasion and conquest, form an awkward point of departure for a national history predicated on that invasion and conquest. It is not surprising, then, that historians and politicians have generally either romanticized the conquest or moved it safely into the past. Some frankly celebrate its violence: "Our ancestors tamed a continent," as the president of the United States put it in 2018.[15] But whether they proceed from that murderous starting point or some other, historians and politicians narrating the nation's history conventionally move Native people offstage as quickly and completely as they can. They learned to do this in the nineteenth century, drawing on the examples provided by Abraham Lincoln, the founding father of the modern American nation, and Frederick Jackson Turner, who transformed the study of American history by arguing that the "American character" had been forged in the struggle against a "savage" wilderness.[16]

Lincoln and Turner represent the forces that drove the American conquest forward while simultaneously erasing or obfuscating Native life and survivance. Both men lived amid the settler conquest, one taking part in it, the other exploring its accomplishments. Both men worked to make Native people disappear from their nation and its history, setting the tone and template for generations of statesmen and scholars. Crucially, both men did so despite their formative experiences among Ho-Chunk people, in the Ho-Chunk homeland. If we want to understand the erasure of Native histories from conventional understandings of U.S. history, the relationship of these founding figures to the Ho-Chunk people and their history provides a matchless illustration.

Lincoln began and ended his career as a fierce proponent of the conquest of Indian Country, and that career began in the Ho-Chunk homeland. As a young man, Lincoln served as a captain in the Black Hawk War of 1832, in an army guided in part by Ho-Chunk scouts. Lincoln's frontier militia represented the shock troops of this phase of "Manifest Destiny." The battles he and his compatriots waged against Black Hawk's band provided the pretext for a postwar occupation of Ho-Chunk territory by U.S. troops. That occupation in turn enabled the United States to extort a vast cession of land from the Ho-Chunk in the Treaty of 1832, the first treaty that explicitly demanded their expulsion. Thirty years later, in the aftermath of the U.S.-Dakota War, Lincoln affixed his presidential signature to legislation that confiscated the Ho-Chunk people's excellent treaty lands in southern Minnesota and banished them to a barren military camp far out on the Missouri River. Lincoln's career touched many Native nations during the Civil War, but few with more searing impact than the Ho-Chunk.

Yet Lincoln had almost nothing to say about the Ho-Chunk, or indeed about any other Native people. He was a settler, and he told settler stories: "Indians" were people of the past, not actors in his nation's history except as impediments to the realization of its promise. Although Lincoln had put his body on the line for settler colonialism, he minimized his youthful contribution. "I had a good many bloody struggles with the mosquitoes," he joked about the Black Hawk War.[17] As president, Lincoln more soberly told members of a Native delegation to the White House that they had two choices: either adopt the habits and customs of American life and become numerous and prosperous like the Americans, or maintain their current way of life and risk annihilation. Either way, Lincoln knew, his settler nation would prevail.[18] He told his own story, and America's, as though Native people were at most a footnote to it.

Lincoln is analyzed and criticized, but mostly sacralized, for his momentous role in the nation's gravest crisis and his part in the abolition of slavery. He gave voice to some of the nation's most resonant ideals of equality and membership in phrases such as "government of the people, by the people, and for the people" and in his embrace, however belated, of African Americans as part of a national "family of freedom."[19] But despite the ceaseless flood of words seeking to make sense of Lincoln, slavery, equality, and the Civil War, only a handful of writers have analyzed Lincoln as a settler and a settler president, a man who never doubted the rightness and inevitability of the nation's expansion across Native people's lands.[20]

Like Lincoln, Frederick Jackson Turner told settler stories, and those stories helped lay the foundation for American history as an academic discipline. Turner was born in 1861 in the part of the Ho-Chunk homeland that Americans called Portage, Wisconsin, and he grew up amid the campaign championed by his father, the editor of the local newspaper, to expel the Ho-Chunk from the state. On the rare occasions that Turner acknowledged that he had grown up among Ho-Chunk people, it was with a mixture of racism and revulsion. He once recalled a boyhood fishing trip on the Baraboo River during which he and a friend stumbled into a Ho-Chunk encampment. Someone had made off with the boys' dinner pail while they were fishing, but although the Ho-Chunks there offered them food, they "did not accept their invitation to dine." On the boys' long, hungry walk home, they were passed by the Ho-Chunk band, now mounted on their horses. Only then did they learn the fate of their own dinner: "One bloodthirsty redskin saluted us from a distance with the assurance 'Heap good pail of grub!' We never went fishing in the Baraboo again."[21]

In Turner's work as a historian, even these fearful, derisive descriptions of Native people disappeared. His career- and field-defining address, "The Significance of the Frontier in American History," delivered at the World's

Columbian Exposition in Chicago in 1893, argued that the encounter with a "savage" frontier broke down the civilizations of European immigrants and forged a new, American civilization. But the "Indians" on his frontier were people without culture or history, except insofar as they helped settlers make one. "Frontier after frontier," he later put it, "the backwoodsmen fought Powhatan, King Philip, Pontiac, Brant, Little Turtle, Tecum[seh], Red Cloud, and Sitting Bull. Each chief in turn rallied his tribesmen and strove to make alliances to stem the tide, but only succeeded in making life in the west a peril, a discipline in courage, a training school for a hardy and conquering stock."[22] Turner could see Native people only as an undifferentiated whetstone against which the American character was honed—a whetstone that by the 1890s, he thought, had been ground to dust. Despite the evidence provided by his own encounter with Ho-Chunk people, he could not imagine them as human beings with histories that continued.

Against the history promulgated by settler statesmen and settler historians, this book explores the history of the United States through the experiences of Native people—people who could not escape being enmeshed in the nation's history but who regarded the nation's assumptions, claims, and transformations with understandable skepticism.[23] The book's premise is that we can best understand the relationship of Native American history to the history of the United States by exploring those connections locally and precisely and by taking the Native history of encounter as seriously as the Native people in that encounter had to. U.S. history, it asserts, would look different if it attended to Native stories—in this case, Ho-Chunk stories—with the same attention that it reflexively pays to men like Lincoln and Turner.

Let us turn away from those iconic settlers, then, and consider what the history of the United States in the era of the Civil War might look like if interpreted through the experiences and struggles of Native people. We can begin by revisiting the Ho-Chunks' 1873 petition, for between its lines we can glimpse its authors' alternative account of the United States, its settlers, and its citizenship. In formal terms, the petition put forward "citizenship," "civilization," "homesteads," and "real estate" as keywords in a lexicon of belonging, one that the United States insisted on and that Ho-Chunk people did not have the power to simply ignore or resist. They offered these words to reassure authorities, to smooth their passage through what they correctly expected to be a desperate season, and to posit a durable place for themselves within and alongside the U.S. nation. But beneath the petition's supplications and promises, its authors offered another account of American history, one that expressed both their sense of themselves as a people and their analysis of the invaders.

In laying out who they were and why they wanted to remain, the petitioners rejected the names, places, and laws by which the United States defined them, offering instead a very different story of themselves. They insisted on their own forms of relation to one another and to the land. "By inheritance and the teaching of parents," they explained, they had "a love for Wisconsin and a dread of new territory." They even rejected their identification with "the Winnebago Tribe of Indians," because that label identified them with the 1837 treaty of dispossession and expulsion, a treaty whose legitimacy they rejected.[24]

"The descendants of Dandy's Band" also pointed obliquely to the other grievous harms they had suffered at American hands. Their petition did not speak directly to the violence they had endured, but it hinted at the ways their status as outlaws left them perpetually on the brink of conflict with settlers. They had "always tried to do right and respect the rights of others," they claimed, and "if any of their young men have done wrong at any time, to any person, they have punished them, and made restitution." This deferential rhetoric focused on their own infractions, implying but not directly naming the converse reality: that the United States and its settlers had abused their persons and property with almost total impunity. As they contemplated the impending arrival of an army of removal, nothing could have been closer to their thoughts than this half-century history of violence.

The 1873 petition did not halt the federal machinery of removal. At the end of that year, U.S. soldiers ventured into the frozen Wisconsin woods to capture and expel the state's remaining Ho-Chunk bands, including the descendants of Dandy's Band. Troops surrounded their winter encampments, took hundreds of people prisoner, drove them to nearby railheads, and deported them to a reservation in eastern Nebraska. Like every prior forced removal, this one brought suffering and death to hundreds of Ho-Chunk people. These losses remain seared into the memory of today's Ho-Chunk communities. But just as with every previous attempt to exile them, Ho-Chunks refused, resisted, and returned.

This time, their survivance, including their mobilization of the histories of "civilization," Reconstruction, land, and citizenship, produced a lasting victory. Soldiers sent to deport the Ho-Chunk discovered that some individuals carried deeds to small parcels of land while others claimed to have been naturalized as U.S. citizens. When soldiers brought Ho-Chunk captives to nearby railroad stops for deportation, local lawyers, judges, and even a crowd of several hundred white settlers came to the aid of Ho-Chunk landowners and their families. Meanwhile, other settlers defended the Ho-Chunk people's rights in the language of Reconstruction and challenged the deportations as a racialized injustice akin to the now-infamous *Dred Scott* decision. "The Indians had rights which we were bound to respect," one state senator insisted, for "they were citizens as much as the negroes." U.S. senators maintained that they could not legally be deported.[25] By 1875, the government gave up. It accepted the right of the Ho-Chunk bands to remain in Wisconsin, subject to state and federal law; it created a homestead policy by which they could obtain land; and it welcomed Ho-Chunk men as voters.

The petition of Dandy's Band hinted at essential features of American history that neither Lincoln's nor Turner's accounts of the nation could acknowledge. Lincoln told a story of a house divided by the sin of slavery, unified and purified in the crucible of war. Turner posited a uniquely American character forged in the encounter with a "savage" frontier. Neither could confront the history lesson that the members of Dandy's Band represented and that their petition implied: that Lincoln's house and Turner's character relied on an ongoing colonial conquest that upended the lives of hundreds of nations and hundreds of thousands of people, and that despite that conquest, Native people remained.

CONFRONTING INVASION

Coming Thunder Winneshiek (Wakąjaguga) was about fifteen years old when he realized the dimensions of the crisis facing the Ho-Chunk world. It was 1827. Over the preceding five years, a growing number of American squatters had planted themselves in his people's lead diggings, violating treaty lines negotiated between the Ho-Chunk and the U.S. government. Squatters robbed, assaulted, and murdered Ho-Chunk men and women with impunity. After Ho-Chunk men committed a few retaliatory killings, those squatters refashioned themselves as a vigilante militia. When one of those gangs came upon Coming Thunder, he was armed and on horseback. He was also alone, separated from the hunting party with which he had traveled from his father's village. The squatters might well have murdered him had they not been accompanied by a white trader who spoke some Ho-Chunk and who induced Coming Thunder to surrender.[1]

The gang's leader, a mining entrepreneur and regional warlord named Henry Dodge, tried to use Coming Thunder to find his father's hunting party, but its members scattered into the woods. The squatters made him take them to his village, but it was deserted. So they brought Coming Thunder back to the squatter capital, the town they called Galena. Coming Thunder remained prisoner there for two weeks as the conflict the Americans called the "Winnebago War" unwound, and he surely learned important lessons about the invaders.[2] They were frank and unapologetic about their designs on his country. They were also numerous and wealthy, with apparently inexhaustible supplies of soldiers and arms: Dodge's hundred-odd armed miners worked in close concert with 600 or more U.S. regulars sent from Fort Snelling, 200 miles northwest up the Mississippi River. With a few more companies, this hastily assembled force would exceed the total number of Ho-Chunk fighters. Coming Thunder must have understood the implications of this might—and of the cooperation between the U.S. soldiers, who were supposed to uphold the treaty relationship between his people and the United States, and Dodge's self-constituted "militia," which openly sought his people's dispossession.

Squatters and soldiers, the founding dyad of settler civilization, brought disaster upon the Ho-Chunk during the second quarter of the nineteenth century. Americans invaded Ho-Chunk lands again and again. Treaties negotiated on terms of coercion stripped the Ho-Chunk of the title to their lands. Little more than a dozen years after Coming Thunder's first encounter with Henry Dodge, soldiers began rounding Ho-Chunks up for permanent expulsion to lands west of the Mississippi River. The violence, hunger, and disease that accompanied invasion and deportation killed well over a thousand of Coming Thunder's people between the late 1820s and the early 1840s. And as the Ho-Chunk reeled under these blows, the invaders claimed sovereignty over the territory and began to establish a new order.

The settlers described their project as "civilization taking the place of barbarism," but from the beginning that "civilization" was rooted in land theft and organized violence. For the new Wisconsin Territory to become the province of self-governing, property-owning white families, millennia of Native life would have to come to an end. The U.S. government and settlers justified this by defining the Ho-Chunk people as "wandering vagrants" who stood outside of American law, order, and property relations and whose presence threatened those forms. Settlers demanded that the law restrain their activities and remove their persons. But when the law moved too slowly for their tastes, settlers turned to vigilante violence to achieve their ends, and they demanded that the government ratify their actions.[3]

The Ho-Chunk fought to stay, and as they experimented with tactics that might secure them the right to remain, they discovered cracks in the settler order. They found spaces at the margins or interstices of settler society where they could continue their seasonal round of activities without provoking dangerous reactions from settler communities. They also learned that while settlers might be of one mind when it came to their right to rule the territory, not everyone sought their immediate expulsion. Long-standing relations of trade and kinship had produced both durable economic ties and people of mixed descent who facilitated those relations. Finally, some Ho-Chunk people began to experiment with American forms of landownership and to claim a legal foothold in the settler grid itself. Together, these tactics enabled a substantial fraction of the Ho-Chunk people—perhaps as many as half— to sustain their material and spiritual lives in a rapidly changing homeland. While the federal campaign euphemistically called "removal" took a grievous toll in death, displacement, and lasting trauma, Ho-Chunk people continued to occupy and use the ceded ground. They persistently returned to the places they cherished and found ways to live alongside growing settler communities, forging ties that cut against the legal and popular demand for their expulsion. All the while, they sustained the relations, practices, language, and stories that made them a people.

On the eve of the American invasion, the Ho-Chunk lived in a world of bands, villages, clans, and families. Their ancestral homeland, much of it a post-glacial landscape of drumlins, moraines, rivers, lakes, and wetlands, lay between the southern half of Lake Michigan and the upper Mississippi River. Countless generations of Ho-Chunk people farmed, hunted, traveled, fought, and traded in this region, many living and traveling across a still wider area.

In the early nineteenth century, approximately 4,500 Ho-Chunk people lived in about forty geographically dispersed bands. These bands organized their lives around villages, where they farmed and stored corn, as well as around seasonal encampments that lay closer to hunting grounds and other important resources. Ties of language and family and the distinct social obligations of their twelve patrilineal clans bound these bands to one another. Long-standing relationships, some friendly and some not, connected them to their Indigenous and European neighbors.

Coming Thunder came of age in a band headed by his father, whose village stood on the banks of the Pecatonica River, a tributary of the Rock River in what is now northern Illinois. Civil leaders like his father came from the Thunder clan, one of twelve affiliations passed from fathers to their children among which Ho-Chunk social and spiritual responsibilities were apportioned. Coming Thunder shared a connection to others in his clan, whether or not they were part of his family or his village. He also belonged to a widely extended family that named and assigned significance to many relationships: for example, he called paternal uncles Jaaji (father) and maternal aunts Nąąnį (mother), and he shared a warm relationship of mutual obligation with the uncles he called Teega (maternal uncles).[4] As many as fifteen or twenty

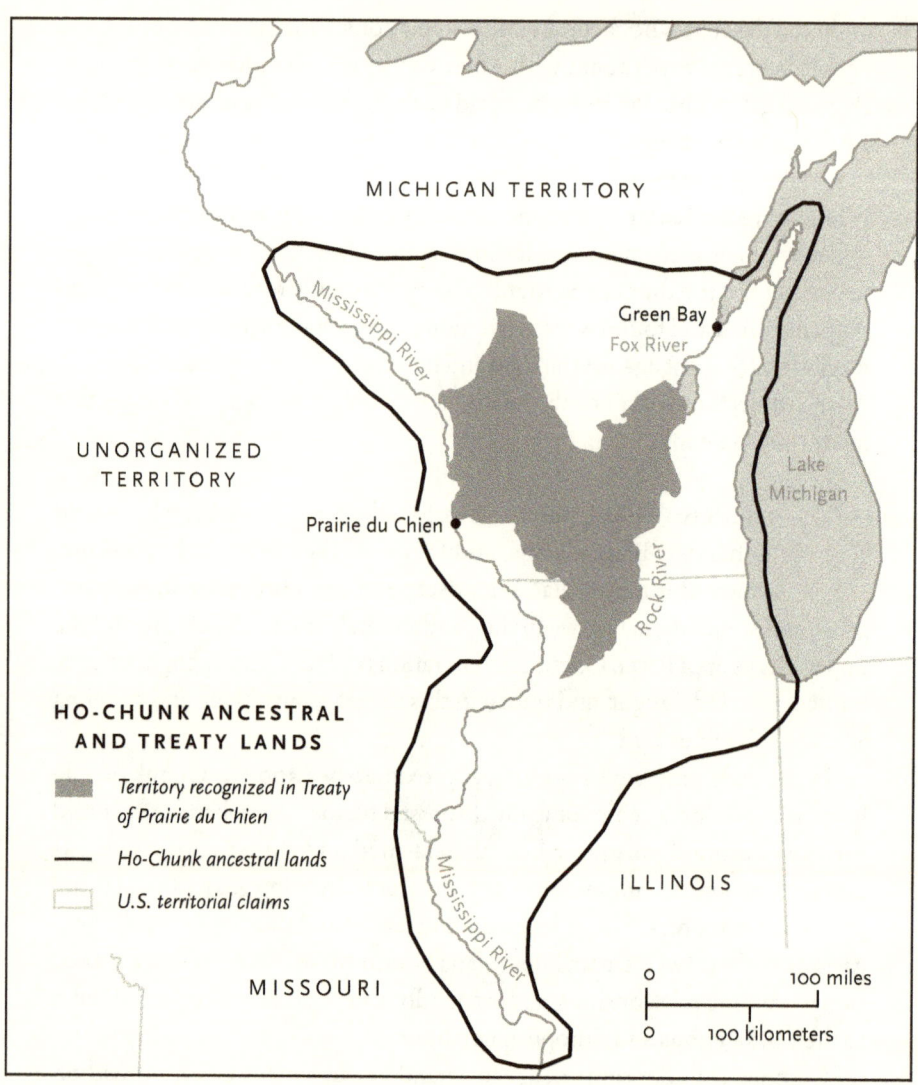

Map 1.1. This map, based on one produced by the Ho-Chunk Nation's Cultural Resources Department, shows both the lands the United States recognized as belonging to the Ho-Chunk in the Treaty of Prairie du Chien, 1825, and the broader area in which Ho-Chunk bands lived. (Ho-Chunk Nation)

members of a family shared a lodge, a large bent wooden frame covered with reed matting or birch bark, with a firepit at the center. A few Ho-Chunk villages consisted of only a single lodge, while the largest, Keecąk (Turtle) village, held thirty-five. Coming Thunder's home village, about thirty miles from Keecąk, numbered perhaps 200 people.[5]

Villages played crucial roles in the Ho-Chunk people's seasonal itinerary, a round of activities that made use of different resources at different times of the year. Villages were generally located on rivers, lakes, or marshes, where fish and small game could be pursued from shore and from dugout canoes. Residents hunted ducks and geese and trapped beaver, muskrat, and other animals for both food and fur, a necessity for the hard inland winter. Children became expert hunters with bow and arrow. But among the most important village activities was the cultivation of corn, one of the Ho-Chunk people's principal foods. Four of the twelve moons in the Ho-Chunk year were named for phases of corn cultivation, an activity mainly conducted by women. Some villages produced a thousand or more bushels annually, storing much of it for winter in underground caches.[6]

Over the course of a year, Ho-Chunk bands might live in their villages during winter and summer months while spending substantial parts of other seasons in smaller camps, pursuing game and other resources. The Ho-Chunk people's quarry had once included the buffalo, which ranged on both sides of the Mississippi. By the nineteenth century, hunters mainly pursued deer and elk, whose annual cycles of growth and mating gave names to four more Ho-Chunk moons. Winter hunting parties sent runners back to their villages with meat, hides, and news before finally returning. As winter stretched on— in the Ho-Chunk homeland it can snow in May—they relied on stores of corn, meat, and other foods. With the early thaws, they tapped maple trees for sugar. Hoohirogįnįnąwiira, the fish-appearing moon, heralded a plentiful new source of nutrition. They readied the ground for planting and waited for larger game to emerge.

The seasonal round of activities, organized around food and other resources, knitted the Ho-Chunk world together. It brought bands into contact with one another, and marriages and other relationships deepened ties of kinship between even distant groups. White Crow, for instance, who grew up in a village at the southern end of Lake Winnebago, about seventy-five miles south-southwest of Green Bay, married a woman from a distant band and resettled at her village at Teejop (Four Lakes), near today's city of Madison.[7] Ho-Chunk people also married, hunted with, and sometimes shared villages with Dakotas, Sauks, Meskwakis, Menominees, and Potawatomis.

Beginning in the seventeenth century, ties among Native groups expanded to include European traders who came seeking furs and in exchange brought useful and beautiful goods, including pots, guns, flints, knives, beads, and cloth. Ho-Chunk parties ranged widely in pursuit of fur for the trade. Regional centers such as Green Bay and Prairie du Chien grew up to connect them and other Indigenous peoples to the Atlantic market. Some Ho-Chunk families made marriage alliances with French-speaking traders and officers and bore names such as St. Cyr and Decorah (from the French Descarrie). The Ho-Chunk homeland was also rich in galena, or lead. Like agriculture, lead digging was primarily the work of women. As one of the era's strategic military commodities, lead yielded huge returns and quickly became central to the economic lives of the region's village bands. By 1810, the hundreds of thousands of pounds of lead extracted annually by Ho-Chunk miners may have equaled in value the tribe's trade in furs.[8]

The Ho-Chunk were deeply rooted in this landscape. They placed their creation in its northeastern reaches, at a place called Red Banks (Moogašuc), near today's Green Bay, Wisconsin. One translation of their name for themselves, "people of the parent speech," names the fact that when other groups speaking similar languages long ago departed this region for new homelands to the south and west, the Ho-Chunk remained. The region was home to thousands of burial mounds, many of them a millennium old, which the Ho-Chunk claim as their patrimony. These included geometric forms—circles or lines—as well as effigies of living or supernatural creatures, including those named in the Ho-Chunk clan system. Some of these effigy mounds were hundreds of feet long, and the wings of the largest, an eagle, stretched nearly a thousand feet from tip to tip.[9]

In the regional wars of the seventeenth century, the Ho-Chunk developed a formidable military reputation. But by the late eighteenth century, their conflicts with other Native nations were generally small-scale, and a well-established tradition of compensatory gift-giving allowed a way out of cycles of retaliatory violence. Warfare took on new modes and meanings as it intersected with the ambitions of European powers for North American resources and territories. Through the middle of the eighteenth century, Ho-Chunk fighters joined the French and their other Native allies in battles against the British. Once the French were defeated and their soldiers withdrew, the Ho-Chunk cultivated alliances with the British. In the half century before Coming Thunder met Henry Dodge, Ho-Chunks took part in British and Native campaigns against rebellious colonists and later the United States.[10]

Alliances with the British and the French enmeshed the Ho-Chunk in new worlds of trade, technology, and diplomacy, but these relationships did not challenge Indigenous cultural self-determination or territorial sovereignty. Little Elk, a Ho-Chunk orator of the early nineteenth century, spoke approvingly of French and British conduct in his homeland. The French, he said, "lived among us as we did," dressing, smoking, and dancing, and often marrying Ho-Chunk women. The British did not assimilate, but they "gave us fine coats, knives, and guns and traps, blankets and jewels" and treated the Ho-Chunk with military respect. No Frenchman or Englishman "ever asked us to sell our country to him!"[11] On some distant mapmaker's table, the Ho-Chunk homeland might bear the label "Nouvelle France" or "Annexed to the Province of Quebec," but these abstractions had no force in Ho-Chunk life. They were only paper.

But Ho-Chunk observers deduced early on that the United States presented a new kind of threat. Unlike the British and the French, the Americans did not come only in search of trading partners or military allies; they coveted the region's resources and its land, and they arrived with the determination and the tools to exploit it for themselves. The Ho-Chunk called them Mąixete, or "Big Knives," a common Indigenous trope referencing a weapon borne by Americans and a synecdoche for the threat they posed to Ho-Chunk life.[12]

In 1783, following the colonists' victory, Britain formally recognized U.S. "ownership" of the empire's vast claims west of the Appalachian Mountains. These included the territory of the western Great Lakes, the homelands of the Ho-Chunk and their neighbors. Under a principle governing relations among European colonial powers, the "Doctrine of Discovery," the Americans now asserted the sole right to negotiate for purchase of these lands from their Indigenous inhabitants, or the right to seize it in "just war." Indigenous people's right to refuse to negotiate was not part of the doctrine.[13] Lawmakers defined Native nations as autonomous for some purposes, but once they set their eyes on a piece of Indian Country, they generally assumed its acquisition was inevitable. Lines drawn on distant maps soon gave way to those drawn on the ground—lines of survey and settlement and of claims to resources: the Land Ordinance of 1784 and the Northwest Ordinance of 1787 imagined the neat division and incorporation of this territory following its acquisition through treaties, devising the grid of townships, six miles square and divided into thirty-six sections, that still define the region when seen from the air.

"Expansion," a euphemism for conquest, waited only for the growth of U.S. populations and a government with the political and military will to transform Indian Country into U.S. territory. At first, the United States lacked the military might to enforce its claims, and it had to keep its long-term goals to itself. In the 1790s, President George Washington warned his staff not to discuss land purchases with Native delegations.[14] But settlers viewed the land between the Ohio River and the Great Lakes as their future home, and a messier and more violent colonialism soon unfolded on the ground. Parties of settlers invaded the Ohio Valley by land and water, paying little mind to U.S. land policy and attacking Native people without regard to their diplomatic relationships with the government. Native people retaliated. These attacks drew in federal forces.[15]

Native nations formed confederations to combat the growing threat, and these alliances clashed with ever-larger U.S. armies in the early 1790s. In one of these battles, in 1791, a thousand-strong army of the Miami Confederacy routed and destroyed a larger U.S. force under General Arthur St. Clair. But the United States mobilized ever-greater numbers of soldiers and dominated the Ohio battlefield. In the 1795 Treaty of Greenville, the United States claimed half of today's Ohio and opened that territory to U.S. settlement. With that opening came further squatting and further conflict with Native people just beyond the treaty line and more ambitious American assertions of authority. In 1800, the United States designated a huge western portion of the Northwest Territory, including the Ho-Chunk homeland, as the Indiana Territory. Policy makers assumed that this area would, after further conquest, new treaties, and sufficient settler population, be divided into new states and incorporated into the nation.[16]

Long before the United States exerted the slightest authority in the Ho-Chunk homeland, Ho-Chunk leaders recognized the threat posed by American territorial ambitions. In 1810, Coming Thunder's father and other Ho-Chunk leaders traveled east to join a new multi-tribal alliance, led by the Shawnee brothers Tecumseh and Tenskwatawa and including the Ho-Chunk people's Menominee, Potawatomi, and Sauk neighbors. The Ho-Chunk members of this alliance, 400 or more in number, lived close to the confederation's capital, Prophetstown, in a village of their own with extensive fields of corn.[17] As this confederation allied with the British against the Americans during the War of 1812, Ho-Chunks fought at Fort Dearborn in 1812, the Battle of the Thames in 1813, and Prairie du Chien in 1814.[18] They suffered great losses in this war. Worse, when the British surrendered in 1815, they essentially abandoned their Native allies, and the victorious United States began to assert itself as the sole imperial power broker in the western Great Lakes.

Coming Thunder was born during this era, perhaps while his father was fighting alongside Tecumseh, and so from his earliest days he learned to see the Mąixete as the enemies of Ho-Chunk sovereignty and the source of his people's suffering. Many Ho-Chunks had come to see the Americans in this way. Although some village leaders from the Wisconsin River area signed a treaty of peace and friendship with the Americans at St. Louis in 1816, others were not ready to accept the new order. One delegation traveled north to a British fort on Lake Huron, hoping to consult with an old ally. The Ho-Chunk spokesman told a British officer that they would "forever detest and hate that bad people, the Big Knives, who are the authors of our misery, as well as that of all our brethren of every nation."[19]

The U.S. government meant conquest to be an orderly national project, one undertaken through treaties in which the government purchased land from Native nations and then required their people to leave. As historian John Bowes puts it, "American expansion on the local, regional, and national levels has always been about Indian removal."[20] Once Native people had been stripped of their title to their lands, orderly American settlement would take place under the terms of land laws passed by Congress. Some early stages of this proceeded as policy makers imagined. In the case of the Ho-Chunk homeland, as in many other moments in early American history, the United States first sought to establish which territories belonged to which Native nations, as it did in treaties in 1816 and 1825.[21]

In practice, American settlement defied these principles. Squatters flooded over treaty boundaries, claimed Native land, stole Native resources, and perpetrated violence upon Native people. When Native people responded in kind, U.S. soldiers sooner or later arrived, sometimes ostensibly to keep the peace, sometimes simply in concert with the squatters' claims. The U.S. government then ratified the new military status quo by demanding that Native nations cede part or all of their domain. Squatters then became legitimate American settlers, and more arrived until they began to press against the new boundaries. And the cycle began again.

In the 1820s, the dispossession and expulsion of Native people for the benefit of white settlers became the basis for a hugely successful political movement. Politicians of Henry Dodge's bent, many of them of even better luck, more powerful connections, or keener political skills, championed the conquest of land and the expansion of rights for ordinary white people—a movement that became the Democratic Party. Andrew Jackson, a westerner equally famous for making ruthless war on Native people in the Southeast and for physically assaulting his political adversaries wherever they were, emerged as this movement's tribune.[22] Jackson relied on men who shared his bloody-minded commitment to a white settlers' empire—men such as Missouri's Thomas Hart Benton, Michigan's Lewis Cass, and soon also Wisconsin's Henry Dodge—to craft the legislation, enact the policies, and command the troops that made this empire possible. This movement helped elect Jackson president of the United States in 1828.[23]

From the late 1820s on, the Jacksonian vision of a white settlers' empire defined the terms of national debate. A crucial turning point came when politicians in the western South, eager to open up land for the production of cotton on slave labor camps owned by U.S. citizens, defied federal authority over treaty relations with the region's Native sovereignties. Between 1828 and 1832, the states of Georgia, Mississippi, and Alabama extended their laws over the Cherokee, Choctaw, Chickasaw, and Creek peoples within their claimed state boundaries, disregarding the tribal sovereignty recognized in previous treaties. The states proffered these Native communities a choice: they could remain within the state's borders and accept the state's jurisdiction over them, or they would be expelled beyond the Mississippi. Either way, their territorial and political sovereignty would be at an end.[24]

The federal Indian Removal Act (1830) ratified this state assault on Native sovereignty. It empowered President Jackson and his successors to oversee transfers of land that these state actions coerced out of Native hands. The Indian Removal Act was controversial, and it came within a few votes of failure in Congress. But within a decade of its passage, effective opposition to "removal" among the white citizens of the United States all but disappeared. Not even the Supreme Court could stand in its way. When the court rejected some state claims to exert jurisdiction over Native people in *Worcester v. Georgia* in 1832, the Jackson administration declared that it would not enforce this ruling.[25]

In the politics of Indian removal, the idea of the United States as a white man's republic could coexist with philanthropic sentiment. Some proponents of "removal" spoke the frank language of Indian-hating. But just as proslavery intellectuals described slavery as the best status for a race of people they deemed inferior, and prescribed "colonization" (deportation) as the only safe outcome for emancipated African Americans, some pro-removal ideologues also represented Native people's forcible expulsion to distant lands as a benevolent project, one that would secure them a future far from the depredations and evil influences of American settlers.[26]

The U.S. government at first moved cautiously into the western Great Lakes, establishing the principle of its imperial power without making direct demands or threats. Land was always at the center of U.S. interests, and the first step in acquiring it was mapping who already owned and occupied it. In 1825, U.S. officials called the region's Native nations together at the Mississippi River trading town of Prairie du Chien to establish geographical lines distinguishing the territory of the region's Ho-Chunk, Potawatomi, Menominee, Sauk, Meskwaki, and Ojibwe peoples. A Ho-Chunk leader protested in vain that hard territorial boundaries did not describe the nature of nationhood in the region, that its lakes and rivers were used in common by many peoples. But the Treaty of Prairie du Chien (1825) drew those lines nonetheless, stating (for the moment) which territories belonged to which Native nations. The Ho-Chunk orator Little Elk foresaw what was to come: "No sooner had [the American] seen a small portion of our country than he wished to see a map of the whole of it; and, having seen it, he wished us to sell it all to him."[27]

While the U.S. government moved carefully, U.S. settlers did not. The American conquest of the Ho-Chunk homeland began in the 1820s, when a trickle of American lead prospectors in the western part of the Ho-Chunk homeland became a squatter invasion. In this "lead rush," U.S. residents by the hundreds, and then the thousands, moved illegally onto lands that the United States formally recognized as Ho-Chunk. Squatters settled, appropriated resources, and resisted Ho-Chunk demands that they leave.[28] They bluntly asserted their mastery of Ho-Chunk territory, in clear violation of the boundaries established in the 1825 treaty. That invasion foretold graver violations in the years to come and land theft on a much grander scale.

From the beginning, squatters relied on both vigilante violence and official force to establish their claim to the territory. First, the squatters threatened, beat, or murdered those who resisted them. Then the U.S. government largely ignored its obligations to restrain its citizens, instead withdrawing its troops from the lead region in 1826.[29] Historian John Hall concludes that the army, while not "a willing party" in the theft of the lead diggings, was "ineffectual" in restoring the treaty order and Ho-Chunk sovereignty. And if it was fruitless to call out the army to restrain the squatters, by the 1820s authorities found it "unthinkable" to call out the militia to evict squatters from Native lands. "The settlers *were* the militia," explains anthropologist Anthony Wallace, "and woe betide any aspiring politician who attempted to set them against their own kind." But the government also encouraged the squatters directly, suggesting how they might transform their land grab into a legal conquest. In

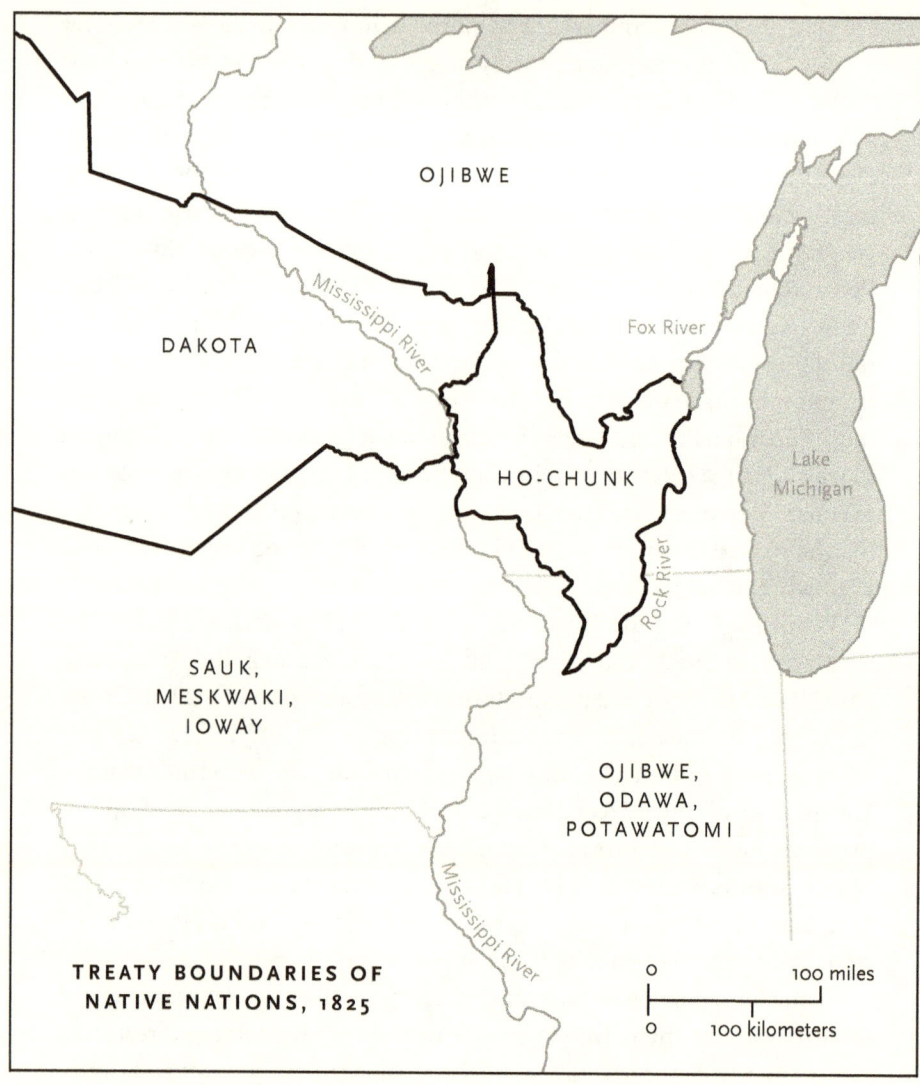

Map 1.2. The Treaty of Prairie du Chien in 1825 was formally known as the "Treaty with the Sioux and Chippewa, Sacs and Fox, Menominie, Ioway, Sioux, Winnebago, and a portion of the Ottawa, Chippewa, and Potawattomie, Tribes." Some boundaries remained only partly defined by this treaty, and some Native nations with claims in the region covered by this map (including the Stockbridge-Munsee Community, the Oneida, the Brothertown, and the Oto) were not represented at the 1825 negotiations.

1826, when the United States withdrew its soldiers from the lead country, it also named Lieutenant Martin Thomas "Superintendent of the United States Lead Mines." When the squatters complained to Thomas that Ho-Chunk residents interfered with their diggings, he told them, "You must remain there untill blood is spilled, & something will be done." That "something" was the redeployment of U.S. forces to defend the squatters and their claims against Ho-Chunk people asserting their ancestral claims and treaty rights.[30]

The rise of squatter-warlord Henry Dodge in the lead country exemplified the dynamics of this invasion. From his earliest days, Dodge acted in the name of the law when it served his interests; when it did not, he became a law unto himself. In 1804, after France formally transferred its claim to the Louisiana Territory to the United States, Dodge's father became sheriff of a vast district on the upper Mississippi River and appointed Henry, twenty-two years old, his deputy sheriff. Within a year of this appointment, the younger Dodge was convicted of assault and battery; this did not prevent him, soon after, from becoming sheriff of the entire district. In 1806 Dodge set out to join Aaron Burr's infamous expedition to seize control of part of the West. When President Thomas Jefferson declared the plan unlawful, Dodge returned home to find that a grand jury had already indicted him for treason. His response was to beat nine members of the grand jury with his fists. But criminal violence was no disqualification for high office: in the War of 1812, Dodge rose to brigadier general and led volunteers in battle against Native nations, including the Ho-Chunk, who allied with the British.[31]

When Dodge arrived in the lead country in 1827 as a private citizen, he continued to bend the law to his interests and his will. The Northwest Ordinance barred slavery from the territory, but Dodge extracted fig leaves of consent from the African American people he held to labor in his lead diggings.[32] Contrary to treaty provisions, Dodge claimed to have paid a local Ho-Chunk leader "rent" on his diggings and then subcontracted the land out to new arrivals. He became a force on the land, overseeing a large group of armed miners who lived in cabins "surrounded by a formidable stockade." The walls of Dodge's own cabin were "well covered with guns." "He said that he had a man for every gun," a traveler reported, "and would not leave the country unless the Indians were stronger than he."[33]

The conflict that Americans called the "Winnebago War" began in 1827 with Ho-Chunk retaliation for years of thefts, assaults, and murders by American squatters. Early in the summer of 1827, Coming Thunder's father met an American official near the territorial boundary established in the 1825 Treaty of Prairie du Chien. He warned the American that whites were pushing his people out of their territory and that "this was the last time they would complain."³⁴ Two new outrages in the weeks that followed pushed several groups of Ho-Chunks past the breaking point. First, a garbled report from Fort Snelling, up the Mississippi River at the site of today's Twin Cities, suggested that two Ho-Chunk men held prisoner by the United States had been surrendered to hostile Ojibwes, who killed them. Second, U.S. soldiers heading up the Mississippi were said to have abducted a group of Ho-Chunk women.³⁵

In accordance with Ho-Chunk values, this violence and violation demanded proportionate retaliation. On June 26, a Ho-Chunk band leader named Red Bird and two companions took up part of this duty, killing several settlers near Prairie du Chien in retaliation for the deaths reported at Fort Snelling. Simultaneously, Ho-Chunk fighters fired on U.S. keelboats as they returned down the Mississippi, killing four soldiers and boatmen. The simultaneous attacks on settler cabins and U.S. boats provoked long-standing fears of a broader Native rebellion against the American invasion. Squatters for hundreds of miles around flew to the shelter of U.S. forts. The attacks also brought companies of U.S. troops and informal militias surging into Ho-Chunk country to suppress the putative uprising. In August, U.S. forces pressed eastward, along both banks of the Wisconsin River, while other troops headed southwest into Ho-Chunk country from Green Bay. Commanders demanded that Red Bird and his confederates surrender. As Lieutenant Thomas predicted, the shedding of American blood had brought U.S. soldiers to defend the squatter forces.³⁶

Ho-Chunk leaders sought peace, but the price was high. In 1828 a delegation of Ho-Chunk negotiators traveled to Washington, D.C., to secure the release of the previous year's prisoners. President John Quincy Adams agreed but required them, in exchange for peace, to hand over the lead country to the United States. They provisionally ceded a portion of the lead region to the United States.³⁷ In the summer of 1829, U.S. negotiators called forty Ho-Chunk leaders to Prairie du Chien and again insisted that they make amends for the Winnebago War, this time by making the 1828 cession permanent and expanding it to include much more territory. In the Treaty of 1829, the United States claimed the whole Rock River country (much of today's northwest Illinois and south-central Wisconsin). This huge area, more than a third of the land the United States acknowledged as belonging to the Ho-Chunk just four years before, was central to the lives of at least half of their population. The details of the 1829 treaty set many of the terms that would govern subsequent treaties, including the promise of annual cash payments ("annuities")—in this case, $18,000 annually for thirty years.³⁸

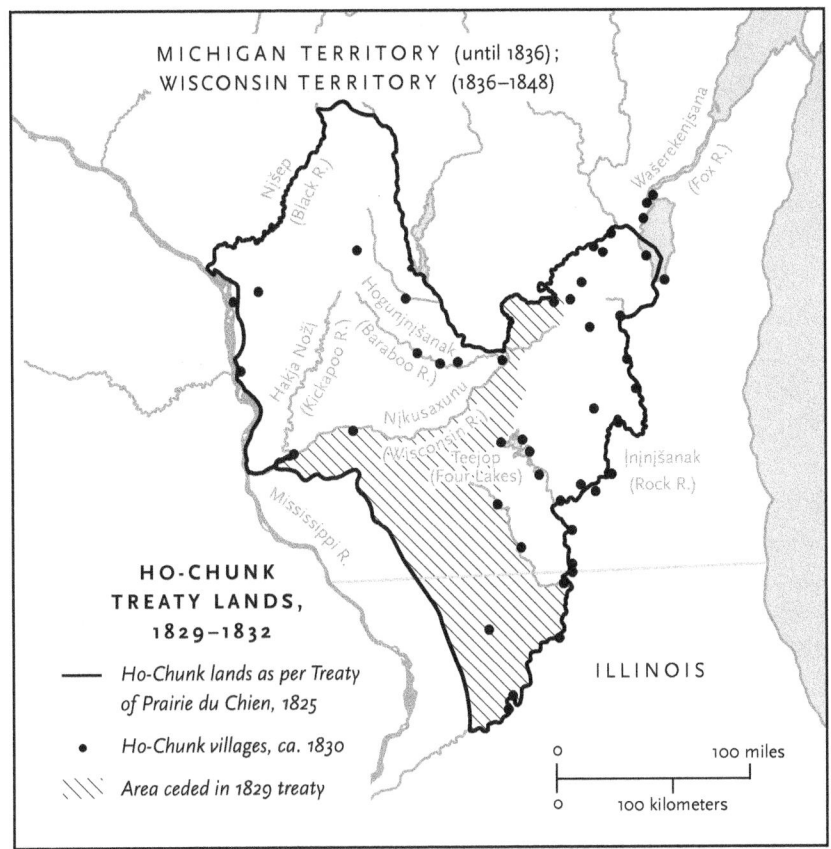

Map 1.3

Ho-Chunk leaders began to fear that the American invasion threatened their total dispossession and perhaps even their extermination. At an 1828 negotiation with Lewis Cass, governor of the Michigan Territory, Ho-Chunk delegates recounted abductions, thefts, and assaults by squatters, none of them redressed by U.S. authorities. Little Elk protested that the United States did not keep its word. "You promised us not to permit one white man on our land; that I heard from you myself, and now they are all over it." Snake Skin complained that "they are working on our land where we used to hunt. Now there are so many on it, that we see no game."[39] It was in a spirit of desolation that another leader, Huujopka (Four Legs), visited a British fort on Lake Michigan to seek advice from a representative of the old ally. He told the British commander that a "black cloud" had surrounded him for the past several years, "so weighty that it has nearly crushed me." "I do not wish to quarrel with the Big Knives," he explained, yet he feared he would not live another year. When pressed to clarify what he meant—what was the "black cloud"?—Huujopka explained that "from what I heard from a Menominee friend, that we have but a short time to live; this friend told me that when the grass would get to a certain height (about mowing time), we would be cut off by the Americans."[40]

How to respond to these dangers became an urgent question in 1832, when another group's refusal to be dispossessed created a new crisis in the Ho-Chunk homeland. Along the southern stretches of the Rock River, ceded to the United States in the 1829 treaty, Ho-Chunk villagers had for years lived with Sauk and Meskwaki people, some of whom had become family. In the late 1820s, on the basis of a fraudulent 1804 treaty, the United States demanded that the Sauk move across the Mississippi River. But some Sauk people continued to return to the Illinois side, occupying their villages and planting corn, which brought complaints and violence from settlers. In 1832, the Sauk leader Black Hawk led a party of more than a thousand back to Illinois to resettle that homeland. Black Hawk, like Coming Thunder's father, had fought with Tecumseh beside the British in the 1810s. The returning party has therefore sometimes been called the "British Band" and the ensuing conflict the "Black Hawk War."[41]

During the Black Hawk War, most of which unfolded across their homeland, Ho-Chunk leaders tried several strategies to avoid shedding American blood. Historian Libby Tronnes argues that the Ho-Chunk goals were to keep the Americans from finding Black Hawk's party, to represent their homeland as impassable and unwelcoming terrain, and to enable Black Hawk's party to begin a quiet retreat toward safety west of the Mississippi River. First, Wabobashiek, a leader of mixed Ho-Chunk and Sauk ancestry whose village lay on the southern reaches of the Rock River, invited Black Hawk's party to live and plant with his people. When American settlers refused to accept this solution, the British Band fled north up the Rock River. As they did, Ho-Chunk bands, including Coming Thunder's, helped guide the party through their territory. Ho-Chunk leaders hoped to keep the U.S. forces from locating Black Hawk's party, thereby preventing the kind of battle that would make their homes into occupied territory. When the British Band arrived in the treacherous marshlands along Lake Koshkonong, Ho-Chunk villagers fed them and hid them from nearby American soldiers, among them Captain Abraham Lincoln. The Ho-Chunk hoped to keep the Americans distracted long enough so that the British Band could escape westward, back across the

Mississippi. Meanwhile, hoping to maintain friendly relations with the Americans, other Ho-Chunk leaders offered aid. White Crow, whose village lay in Teejop, guided U.S. forces through ceded and unceded Ho-Chunk territory as they pursued the fleeing band. Tronnes argues that Ho-Chunk "aid" to the Americans may not have been quite what it appeared to be. Much of what looked like Ho-Chunk cooperation was in fact misdirection: White Crow and other scouts deceived and stalled U.S. forces in an effort to give the British Band time to escape. For several weeks, they succeeded. Regulars, militiamen, and more than one future president floundered in unfamiliar woods and swamps, only miles from their quarry but in total ignorance of their location.[42]

If this was the gambit, it nearly worked. But when U.S. forces chanced upon the British Band's trail and gave chase, a few Ho-Chunks continued to play the role of ally. Several Ho-Chunk fighters were among the combined U.S. and Native force that pursued and attacked the fleeing band as they tried to escape across the Mississippi, a massacre that Americans called the "Battle of Bad Axe." In the aftermath, however, U.S. interrogation of its captives suggested that other Ho-Chunk fighters—including Coming Thunder—had given aid and comfort to Black Hawk's band all along. Having failed to prevent a war, the Ho-Chunk people now found themselves objects of American suspicion and hostility. Coming Thunder was not only interrogated but imprisoned in St. Louis's Jefferson Barracks for a year after the war's conclusion.[43]

U.S. negotiators then demanded half of the remaining Ho-Chunk homeland, on what one official bluntly called "the blended grounds of conquest & contract."[44] The phrase perfectly captures the double character of American treaty-making with Native nations. On the one hand, the treaties formally represented the United States and Native nations as equal contracting parties, laying out in precise terms what the United States would provide in exchange for land: these could include annual payments of currency ("annuities"), provisions and other goods, the services of blacksmiths and teachers, money to cover Native people's debts to traders, and special allocations of money or land to the mixed-descent family members of Native people. They were contracts, and they made the transfer of title concrete, permanent, and (in American eyes) just.

On the other hand, treaty negotiations almost always took place under highly coercive circumstance—if not literally at the barrel of a gun, always with the more or less explicit threat that the alternative to ceding land was renewed violent conflict in which the United States could not be expected to take sides against its own citizens. In this case, the United States had just made its commitments plain. In June 1832, as the Black Hawk War began,

Superintendent of Indian Affairs William Clark (of Lewis and Clark fame) hoped for the "destruction" of the British Band in a "War of *Extermination.*" A few months later, the massacre at Bad Axe affirmed that this was not just bluster. The army of the United States occupied the Ho-Chunk homeland, and the Ho-Chunk owners of that land were imprisoned, demoralized, and in disarray.[45]

"Conquest & contract" became "conquest by contract." Calling more than forty Ho-Chunk civil and military leaders to Prairie du Chien, U.S. authorities laid claim to half of the remaining Ho-Chunk lands: everything south and east of the Wisconsin River, including the watersheds of the Rock and Fox Rivers, and the lakes, rivers, wetlands, and hills of Teejop, the Four Lakes. The Treaty of 1832 dispossessed more than half of the Ho-Chunk people.[46] It required them to move either to the less fertile lands north of the Wisconsin River or to the "Neutral Ground" on the western banks of the Mississippi, a large tract between the territories of rival Sauk and Dakota peoples embracing much of today's northeastern Iowa and adjacent parts of Minnesota. Henry Dodge urged the rapid execution of this stipulation. "I think it is important to the peace of the country," he wrote in 1833, "that the Winnebagoes should be forced to leave the country ceded to the U States."[47]

As the Ho-Chunk felt settler society extend its grip over their lands, they experienced the worst hardships in living memory. The Black Hawk War displaced them from their villages during the summer growing season, and provisions promised in the 1832 treaty were delayed by iced-over rivers. Many of them were left destitute and hungry during the winter of 1832–33.[48] In 1834 came the worst: a smallpox epidemic killed well over a thousand people, perhaps a quarter of the nation. They reeled beneath the blows.[49]

Stripped of their claim to the land, the Ho-Chunk people found themselves in the dire position of what Anglo-American law called "paupers" and "vagrants." For centuries in England and its colonies, paupers, beggars, vagrants, and other people without fixed residence or employment had been vulnerable to exclusion, punishment, imprisonment, or forced labor. This tradition persisted in the common law and statutes of the United States. The nation's first constitution, the 1781 Articles of Confederation, granted the free inhabitants of every state "all the privileges and immunities of free citizens in the several States," establishing that the former colonies were a single nation, but it excluded from these privileges and immunities "paupers, vagabonds, and fugitives from justice." The Constitution of 1787 did not repeat this phrase, but the principle was well established in state and federal law that localities and states had "police power" to exclude such people as undesirables. From

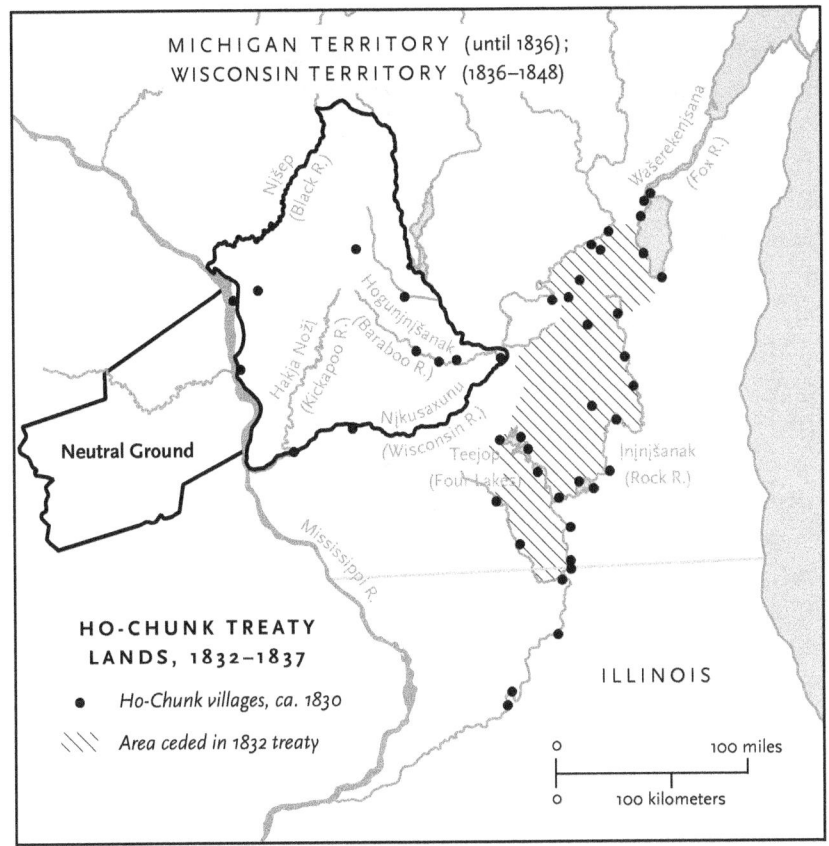

Map 1.4

the beginning of the United States through the Civil War, this power was particularly employed to set limits on the rights and residency of free African Americans, whom white communities frequently viewed as intrinsically slave-like, incapable of proper social and economic lives, and a danger to the white people around them.[50]

Native people who remained in their homelands after being stripped of their title to land fell into the same category as paupers, vagrants, and free African Americans: they stood outside the bounds of the community and its laws and became vulnerable to the harshest forms of vigilante violence.[51] Desperate people stole livestock and goods from settlers; in retaliation, settlers shot and whipped them and seized their guns.[52] "Now that the Indians have lost the power to be formidable," explained one observer, "they are

Confronting Invasion

regarded as wandering vagrants, whose irregularities and encroachments are to be corrected and restrained by the law of the club and lash."[53] By 1836, their longtime agent on the Rock River, Henry Gratiot, described "men who were once proud warriors ... now despoiled of their guns and blankets.... Several of this tribe were found dead within the last month, and their appearance too plainly indicated that hunger, united with inclement weather, was the cause of their death."[54] Wakan Decorah stated the results bluntly in a council with the territorial governor that same year: "Since the whites have come among us ... we do not know what will become of us."[55]

Meanwhile, the one set of rights the Ho-Chunk could claim in relation to the American state—the provisions of the treaties—also became the means of their coercion. The federal government and its agents took merciless advantage of their desperate circumstances. The annuities guaranteed by treaties had become an essential lifeline, so U.S. officials withheld them or changed the location of their distribution in order to keep the Ho-Chunk moving west, out of the ceded territories. They did so even when it violated treaty stipulations.[56]

In 1837 the U.S. government used its power over annuities to coerce a new treaty out of the Ho-Chunk, one that would cede all their remaining lands east of the Mississippi. They demanded that the Ho-Chunk send a delegation to Washington for this purpose. At a council called by the federal Indian agent to the Ho-Chunk, Roaring Thunder refused. Then a young man, he had joined his father in the 1828 delegation to Washington that signed the first fateful treaty of cession. He knew that the government did not keep its promises. What, he now asked, could it possibly want from them other than their land? "We do not wish to go at all," he informed the agent. "We have been at Washington once and heard the words of our Great Father and remembered them. We do not wish to go again."[57] But the government's control over the nature, timing, and location of annuity distribution gave it substantial coercive power, and not all Ho-Chunk leaders could follow Roaring Thunder in refusing to go to Washington. Those who did send representatives tried to forestall disaster by assembling a delegation whose members were mostly not Bear clan, the division of the nation responsible for land. In the end, twenty band leaders and other leading men and women traveled to Washington in the fall of 1837.

Once in Washington, they were threatened, bullied, and refused passage home until they signed a treaty giving up their remaining Wisconsin lands. In the months, years, and generations to come, they remembered the treaty as the product of coercion and fraud. Roaring Thunder first rejected the treaty because only one band leader from his region had attended the negotiation, and that man did not belong to the clan empowered to negotiate about land.[58] But Roaring Thunder's conversations with the signatories soon convinced him that, in an even deeper way, "the treaty was not regularly made."[59] The agent, he said, refused to tell the members of the delegation what was in the treaty "for fear they would object."[60] That man had also threatened that "if they did not sign the treaty he would put them into a house or on board of a boat, and kill them."[61] When the terrorized delegates did agree to make their marks on the treaty paper, they tried to insist on a long grace period—four years in which to get their affairs in order. The one delegate from the Portage-area bands, Little Soldier, later told Henry Dodge that "I touched the pen amongst the rest ... and I asked that we should have four years to remove in." Blind DeKauri was told "that we were to remain four years on the land—that he had pity on our old men and women, and we came back under this belief." The Snake remembered the last signer, "when he took up the paper, ask[ing] that four years should be given to remove in."[62]

Fraud and theft of this magnitude were baked into the treaty system, in which the United States actively chose which Native people to negotiate with, ignoring (often deliberately) whether the people they were dealing with adequately represented the nation whose territory they were trading—or even whether they represented that nation at all. The 1837 treaty was one of several treaties signed under fraudulent circumstances that year, including another affecting Native nations in the Wisconsin Territory. In the Treaty with the Chippewa (Ojibwe) at St. Peters, bands living west of the Mississippi River were induced to sign away lands that belonged to bands living east of the river.[63] Signatures could be just another fig leaf of consent, legitimating theft by putting it in the form of a contract.

The 1837 treaty remained a persistent point of anger among the Ho-Chunk people. It ceded the remainder of the Ho-Chunk lands east of the Mississippi and required the entire tribe to move across the Mississippi to the Neutral Ground. It promised the Ho-Chunk annual payments of $55,000 in provisions, goods, and cash for the next twenty-two years—like the preceding treaties, until 1859. It allowed them just eight months to leave Wisconsin. When the returning delegates protested their treatment, the territorial governor of Wisconsin brushed away their accusations of coercion and fraud. When they had asked for four years, the governor said, they had been informed that the treaty required them to leave in eight months. If they had been told that, DeKauri replied, "it was in English and not in Indian."[64]

The territorial governor who dismissed the Ho-Chunk delegates' objections was none other than Henry Dodge, one of the chief architects of their decade of disaster. In the aftermath of the conflict, the U.S. Army incorporated his band of lead-country squatters as the First Regiment of U.S. Dragoons, with the squatter king himself as the regiment's commander.[65] But Dodge's thoughts and interests remained closely tied to the territory he had done so much to take. As the eastern part of the Michigan Territory prepared for entry as the new state of Michigan in 1837, the United States rechristened what remained, west of Lake Michigan, the Wisconsin Territory. To no one's surprise, Dodge was named its first governor. The vigilantes had become the army, and their leader had become a chief executive.

At the same time, squatters had become legitimate settlers. They accomplished this in a host of ways, but the most important concerned how land would become available for sale. Squatters and settlers asserted their local authority over how land became available for sale both before and after its formal acquisition by the United States. Across a broad sweep of the West, from Indiana to Wisconsin and as far west as Oregon, squatters established "claims clubs" to ensure that the people already asserting ownership would retain it. As historian John Suval puts it in his study of the squatter in American political culture, they did so "in places where the federal government had yet to set up shop, run survey lines, or even negotiate with Indians for land."[66]

The federal land policy called "pre-emption" retroactively ratified the actions of squatters. The 1830 federal Pre-emption Act allowed squatters the right to claim lands they had improved prior to survey and sale and to purchase them at the government price ahead of claims that other settlers might seek to make.[67] These laws encouraged further squatting, bringing illegal settlers into conflict with Native people in other unceded territories. The expectation rapidly developed that wherever squatters planted themselves, the government would eventually follow to ratify their claims, and they in turn would become the sovereign people of that territory, charged with self-government. Squatters themselves echoed this judgment, representing preemption laws not as "reward of crime" but as vindication of their labors and a validation of "their just rights."[68]

The essential first step in confirming settler claims was making that land legible to buyers and sellers through surveys and maps. During the 1830s, American surveyors crisscrossed the Ho-Chunk homeland with stakes, chains, and sextants. They followed the plan laid out by Thomas Jefferson in the Northwest Ordinance and other land laws adopted fifty years before. Jefferson's plan for the future settlement of the vast area—encompassing today's states of Ohio, Michigan, Indiana, Illinois, Wisconsin, and Minnesota east of the Mississippi River—reflected the Enlightenment imperative of imposing order on nature: a rigidly methodical grid of townships, six miles square, each containing thirty-six sections of 640 acres. Each section could be further divided and sold in lots of 40, 80, or more acres.

The system offered formal regularity: these surveyed acres, now the "public lands" of the United States, were available for purchase at regional land offices. After 1830, the right of preemption meant that squatters could claim priority on any 160-acre tract they had occupied and farmed, and fraud and conflicting claims inevitably followed. A larger problem for settlers was the cost. Although federal land laws continued to encourage settlement, at $1.25 per acre, with a minimum acreage of eighty, the price was too high for many prospective settlers.[69] Thomas Hart Benton's "Graduation Bill," had it passed, would have priced unsold federal lands lower each year until they were all sold.[70] Later still, the Homestead Act waived everything but a small filing fee for settlers who improved the land for five years.

Once settlers purchased these lands, the imaginary grid took legal, physical, and symbolic form. Patents and deeds conveyed the owner the exclusive right to use, occupancy, and profit. Settlers built fences and roads dividing one claim from another, etching the principle of private ownership on the landscape itself. Financial instruments such as mortgages transformed the land into collateral, the basis for loans with which the owner could improve the land or buy more. Tax assessments drew a portion of the landowner's wealth back to the state to fund its operations. And the proceeds from one section in each township were dedicated to public education, reflecting Jefferson's hope that the Northwest would be the home of public virtue as well as private initiative, and building state institutions that would bind these landowners and their children together.

A fundamental alchemy was at work: the reimagining of Ho-Chunk places as American lands, exchanged on American terms, and soon bearing American names. By the mid-1830s, if an American settler came to the federal land office at Mineral Point in the Wisconsin Territory and put down his cash for eighty acres of land in the Four Lakes region, he did not describe himself as a Ho-Chunk person might, as residing in Teejop. Rather, he now laid claim to a plot of land according to its place on the settler grid—for example, in the jargon of the General Land Office, the eastern ½ of the southwest ¼ of section 5, Township 6 North, Range 10 east. And as the settler on that tract heard the distant hammers of workmen erecting the territory's first capitol building, he learned to call his new home part of "Madison." Legally, materially, and symbolically, these forces reimagined the Ho-Chunk homeland as a settlers' republic.

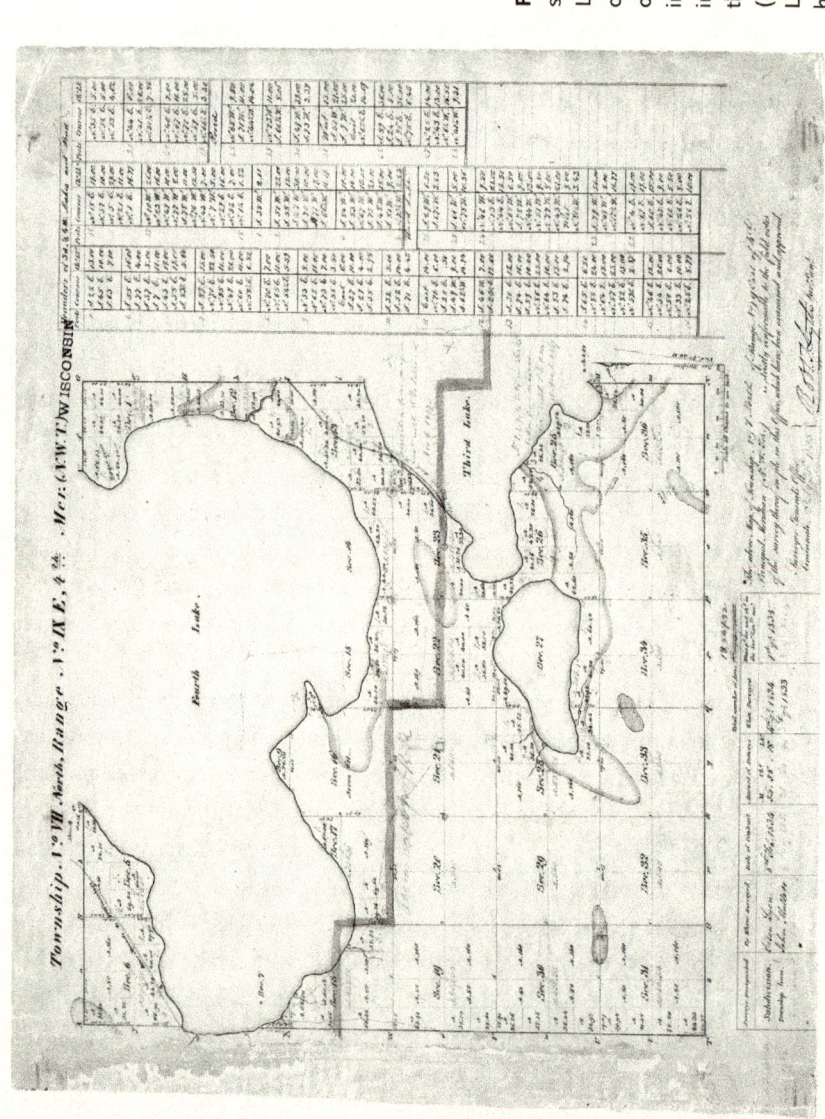

Figure 1.1. The 1835 federal survey of part of the Four Lakes region (Teejop). A grid of section lines is plotted over the region's landscape, in preparation for the sale of individual parcels through the federal land office. (Records of the General Land Office, searchable at https://glorecords.blm.gov/)

Settlers depicted their conquest as the inevitable triumph of "civilization" over "barbarism." The seal of the new Wisconsin Territory claimed that transformation as its motto, and it left no doubt what, or who, stood at the center of that project. Just above words identifying the territory's founding with the nation's—"Fourth of July 1836"—the seal featured the figure of a white man breaking the land with team and plow. This virtuous yeoman was surrounded and encouraged by a sailing ship, lighthouse, and steamboat, elements of a modern commercial economy. The seal imagined a new society in the model of the old, with room for ambitious white men to plant themselves, establish households and farms, prosper as property holders, and govern together as citizens. Here, in the laws and assumptions undergirding this next phase of colonialism, the settler emerged as the key actor in the drama of "civilization." Meanwhile the old order, represented by a crudely drawn Indian figure, gazed west across the Mississippi, where his new home presumably lay. Reflecting on the invasion a half century later, a surveyor turned frontier politician depicted this settler-colonial replacement as preordained: "The law of destiny demands that the aboriginal Mongolian inhabitants of the cultivable portions of the North American continent, should give place to the advancing civilization of the Caucasian race."[71]

"Civilization" denoted private property and sedentary households with an implied gendered division of labor. It was not an accident that the territorial seal placed a male settler and his productive use of the land at its center, for the laws and customs of settler society emphasized the public and productive roles of white men. But the gendered order that prized men's agricultural and other remunerated labor also celebrated and required women's work of domestic production and reproduction. Native societies such as the Ho-Chunk, organized around seasonal itineraries, mixed production, and women's agricultural work, inverted American proprieties. Their systems of ownership and use, like their household arrangements, constituted "barbarism" in American eyes.[72]

Through the same alchemy that transformed coercion into contract and conquest into destiny, these squatters—native-born, naturalized, and alien—gradually refashioned themselves into the citizenry of an American territory.[73] In the first decades of American settlement in Wisconsin, the meanings of "citizen" were more rhetorical than legal. In fact, the white men at the literal and figurative center of the seal's "civilization" did not actually have to be citizens to be integral parts of the settler project—at least, they did not have to be citizens yet. Many laws for the western states and territories sought to draw

Figure 1.2. Seal of the Territory of Wisconsin, July 4, 1836, representing the forms of "civilization" that its founders hoped would replace what they understood as Native "barbarism." (Wisconsin Historical Society, WHI-64629)

eligible white immigrants into the process of conquest and settlement and expand the reach of the American order.

Noncitizens could stake many crucial claims, literal and figurative, to belong in the territory. To begin with, the federal militia law of 1792 demanded service of every "free able-bodied white male citizen," but white noncitizens also served. For example, the Illinois militia that invaded the Ho-Chunk homeland in pursuit of the British Band—Abraham Lincoln's militia—enrolled "free, able-bodied men" regardless of their national allegiance, but not "negroes, mulattoes, and Indians."[74] The early land laws for the Northwest Territories cast aside eastern states' prohibitions on alien ownership and transmission of real estate. Instead, they made land available for settlement and purchase by "inhabitants." Next, territorial boosters in the region began to offer the privileges of landownership to any noncitizen who was eligible for naturalization—"free white persons," in the language of federal naturalization law. Preemption laws followed suit with regard to the federal government's public lands: the act of 1830 and its revision in 1841 granted preemption rights to squatters who were already citizens, but it also welcomed preemption claims from "free white persons" who had declared their intent to naturalize, which eligible immigrants could do immediately upon arriving in the United States.[75]

Finally, while some white settlers began to make political claims in the name of "the citizens," a growing number of western territories and states granted voting rights to free white immigrant men who had declared their intention to become citizens.[76] In 1840 the Illinois Supreme Court ruled that even if men were "neither native nor adopted citizens," when they "by habitation and residence identified their interests and feelings with the citizen," they were "upon the just principles of reciprocity between the governed and governing, entitled to a voice in the choice of officers of the government."[77] Wisconsin was one of many western states to take a similar step. Although the congressional act creating the Wisconsin Territory in 1836 restricted voting rights to U.S. citizens, by the time territorial leaders passed the 1848 state constitution, they enfranchised all white male adults whether citizens or not—and, as we will see, some others as well.[78] As legal scholar Jamin Raskin puts it, "*Non*citizen voting became *pre*-citizen voting."[79]

Settler society grew through reproduction as well as immigration. Whether or not immigrant settlers finally naturalized as citizens, their American-born children were understood to be citizens of the nation and of their state. Although birthright citizenship is conventionally described as following from the citizenship language of the Fourteenth Amendment—"all persons born"—it was a well-understood principle decades before the Civil War, one widely embraced with reference to the children of white immigrants and doggedly claimed by African Americans.[80]

These mechanisms for incorporating noncitizens, extending privileges to them, and conferring citizenship upon their children were predicated on one critical attribute: that the prospective citizen met the requirements of the state's laws of settlement. In Wisconsin's early days, just who could gain a settlement remained somewhat unclear. In Wisconsin's 1849 code, one year's residence established a presumption of legitimate membership in a town or county and made the resident eligible for poor relief.[81] That residence was not explicitly limited by race: unlike Michigan to the east and Iowa to the west, Wisconsin's early statutes did not seek to forbid or deter free African Americans from gaining a settlement.[82]

Some free people of African descent did settle in Wisconsin in the decades before 1865. More than thirty households headed by people census takers designated as "colored," "negro," or "mulatto" dotted the territory and state, and several settlements within the Ho-Chunk homeland—Cheyenne Valley in Vernon County and Pleasant Ridge in Grant County—included multiple families with origins in the eastern slave states. Some were of mixed African and Indigenous ancestry and maintained kinship ties with Native relatives in North Carolina. But in the racial order of mid-nineteenth-century Wisconsin these families seem to have figured (and represented themselves) as Black. Permitted to settle in Wisconsin, if not to vote, these Black settlers saw the territory as a place where they might build lives and communities comparatively free from the strictures imposed by most states outside New England.[83]

Finally, as we will see in the next chapter, those statutes even imagined certain classes of Native men as eligible to vote, making it clear that there was no hard-and-fast bar to exclude them from civic membership solely on the basis of American ideas about race. But it remained unclear whether or how Native people could, if they wished, achieve the same settlement, and right of membership, available to non-Native migrants to the state. As settlers flooded into the southern portion of the Wisconsin Territory, Native people occupied an increasingly precarious place, not just on the territorial seal but in the lands they called home.

The claims of settlers, including their territorial seal, evaded a crucial truth: in 1836, most of the region the United States called the Wisconsin Territory remained in Native possession. To the east and northeast, the state's population included Potawatomis as well as Native migrants pushed out of eastern states during the preceding decade—the Oneida, Stockbridge-Munsee, and Brothertown peoples. To the north and west, Menominee and Ojibwe peoples remained the great majority of the population and the owners of the land. Even after the Treaty of 1837, as territorial leaders constructed a new capitol building in the Four Lakes region, many Ho-Chunk people remained resident in the place they called Teejop. The territorial seal seemed to contemplate ethnic cleansing, but it was far from accomplished.

Despite the terms of the Treaties of 1832 and 1837, the Ho-Chunk did all they could to remain in their homeland and reconstruct the rhythms of their lives.[84] In the absence of a concerted federal military campaign to expel them, their determination was sometimes enough. In 1833, a U.S. officer passing through Teejop—part of the 1832 cession—found many Ho-Chunks residing in well-established villages. "A great part of them," he wrote, "returned to their old camping ground, near the Four Lakes, and are engaged in gathering rice and hunting as formerly."[85] In 1836, another U.S. official estimated that half or more of the Ho-Chunk people continued their seasonal rhythms of residence and subsistence in the territories they had already ceded.[86]

Many settlers hoped to follow conquest with expulsion. Governor Dodge warned federal officials and territorial legislators that settlers resented the Ho-Chunk people's continued residence. He asserted that their "depredations on the stock and property" had been so egregious that "it has been with great difficulty that the Citizens ... could be restrained from killing them."[87] He urged the deportation of the Ho-Chunk as the only way to ensure a peaceful settler order. But deportation required federal military action, and as a military man Dodge was aware of the challenges this presented. To expel the Ho-Chunk and keep them expelled would necessitate cooperation among U.S. territories and the federal government. "It will require a strong mounted force to remove them in the Spring," he warned the commissioner of Indian Affairs in 1839.[88] The U.S. agent to the Ho-Chunk, Rev. David Lowry, warned that even if the United States did deport the Ho-Chunk west of the Mississippi River, the government could not expect to keep them there without continually resorting to force.[89]

The U.S. effort to expel the Ho-Chunk from Wisconsin in the spring and summer of 1840 followed a predictably deadly pattern and marked another season of horrific loss for the Ho-Chunk people. More than 400 U.S. troops gathered up Ho-Chunk families and bands from the Rock River and Wisconsin River country and took them to Prairie du Chien for transportation across the Mississippi River. Dysentery and other diseases killed hundreds of them as they waited in these camps. The old and the very young suffered the worst, layering the emotional crises of sick and dying children upon the loss of experienced political and diplomatic leadership.

Ho-Chunk people pleaded for mercy. A fur trader working as an interpreter for the government described the scene at a camp on the Kickapoo River in western Wisconsin, where three elderly women "came up, throwing themselves on their knees" before the soldiers, asking for death rather than deportation. "They were old, and would rather die, and be buried with their fathers, mothers, and children, than be taken away," they said. "They were ready to receive their death blows."[90] The son of a band leader appealed to Governor Dodge for a less stringent policy, explaining that "since we left the Portage my mother and two brothers have died, and now I am left alone with a little brother and sister, both of whom are sick." Only a few leaders could come to plead with the governor; "all the rest are sick."[91] Coming Thunder, now a young man, warned the U.S. agent that so many people were sick and unable to walk that it would cost the tribe their whole annuity to hire the wagons necessary to haul them to the Neutral Ground.[92]

Their misery matched that of other victims of "removal." As historian Claudio Saunt reminds us, "removal" was a contemporary term of art, a word that did not clearly connote coercion or violence. He urges us to look past this euphemism to the intentions and effects of the policy itself: deportation, expulsion, and extermination.[93] "Extermination" is another hard word, but there is no denying the murderous results of the policy. U.S. soldiers rounded up many thousands of Cherokees in 1838, beginning a deportation of 800 miles from the hill country South to Indian Territory, across the Mississippi River. The government had had ample time to plan for this forced migration, but thousands died of hunger and disease before this Trail of Tears concluded in 1839. Some 88,000 Native people were expelled from eastern homelands during the two decades after the Indian Removal Act, and historian Jeffrey Ostler estimates that between 12,000 and 17,000 died. Policy makers in 1830 could plausibly hypothesize that removal would not be unduly dangerous, he notes, but "as the death toll mounted, American leaders had a choice." They chose to continue the policy. Ostler suggests that in this context, the term "genocide" is apt.[94]

From the beginning, many Ho-Chunks actively resisted deportation. The so-called Neutral Ground to which the 1837 treaty assigned them was hardly a safe harbor; at the end of 1839, a Sauk attack on a Ho-Chunk camp left twenty dead.[95] More important, though, the Neutral Ground was not home. Roaring Thunder repeatedly asserted his people's right to remain in their homeland. As early as 1838, he told John Kinzie, the former U.S. agent, that he and his band would not leave Wisconsin. "The Indians on the Upper Wisconsin are much dissatisfied with the late treaty," Dodge warned the commissioner of Indian Affairs, and "they will resist, as far as in their power, any attempt to remove them from that country."[96] He tried but failed to secure Roaring Thunder's arrest. Authorities did jail another leader, Yellow Thunder, for presenting a "great obstacle to a free and peaceable removal." In a highly unusual move, they also imprisoned Yellow Thunder's wife. Known by the Ho-Chunk birth-order name Wiihąga, she had previously been called "Washington Woman," because she had joined the 1837 delegation to the U.S. capital. Now, for her obstruction of the federal deportation, officials dubbed her "an exceedingly troublesome woman."[97]

The Ho-Chunk were able to trouble the deportation so gravely in part because their circumstances differed in a crucial respect from those of the Cherokee, Potawatomi, and other groups subjected to similar policies: only the Mississippi River separated their new territory from their homeland, and many of those forcibly expelled from the territory in the early 1840s soon returned. Ho-Chunk people often crossed the Mississippi River back into Wisconsin. They established villages and camps on both banks of the Mississippi and on islands in the river.[98] Wisconsin's territorial governor estimated in 1843 that, despite the treaties and removals, "very nearly one half of the Winnebaygo nation now [reside] east of the Mississippi river."[99]

Settlers charged that the resistant Ho-Chunk posed an immediate danger to American settlement. Officials attributed "the return of emigrants to their old haunts, on ground they have ceded to the United States," to their "reckless disposition and vagrant habits."[100] The governors of Wisconsin, Minnesota, and Iowa exchanged sharp letters about what they were hearing.[101] Iowa's governor told a fearsome tale of Ho-Chunks "destroying large quantities of valuable timber," removing the section corners placed by surveyors, and "demand[ing] rent from persons living on said land." They were undoing the American order of property relations, he thought, and seeking to unmake the settler grid.[102]

But the Ho-Chunk people's movements were purposeful, not vagrant. They lived where they could plant corn, hunt, and carry on as much of their accustomed seasonal rhythm as possible under the dire circumstances of their dispossession.[103] In fact, the commissioner of Indian Affairs' own account of their "wandering" acknowledged this: he noted that they cultivated corn on their riverfront lands but spent the winter to the south and east before returning in the spring.[104] Even those who remained west of the river generally did not live where the government intended; instead they chose lands that suited them better, either at the eastern edge of the Neutral Ground near the Mississippi River, or north of there in Dakota country.[105]

The expulsion of the early 1840s finally faltered because the federal government was less interested in a short-term containment of the Ho-Chunk in the Neutral Ground than in a long-term solution: their removal to a more distant and (ostensibly) permanent homeland to the north or west. Beginning a campaign that would not end until the 1870s, officials urged Ho-Chunk delegations to visit the part of Indian Territory southwest of the Missouri River. Officials hoped to secure at least their nominal agreement to move there, after which they could put the machinery of treaties, appropriations, and soldiers in motion.[106] The Office of Indian Affairs also dreamed up plans for a northern Indian Territory in today's southern Minnesota, perhaps 5 million acres that would provide permanent homes for 50,000 Native people, including the Ho-Chunk. Once the Ho-Chunk were located in one of these places, as "wards" of the government, authorities believed they could be "civilized"— led "from their present wild lives to habits of agriculture."[107]

Given the grand strategy of a consolidated removal, it made sense for the United States to bide its time and to tolerate Ho-Chunk bands' decisions to locate themselves far from their assigned lands. Less than a year into the military removal, the secretary of war told officers to let those Ho-Chunks living in Wisconsin to remain there, but to try to prevent them from annoying settlers or encouraging others to cross the river. As Washington officials explained to officers on the ground, "It is the policy of the department to conciliate those

Indians, and to allay their present excitement and irritation with a view to the most favourable arrangement for their removal and permanent settlement in the country which may be assigned to them." The government would force the Ho-Chunk to move, but on its own schedule.[108]

Despite the treaties demanding their expulsion, well over a thousand Ho-Chunk people continued to live in Wisconsin through and after the deportations of the early 1840s. There, they sought to carve out a permanent place for themselves and sometimes even exerted sovereignty in ways that competed with settlers' claims.[109] These strategies could work so long as Ho-Chunk people and settlers did not come into sustained conflict over the same acres or resources. Other Ho-Chunks developed more complex relations with the growing settler society around them. Some of these relations were rooted in histories of trade, marriage, family, or other alliances; they could be essentially exploitative, aimed at extracting wealth from Native people through debts to be repaid with annuity money. But whatever their motivations or dynamics, these relationships cut against demands that Native people simply disappear.[110] Meanwhile, a few Ho-Chunk people began to experiment with the power of American forms of landownership, and even "citizenship," to secure a foothold in their homeland for themselves and their relations.

The Ho-Chunk who persisted in Wisconsin after treaties of cession and removal were not the only Native people to do so in this era. Miamis employing the same array of tactics persisted in Indiana in the 1840s despite the terms of earlier treaties. Potawatomi communities responded to local interests and dynamics across several northwestern states and territories, and several managed to establish a right to remain in the region. But as historian John Bowes cautions, evading removal "did not indicate that the struggle had ended."[111]

Settlers longed to perceive the Ho-Chunk as wanderers and vagabonds with no meaningful claim to any piece of land. But they could not ignore what one agent referred to as "the Indian's attachment to the home of his childhood, and his reluctance to abandon to a stranger's keeping the graves of his fathers."[112] This hackneyed idea—"proverbial," an official called it—was also a literal description of an ongoing social conflict. In the 1850s, in a part of Sauk County thinly settled by whites, a settler named Abraham Ackerman desecrated a Ho-Chunk grave, stealing a pipe, beads, and knives. When Ho-Chunk companions of the deceased visited the grave, they were outraged. They "demanded Ackerman and boldly told the settlers that if he were not produced a raid would be made upon them." Ackerman had already moved west, making restitution difficult. The matter was finally settled, according to the memory of a local settler, "by the whites in the neighborhood signing a statement that no other graves would be disturbed."[113]

But where settlers gathered in larger numbers, Ho-Chunk power dissipated. Not far from the site of Ackerman's desecration, in the growing village of Reedsburg, a settler destroyed a Ho-Chunk cemetery when clearing a lot for his new house. The settler's daughter remembered that he took away "a half pint of beads" and cloth whose condition indicated the graves were recent. When Ho-Chunk relatives returned to town and discovered the desecration, they "vigorously protested," but it is not clear that they were able to extract any concessions from the perpetrator.[114]

No one better represented "vigorous protest" in this era than Roaring Thunder. His impulse to reject the Treaty of 1837 was confirmed in the spring of 1838, when his band returned from their winter hunting camp to find settlers claiming and clearing their village site. Furious, Roaring Thunder challenged the soldiers at Fort Winnebago to remove these invaders before his "young men" did the work for them.[115] He did not make good on this threat, but his band and several others continued to live seasonally on the Baraboo, Wisconsin, and Fox Rivers, provoking petitions and complaints from some white residents.[116] Roaring Thunder remained the face of Ho-Chunk persistence and resistance for the next three decades.

During those decades, the threat of settler vigilante violence was never far from the surface. In October 1845, fifty Ho-Chunks traveling east on the Wisconsin River encountered a hostile party of white settlers. They presented papers speaking to their peaceful intentions: one from their agent in the Neutral Ground and another from an official of the American Fur Company. The settlers tore up their papers and hustled them back downriver, a warning of a fiercer conflict to come. That winter, two Ho-Chunks used a Wisconsin settler's canoe without permission; when pursued by angry settlers, the Native men hid in the house of a friendly white man in the town of Muscoda. An impromptu community meeting resolved to drive them out, and local men seized and beat the two Ho-Chunks. The struggle drew in larger parties of armed white and Ho-Chunk men, who briefly exchanged fire. Settlers killed at least two Ho-Chunks before the day was done.[117]

This conflict provided a new opening for the forces of expulsion. Governor Henry Dodge called for troops, departed immediately for the scene, and, as in the lead diggings in the 1820s and the Black Hawk War in the 1830s, took personal command of the settler army.[118] Meanwhile, similar complaints farther west prompted military action against Ho-Chunk bands, including their forcible removal from camps on the banks of the Mississippi River and islands in the river.[119] Dodge approvingly informed the commissioner of Indian Affairs that the violence "has had a good effect in restraining the Winnebagoes and keeping them more within the limits of their own country."[120] A company of dragoons and other U.S. forces searched Wisconsin; they even captured Roaring Thunder, with a view to holding him hostage until his band surrendered and departed the territory.[121]

But the stories that followed Roaring Thunder's arrest reflected some settlers' complex and even conflicted feelings about the Ho-Chunk people living among them. They understood Roaring Thunder to be a militant leader, a person others might follow into open conflict with settler society. Even twenty years later, amid a settler panic about a possible pan-Indian rising, agents and authorities imagined Roaring Thunder as the architect of the trouble. But at the same time, many regarded him with feelings other than fear. Some admired him; others professed to be amused by him. In both ways, perhaps because his challenge to settler authority was so persistent, settler stories sought to domesticate him. In any case, settlers could not stop thinking about him.

Settler commentators focused first on Roaring Thunder's elaborate and culturally significant clothing, accoutrements, and pigment, for which they nicknamed him "Dandy." In the early 1840s, an eastern painter named Charles Deas traveled down the frozen Rock River and then returned to paint portraits of the Ho-Chunk leaders he met. His first oil sketch of Roaring Thunder (mistranslated as "Rolling Thunder") captured the young man elaborately painted and outfitted for a formal interaction.[122] Others who met him around the same time offered even greater detail. Juliette Kinzie, wife of longtime Indian agent John Kinzie, remembered Roaring Thunder vividly in her 1856 memoir *Wau-bun*. "His dress was of the most studied and fanciful character," she wrote. "A shirt (when he condescended to wear any) of the brightest colors, ornamented with innumerable rows of silver brooches, set thickly together; never less than two pairs of silver arm-bands; leggings and moccasins of the most elaborate embroidery in ribbons and porcupine quills; everything that he could devise in the shape of an ornament hanging to his club of hair behind ... [and] the variety and brilliancy of the colors upon his face."[123]

American stories about Roaring Thunder sometimes turned him from insurgent to trickster. When officials brought Roaring Thunder to Madison in chains in 1846, Governor Dodge insisted that Roaring Thunder lead his people out of Wisconsin and into the Neutral Ground, to the agency established for them there at the Turkey River. A journalist enjoyed recounting the exchange that followed. Picking up a Bible, Roaring Thunder inquired

Figure 1.3. Wakąjaxetega (Roaring Thunder) in a naturalistic rendering. (Charles Deas, *Wa-kon-cha-hi-re-ga "Rolling Thunder,"* ca. 1840–1841. Oil on paper, 8 ¼ in. × 6 ¼ in. Colby College Museum of Art. The Lunder Collection. Accession Number: 2013.105)

Figure 1.4. Wakajaxetega (Roaring Thunder) in painter Charles Deas's moodier and more romantic second rendering, ca. 1841. (From the collections of the St. Louis Mercantile Library at the University of Missouri–St. Louis)

through an interpreter, "If a man would do all that was in that book, could any more be required of him?" No, replied Dodge. "'Well,' said Dandy, 'look that book all through, and if you find in it that Dandy ought to be removed by the government to Turkey River, then I will go right off; but if you do not find it, I will never go there to stay.'"[124] The furious governor sent him off to be held at a fort, to wait there as a hostage until his band came in to be removed.[125]

Settler accounts such as this—including many other poorly documented and less likely stories—treated Roaring Thunder as essentially harmless and even amusing.[126] Even Roaring Thunder's subsequent escape from American captivity could be rendered in comic terms. One telling version went this way: By the time his escort brought him to his prison, he seemed a pathetic figure. Apparently hobbled by weeks in chains, he begged the soldiers accompanying him to let him use the privy, then set off groaning toward the shack. But halfway across the enclosure, he bolted for the gate. He eluded one pursuer, tripped another, and made good his escape.[127] He would not be in U.S. custody again until 1863.

In settler imaginations, this version of Roaring Thunder became a carefully encapsulated figure of a domesticated "Indian frontier"—an object of interest and even fascination. The painter Charles Deas underscored this tendency with a second rendering of Roaring Thunder. Having apparently concluded that his first likeness lacked a certain romance, he tried again, this time producing a more vivid, energetic, and somber figure, his body now poised for movement and his expression thoughtful, perhaps even sad.[128]

Even as settler interpreters sought to contain Roaring Thunder, the facts told a different story. In 1850, amid another wave of settler demands that the Ho-Chunk be expelled from Wisconsin, U.S. Indian agent Joseph Fletcher made the long trip from central Minnesota to Roaring Thunder's camp on the Baraboo River. His mission was to induce the dissident to surrender and bring his band to join the half of the Ho-Chunk people in those years officially located at Long Prairie, on the upper Mississippi River.[129] But when confronted with this demand, Roaring Thunder did not play the dandy, the trickster, or the figure of frontier romance. Instead, he was "very abusive indeed, telling Mr. F. that he would not go."[130] The 1873 petition of "Dandy's Band" puts a period on this claim: he never did. Roaring Thunder remained the leader of a band living outside the settler order and outside the law, defying officials and escaping all punishment.

While Roaring Thunder's band carefully remained at the far outskirts of white settlement, other Ho-Chunk people established or maintained more intimate relationships with settler society. The 1832 treaty envisioned the ultimate migration of the Ho-Chunk across the Mississippi, but the fur trade, even in its waning days, provided a counterweight: as soon as the treaty was signed, agents and allies of the American Fur Company began encouraging Ho-Chunk bands to establish villages just north of the Wisconsin River, in their remaining unceded territory.[131] Traders—some of them of Ho-Chunk descent, some married to Ho-Chunk women, some unaffiliated by kinship—eagerly sought their furs, blankets, and horses.[132] After 1840, when the area north of the Wisconsin River had been seized by the United States and Ho-Chunk people generally had no right to reside, hunt, plant, or trade in any part of Wisconsin, these relationships helped secure their ability to return or remain. A frustrated agent concluded that they "are encouraged to remain there, by the citizens, in whose community they live."[133] They lived mainly in places with few whites, the agent explained—at the margins of the grid.[134] But some elements of settler society welcomed and even relied on the goods they brought to market.[135] Upon hearing reports of several hundred Ho-Chunk "strolling through western Wisconsin," another official fumed that "it would be useless to remove them again as long as the citizens invite them to come back." Until the department could dissuade these "citizens from inducing them to leave their new homes" for purposes of continued trade, it was pointless to take further action.[136]

These complaints pointed to cleavages within settler society—among its "citizens" and even its leadership. Experienced observers made a distinction between new arrivals, who feared Native people, and the old settlers, "who represent the Indians as peaceable and well disposed."[137] Traders in the longtime entrepôt of Prairie du Chien even cooperated with Ho-Chunk leaders against federal Indian agents whom the two groups did not like.[138] Not surprisingly, officials who sought the Ho-Chunk people's removal resented the traders' countervailing influence and described them as "the worst enemies, which the Indians have."[139] Governor Dodge put it bluntly: "The old established traders ... will be opposed to the removal of these Indians" and would dissuade them from leaving.[140] He saw the traders as a force that must be "neutralized" before expulsion and relocation could go forward.[141] Some officials claimed that the Ho-Chunk received nothing from their bargains with the traders but whiskey, and that this led to poverty, theft, and friction and violence between them and white settlers.[142] But not every settler official agreed. Even amid an expulsion campaign in 1841, Wisconsin territorial governor James Doty reminded the legislature that American traders had more than a million dollars invested in the fur trade—a trade that relied on Indigenous labor.[143]

Many of the relationships that tied Ho-Chunk bands to settler communities were more local. As a settler village sprang up in Madison, the new territorial capital, Ho-Chunk people continued to live nearby in large numbers.[144] Some spent spring and fall months making maple sugar and hunting and trapping muskrats, which they traded with downtown storekeepers.[145] But this was incidental to their rich and continuing lives in the place they still called Teejop. Even after a capitol building rose between the largest of the four lakes in 1837, extensive summer villages persisted on the nearby shores. Ho-Chunk people continued to hunt ducks with bow and arrow from fine wooden and birch bark canoes, to trap muskrats for food and furs, and to weave rush mats. Children competed to see whose arrows flew straightest, while adults wagered muskrat skins on games of chance. American visitors were welcome in these villages, even if they had nothing to trade.[146] Some settlers feared and gave chase to them as they continued their seasonal pathways through the territory. But others regularly exchanged goods and labor.[147]

The continued coexistence of Teejop and Madison during the middle decades of the nineteenth century was smoothed by the difference between Ho-Chunk and settler uses of the land. American settlers generally wanted to clear and cultivate large fields that would not flood. They were less interested in the wetlands, riverbanks, and shorelines where Ho-Chunk villagers sought wild rice, reeds, ducks, muskrats, and other resources. This was how a summer village holding hundreds of people could exist less than two miles from the territorial capitol building: the village lay on the marshy lakeshore, terrain that held little interest for settlers. Elsewhere in the region's woods and marshes and on its lakeshores and riverbanks, Ho-Chunk bands spent weeks or months hunting deer in early winter, or fishing and farming in the summer, and relations remained generally amicable.[148] Some settler families allowed sojourning bands to store their pots and traps in settlers' barns when they left for the season.[149] These patterns continued in some places into the twentieth century.[150]

But coexistence had its limits, and the growth of American settlement in the 1840s forced the Ho-Chunk to adjust. This was especially true in the most densely settled parts of their homeland, including Teejop. Ho-Chunk people's late-fall deer hunt in the woods just east of Madison began to provoke settler complaints that they "annihilated" the herd.[151] And the construction of downtown houses and businesses disrupted their cornfields and destroyed their burial mounds. But the most consequential change came when settlers began to transform the lakes themselves. In the late 1840s, American engineers built a dam and lock on the river that crossed the isthmus, at the site of a large

Ho-Chunk summer village. The dam raised the water level on the largest lake, Wąąkšikhomįkra (The Lake Where the Man Lies Down), by at least two feet; later construction would raise it still higher. This expanded the lake's footprint and flooded some of the wetlands the Ho-Chunk relied on for waterfowl and wild rice.[152] When the American promise of "civilization succeeding barbarism" took this kind of dramatic physical form, Ho-Chunk life became much harder to sustain.

A few Ho-Chunk people tried a different strategy to remain in Wisconsin: landownership on American terms. In 1840, amid the first full-scale removal campaign, "Peter De Kori a Winnebago Indian" asked Governor Dodge's permission for himself and his family "to remain on the Barraboo [river] and to become a Citizen of this Territory." Peter Decora belonged to a prominent Ho-Chunk lineage (which Americans also spelled Decora, Decorah, Dekorra, DeKauri, De Korrie, and De Korri) that descended from the early eighteenth-century marriage of a band leader's daughter, Glory of the Morning, to a French officer, Sabrevoir Descarrie.[153] Many members of the family were Catholic, and this Decora professed Christianity.[154] He presented a letter from prominent white citizens attesting to his character, and he impressed General Henry Atkinson in a personal interview.[155] Governor Dodge, Atkinson added, "speaks in very high terms of him."[156] This Christian man of mixed descent who claimed to have "given up his Indian ways" seemed a welcome neighbor, one who merited incorporation rather than expulsion. General Atkinson and Governor Dodge both endorsed his petition "asking to become a Citizen of the Territory and to remain on the land he now occupies."[157]

The Native people who most easily imagined and embraced the title or forms of citizenship were, like Peter Decora, people of mixed descent who were already situated as cultural intermediaries and brokers. Decora's successful claim reflected the ties developed over several centuries of the fur trade. Families descended from French traders and Ho-Chunk women, such as those of Michel St. Cyr, Pierre Paquette, and Catherine Myott, positioned themselves as traders, agents, brokers, translators, and intermediaries of various kinds. Described in the record as "half-breeds" or "mixed-bloods," and later sometimes as "métis," these people could sometimes turn American processes of law and property to their families' advantage. People of mixed Ho-Chunk and Euro-American descent received special allocations of cash in the Treaty of 1837, for example, and elsewhere reserves of land were set aside for sale or settlement by such people.[158]

But Peter Decora turned out not to be quite what Henry Dodge expected. White settlers in Decora's neighborhood soon began to complain that officials

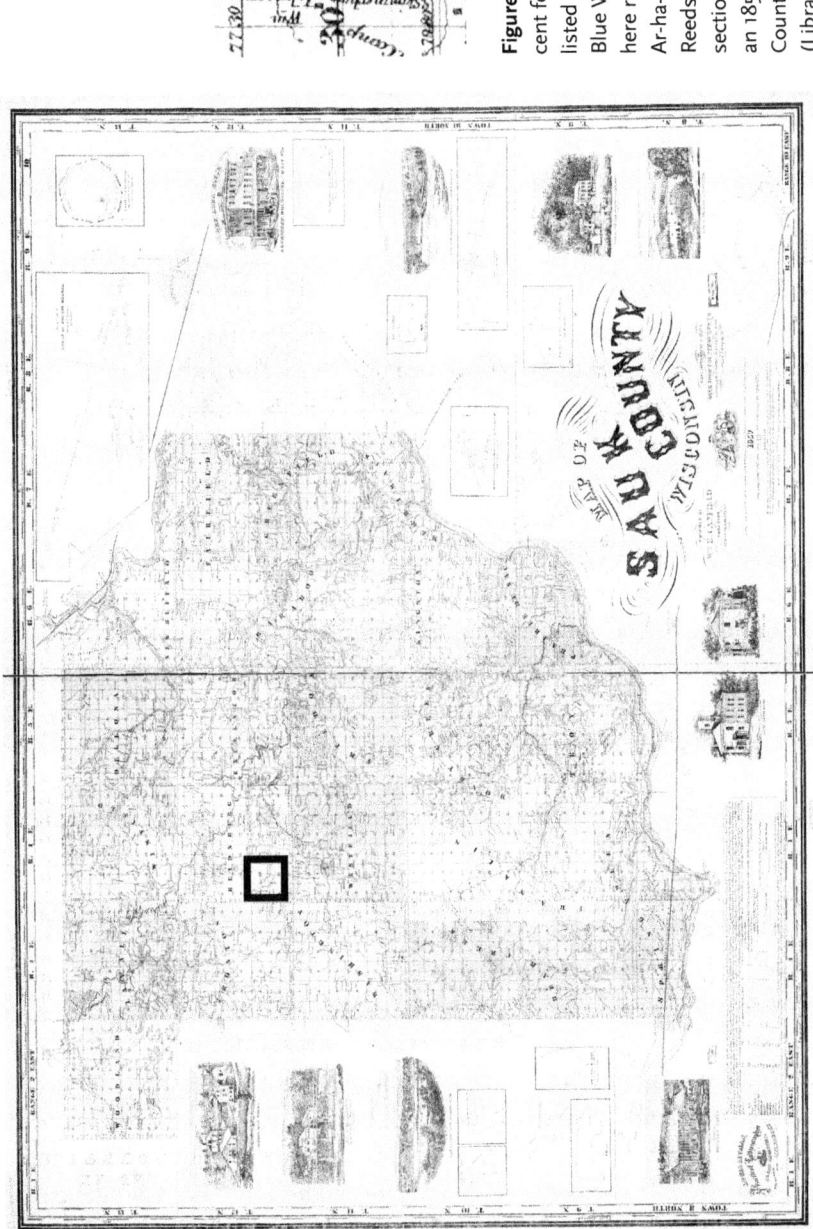

Figure 1.5. Three adjacent forty-acre parcels listed as the property of Blue Wing (Aahucoga, here rendered "Indian Ar-ha-choker") in Reedsburg township, sections 29 and 30, on an 1859 map of Sauk County, Wisconsin. (Library of Congress)

had opened a floodgate to an endless stream of Ho-Chunk sojourners. "The Indians visiting that part of the country say they are *the relations* of the family, and claim the privilege of visiting and remaining with them."[159] Despite this, however, Decora remained in the governor's good graces. In 1844, caught in another military campaign to expel the Ho-Chunk from Wisconsin, Decora was sent to the Neutral Ground. Dodge asked the commissioner of Indian Affairs to allow him to return, and the commissioner agreed. But he warned that Decora should time this so as not to encourage the rest of the recently expelled Ho-Chunk to try to return as well.[160] The whole affair must have raised troubling questions. What had been Decora's actual intentions? What did it mean that the Christian man's "family" extended to scores of others, whose activities gave rise to angry petitions from settler citizens? Did his profession of Christianity and nominal desire to be a "citizen" imply a commitment to settler "civilization"?

Other Ho-Chunk people began to follow in Decora's footsteps. Around the same time that officials were confirming Decora's right to remain in Wisconsin, Ho-Chunks living in the Neutral Ground began to inquire how they could purchase Wisconsin lands, and a few were able to establish themselves in Wisconsin by buying land through the General Land Office. The people who did this, the ways they did it, and the worlds they created told a very different tale from the one Peter Decora promised the governor.[161] Yellow Thunder, for instance, was a resistant band leader, a cohort of Roaring Thunder's and the husband of the "troublesome woman." Yet in 1849, he too seems to have arrived at the conclusion that landownership was his best chance to create a permanent foothold in Wisconsin. To do this, he drew on long-standing relations of trade and family. He persuaded John De La Ronde—a white employee of the American Fur Company, a fluent Ho-Chunk speaker, and the husband of a woman from the Decora family—to accompany him to the land office. With De La Ronde's help, Yellow Thunder purchased forty acres in Sauk County, near Portage.[162]

Another Ho-Chunk landowner, Blue Wing (Aahucoga), seems to have taken Peter Decora's example to heart and to have enacted it even more successfully. In the 1850s he purchased three adjacent forty-acre parcels in a little-settled part of Sauk County.[163] As with Decora's tract, Blue Wing's lands did not become an American homestead but a Ho-Chunk village. A natural spring provided water for the inhabitants of ten or more permanent lodges, and more residents erected ciiporoke (wigwams) during the winter months. All told, there may have been several hundred Ho-Chunk people residing on these lands at least part of the year during the 1850s, among them

Figure 1.6. Aahucoga (Blue Wing), an early Ho-Chunk landowner, whose community flourished in Sauk and Monroe Counties during the middle decades of the nineteenth century. (Sauk County Historical Society)

another Ho-Chunk landowner whose patent named him only as "Decorah." The available sources cannot confirm whether this was Peter Decora himself. In any case, as with Decora's land, Blue Wing's Ho-Chunk village also served as a seasonal base for a large group's more extensive subsistence practices. Hunting parties ranged across the surrounding settler townships. Hundreds of Ho-Chunk people gathered at the village for ceremonies and celebrations; these "were often visited by the early settlers."[164]

In 1861 Aahucoga sold the land to a white settler, but not in order to move farther from white settlement. In fact, his band relocated to a site on the Baraboo River only two miles northwest of the town of Reedsburg. Their dozen lodges in that new location constituted a substantial village whose residents continually interacted with the growing white settlement just downstream, selling goods and baskets. Aahucoga "frequently associated with the whites and kept himself informed on the events of the day which affected the territory occupied by his tribe," recalled town historian F. D. Hurlburt. Settlers "usually received him with a warm welcome.... They sometimes invited him to remain over night."[165]

Recollections of early, amicable relations may be clouded by sentiment or nostalgia, but the facts suggest that landownership enabled a few communities such as Blue Wing's to sustain Ho-Chunk ways of being in post-removal Wisconsin. Those residing in Blue Wing's settlement clearly did not live in fear of their white neighbors, and Blue Wing himself may well have been welcome in town. Nevertheless, his precise status was unclear. He was neither a citizen nor an immigrant eligible for naturalization. He belonged to a nation that by the 1837 treaty "agree[d] to remove ... west of the Mississippi."[166] Absent the sort of official dispensation provided to Peter Decora, did landownership actually guarantee him a right to remain?

In the world just beyond Blue Wing's settlement, such questions were beginning to resonate more loudly, often in relation to the title Decora had sought: citizen. What precisely that word meant remained as murky as the fact of landownership was clear. Yet in laws and treaties with Native nations in Wisconsin and many other places, governments were beginning to consider the relationship between land and citizenship. Meanwhile, some Native nations pondered how the statuses of citizen and landowner together could create a durable path by which they might remain in their homelands, defy the charge of being "wandering vagabonds," and gain a measure of protection against settler vigilantism. But as some Native people experimented with these new forms over the ensuing decades, other Native people, including Coming Thunder Winneshiek, confronted their costs.

ALLOTMENT AND ITS DISCONTENTS

It was in the summer of 1861, on the lush lands of southern Minnesota, that Coming Thunder Winneshiek reached the end of his rope.
    For two decades, across three successive reservation homelands and the spaces in between, he and the rest of the Ho-Chunk people west of the Mississippi River had tried to live as they preferred. Instead of settling on tracts near Indian agencies and adopting American forms of agriculture, as American authorities wished and planned, they adapted their seasonal round to new environments. In the mid-1850s, Coming Thunder had even helped to engineer a removal the Ho-Chunk actually wanted, in which they swapped undesirable lands in central Minnesota for richer acres at Blue Earth, in the southern part of the territory. But throughout this period, he also watched with alarm as policies of so-called civilization moved from scattershot efforts toward a concerted policy that posed a direct threat to Ho-Chunk ways of being.
    Now that threat had arrived on the Ho-Chunk reservation in the form of surveyors and census takers, whose instruments and notebooks were daggers aimed at the heart of his people's common life. Coming Thunder knew that once the government had precise knowledge of the number and size of Ho-Chunk households, it could begin the process of dividing their common lands into household plots "to be cultivated and used," as the most recent treaty put it, "for their own individual use and benefit."[1] Once their collective

Figure 2.1. Coming Thunder Winneshiek (Wakąjaguga). Photograph likely taken in 1863, during the deportation from Minnesota to Crow Creek. (New York Public Library Digital Collections)

use of land was undermined in this way, it would be a short step to the dissolution of self-government and absorption into the United States. Those fatal transformations—what finally drove Coming Thunder to the breaking point—could be summed up in a handful of words: civilization, allotment, and citizenship.

So Coming Thunder confronted American power directly. The Ho-Chunk were assembled for the distribution of annuities when U.S. officials began moving them into the agency stockade to take a census of the tribe. Coming Thunder and his allies "proceeded among those who were in the yard, vociferating at the top of their voices, and in a short time a large number came pouring out and began to disperse." The census was a failure, and agents held Coming Thunder responsible. Two weeks later, he again defied a representative of American power, the surveyor sent to mark the reservation for division into individual plots. He and his allies blocked the surveyor, "attempted to seize and carry away [his] surveying instruments," told him to leave that part of the reservation, and threatened to "stick" him if he did not.[2]

Coming Thunder's rebellion reflected broader dynamics that had been unfolding over the past several decades on the border of U.S. and Native homelands. Between the 1830s and the 1860s, the U.S. government refined a matrix of policies aimed at transforming Native life. Allotment demanded the alienation of Indigenous people's common land and its transformation into real estate that American settlers could purchase. Detribalization pursued the dissolution of Native governments and the incorporation of Native people under the jurisdiction of the United States. These policies did not supplant efforts to push Native nations farther west, especially into Indian Territory, but they did allow the possibility that the United States could absorb both Native land and Native people. And the most common name for that proposed absorption of people was citizenship.

Citizenship's boundaries and meanings remained unclear throughout the decades preceding the Civil War, but from the first, Native people encountered it as a feature of conquest. Citizenship typically portended the loss of political and territorial sovereignty and the transfer, by one means or another, of a great proportion of tribal land to settlers' hands. From the first treaties that used the word in the 1810s, all the way to the Dawes Act seventy years later, the United States imagined citizenship as a way to individualize Native people, slipping them out of the category of foreign nations that must be dealt with collectively through treaties and transforming them into individuals whose persons were subject to American laws and whose lands were available for sale. From this perspective, citizenship was a mechanism of settler-colonial elimination, part of a repertoire of policies that together sought to replace Indigenous societies with a settler society. The Native history of U.S. citizenship in this era asks us to imagine incorporation into the nation not as a right or privilege but as something to be resisted or managed. It also underlines that one means of incorporation into a nation is, simply put, coercion.[3]

Despite this history, a variety of Native groups experimented with the institutions, laws, and rhetoric of citizenship in order to bolster their claims to ownership, residency, or cohabitation in relation to settler society. In the 1840s and 1850s, as the meanings of citizenship for Native people orbited ever more closely around the policy of allotment and the private ownership of land, some Native nations seized on that policy matrix as a means of slowing or halting their dispossession. Native people's embrace of citizenship was often skeptical or tentative, undertaken in the knowledge that Americans first and foremost coveted their land. Citizenship unfolded in the shadow of conquest, dispossession, and expulsion, and it frequently bore bitter fruit. But it did enable some individuals and communities to set limits on their dispossession and to carve out spaces within settler society that they could continue to fill according to their own values and desires. So even as Coming Thunder defied the forces of "civilization," other Ho-Chunk people were coming to different conclusions.

The questions of land and citizenship that the Ho-Chunk confronted in the 1840s and 1850s took shape in close relation to the great struggle within the United States over the future of slavery in the West. That struggle consumed American politics in the 1850s, creating a deadlock that slowed settlement, railroad development, and the formation of new territories and states. Questions of status and citizenship surged through these territorial conflicts, most famously in *Dred Scott v. Sandford* (1857), in which the Supreme Court held both that African Americans were racially ineligible for national citizenship and that the federal government could not bar slaveholding in its western territories. But other perspectives shaped national politics as well, including the increasingly popular "free soil" claim that slavery should be barred from the West. The stakes of these arguments went back to the republic's founding and raised essential questions about its nature and composition: Was the United States essentially a white republic in which non-whites—both African Americans and the American racial category "Indians"—could hope at best to be inhabitants or denizens? Or could American "civilization" belong to anyone who accepted fundamental premises of landownership, individual rights, and republican government?

Native people approached these conflicts over the future of the West and the nation from a very different standpoint than did "free soil" politicians or proslavery ideologues: their fundamental imperatives were organized around the land they still held, the very same land whose future those other forces were debating. Yet Native people on the borders of U.S. settlement—people such as the Ho-Chunk—could not avoid wrestling and reckoning with the question of citizenship as well, especially as policy makers tied that status ever more tightly to the individual ownership of land.

That Native people should in general be dispossessed of their land was as close to a consensus as Americans came during the Civil War era. After a sharp congressional debate over the Indian Removal Act of 1830, expansionism without regard to the prior claims of Native nations became the dominant strain in U.S. western policy. Debates over Texas annexation, the status of the Mexican Cession, and "Bleeding Kansas" in the mid-1850s concerned the terms of U.S. expansion much more than its wisdom or justice. And throughout the crisis of the Union in the 1850s, both proponents of "Free Soil" and their "Southern Rights" foes understood the acquisition and absorption of Native homelands as essential to their projects, even if they rarely argued about it in those terms.

But how exactly those homelands should be acquired and absorbed, and what should happen to their people, remained complex questions. The U.S. presumptions of cultural superiority and right of conquest help explain the formulation "domestic dependent nations," which the Supreme Court settled on in the 1830s to define the status of Native sovereignties within the claimed borders of the United States. That phrase represented Native sovereignty as conditional and as constrained by U.S. power. Territory occupied by Native people, whether under treaty or beyond treaties' purview, remained "foreign" only so long as the United States did not want it; in that sense, it was not as "foreign" as other territories. Yet if Native territory was only conditionally foreign, Native people as individuals were treated as more "alien" than European immigrants. Their allegiance to their own nations was presumptively definitive, and no national law allowed them to naturalize as citizens. They were even more alien than non-white immigrants such as the Chinese. Although Chinese immigrants were ineligible to naturalize as citizens, the small number of children born to Chinese residents on U.S. soil in this era (like the much larger number of children of other non-naturalized immigrants) could and did claim birthright citizenship. Native Americans could not claim that status as a matter of birth, no matter where they were born.[4]

It was not just that Native people were not birthright citizens. Like African Americans, they featured in American politics and culture as anti-citizens—as potential threats to the peace and security of the legitimate citizenry. And a full understanding of how citizenship evolved in this era requires that we consider the faces of anti-citizenship.

Enslaved people, of course, were not citizens. They were, in the oblique language of the Constitution, "other persons," a domestic population that bore neither rights nor obligations. Enslaved men were not enrolled in state militias; indeed, one of the purposes of those militias was to guard against enslaved people's rebellions. But the stigma of slavery attached to free people of African birth or ancestry as well, and the laws of most states and territories treated free African Americans as an inferior caste. Even where they came closest to formal equality, in Massachusetts, they were barred by law from militia service and in practice from juries and most professions. Roger Taney's opinion in *Dred Scott* in 1857, that as a matter of history "the black man had no rights which the white man was bound to respect," ratified his long-standing view, shared by many Americans, that African Americans generally were a "degraded class."[5] Not every white person fully subscribed to this view, but not even every white abolitionist entirely rejected it.

Rules for the incorporation of African Americans were shaped by the imperatives of maintaining racial slavery, but also by a growing movement among free African Americans and some whites for nonracial freedom and equality. The national citizenship status of free African Americans remained unclear until the end of slavery. It is often assumed that this citizenship was bounded from the beginning by race, but such an interpretation accepts Taney's bad history in the *Dred Scott* decision as fact. In fact, while the early laws of the United States restricted key elements of national belonging such as naturalization and militia service to white persons, neither the Articles of Confederation nor the Constitution contained racial prohibitions on citizenship. And at the very moment that Article IV, Section 2, defined the rights of citizens of any state as having implications for their national status, some states clearly acknowledged African Americans as citizens. Contrary to Taney, in the early years of the republic it was not at all clear where the racial borders of national belonging lay.

Free African Americans responded to this ambiguity by asserting their birthright citizenship, in the hope that it might mitigate some of the threats to their liberties and lives. They often called themselves "colored citizens" in terms that asserted their right to residence on the nation's territory and the right to move freely across it. State citizenship, which some of them clearly possessed, offered a potentially fruitful basis for such claims, since the Constitution seemed to guarantee that as citizens of a state they had those privileges throughout the nation. Free Black sailors, jailed in Southern ports by state laws that treated them as vectors of dangerous liberatory ideas, tried to claimed freedom on this basis. The even graver challenge of the movement called "colonization" evoked similar responses. "Colonization" imagined the ethnic cleansing of the United States by the liberation and deportation of African Americans to Africa or other foreign destinations. Black activists responded by asserting their citizenship and imbuing that status with meaning. David Walker's *Appeal to the Coloured Citizens* (1829) nowhere defined that term, but it put forward a claim, rooted in birthright and sweat equity, to residence and membership in the United States.[6]

Ideas of anti-citizenship sometimes attached to disfavored white people, but not with the same existential implications represented by Negro Seaman laws or "colonization." Many Anglo-Protestants fearfully regarded Catholic immigrants, especially Irish Catholics, as drunken and disease-ridden creatures of a sinister Vatican cabal: a danger to law and order, to the public schools, and to the republic itself. By the 1850s, nativist efforts to restrict their immigration, political power, and cultural impact animated the "Know Nothing" movement, which sought to curtail immigrants' rights and diminish their influence on society. But the anti-citizenship that these immigrants' foes attached to them differed dramatically from that confronting African Americans. Rules for the incorporation of immigrants were shaped by the ceaseless flow of Europeans into (and out of) the United States—a flow that antebellum law generally encouraged. Immigration officials did not doubt that Irish immigrants were white people eligible for naturalization. The Democratic Party recruited them as voters. And as we have seen, even before such immigrants became citizens, many western states allowed them to assume the prerogatives of full membership, including preemption, voting, and militia service.[7]

Native anti-citizenship, by contrast, was rooted in the threat that Indigenous people's territorial sovereignty—indeed their very existence—posed to U.S. territorial ambitions. This was so from the very beginning.[8] The Declaration of Independence indicted the king's Native allies as "merciless Indian savages." As historian Gregory Ablavsky points out, when the American Revolution turned British "subjects" into American "citizens," it conspicuously excluded the Native residents of North America whom the Crown had previously claimed as subjects. In the eighteen treaties between the United States and Native nations before 1800, Ablavsky concludes, the word "citizen" "served as a term of art" to denote non-Native members of the new American polity. Similarly, the first Trade and Intercourse Act (1790), which defined the terms of U.S. authority over relations with Native people, distinguished between two basic categories: "Indians" and "citizens or inhabitants." So from the beginning of the United States, the term "citizen" explicitly counterposed "American" and "Native" in matters such as jurisdiction and trade.[9]

Yet despite the ideology of conquest and the broad view of Native Americans as culturally incompatible, the incorporation of Native people as members of American civic and political life persisted as a possibility. For Thomas Jefferson, "the ultimate point of rest and happiness" for Native people would be "to let our settlements and theirs meet and blend together, to intermix, and to become one people."[10] This vision of peaceable incorporation was of course predicated on Native people's assent to U.S. ideas of what constituted proper "settlement" and their future political status as part of "one people." These ideas certainly demanded an end to Native political sovereignty and probably to most forms of Native culture as well. It was a vision of assimilation and absorption.

A few Native people took this path, a fact obliquely recognized by the early laws of the United States. In 1781, the Articles of Confederation gave the new Congress the power to manage trade and relations with Indians who were "not members of any of the States," an acknowledgment that some states already embraced some people of Native descent as their citizens.[11] The Constitution's exclusion of "Indians not taxed" from enumeration for taxation and representation likewise implied the existence, somewhere, of another group—"Indians taxed"—who did belong within the American economic and political community. The policy of "civilization" pursued by early national administrations contemplated the same possibility. From the dawn of the United States, presidents and congresses allocated funds and sent agents into Indian Country to teach, persuade, and exemplify a new order of things for Native nations.[12] For Jefferson, the endpoint of his imagined happy "blending" was Native people "incorporating themselves with us as citizens of the United States."[13]

Citizenship was a weak and poorly defined category in the early decades of the American republic, less important than other criteria for determining status and membership such as age, gender, race, and able-bodiedness.[14] It remained so for the first two-thirds of the nineteenth century. When Attorney General Edward Bates wrote of the vagueness of citizenship's definition in 1862, he recognized that the history of the United States was saturated with unequal statuses—for African Americans and women, especially—and that "citizen" could not be said to mean more than bare membership in the political community. Whatever the historic connotations of the word, he explained, in practice the status conveyed no equal rights or privileges.[15]

Citizenship existed in an unsettled relationship to property ownership, on the one hand, and state laws of settlement, on the other. States and localities possessed broad latitude, under their "police powers," to "regulate and remove people considered threatening to the public peace," including paupers, vagrants, "vagabonds," fugitive slaves, and others deemed undesirable.[16] But a person's ownership of real property created a strong presumption that they stood outside those proscribed categories. Among the first laws enacted in the Northwest Territory in 1795 was the principle that owning property or paying substantial rent entitled one to a "settlement"—formally recognized residence in the area.[17] Even when states and territories discriminated against non-white residents (as New York did for the right to vote and Michigan did for the right of settlement), those residents could sometimes escape those prohibitions by owning real estate or putting up surety bonds. Landownership continued to serve this legitimating function—not everywhere, and not all the time, but consistently enough to be closely associated with a right to remain in a community or to claim that right against countervailing forces of exclusion and expulsion. And that right to settle and remain orbited closely around the ill-defined term "citizen." Over the next half century, several justices of the Supreme Court went so far as to suggest that if a citizen of one state settled in another with the clear intention of establishing residence, that was enough to define that person as a citizen.[18] So while the exact relationship of land, property, and settlement to citizenship remained unclear during the first half of the nineteenth century, it was impossible to miss the potential of the nexus of property and residence for transforming noncitizens, perhaps even anti-citizens, into citizens.

Before Reconstruction, states determined most questions of membership, inclusion, and exclusion, and it was these policies, as much as or more than federal law, that shaped the lives of Native people within a state's borders. Between the 1820s and the 1860s, those state policies unfolded in terms that ranged from bleak to disastrous. Some states bulldozed over Native sovereignty, secured federal cooperation, and presented Native people with a choice: incorporation as unequal inhabitants or expulsion at the hands of federal troops. On the Pacific coast the terms of conquest could be even harsher and in the 1840s and 1850s sometimes met modern definitions of genocide. Native people living in the western Great Lakes, including the Ho-Chunk, evaluated their own choices and constraints in the light of these fearful possibilities.

As we saw in chapter 1, the Indian Removal Act of 1830 meant that Native people who refused to be removed became subject to state law. To understand the risks inherent in this, it is important to put aside post–Civil War understandings of what civic membership means. Today, under the terms of the Fourteenth Amendment, states may not deny any person in their jurisdiction "equal protection of the laws." But before that amendment defined the rights of persons and citizens in these unequivocal and egalitarian terms, states and territories established a wide array of different legal statuses for their residents. This was especially true with regard to free African Americans. Many slave states' laws restricting Black people's movement and assembly covered free as well as enslaved people. In general, those states did not permit free Black people to give testimony against whites. But states that had abolished slavery also enacted "black laws" that substantially limited free Black people's rights or even formally barred them from entering the state. New York's constitution allowed all adult white men to vote but extended that right only to those Black men who owned substantial real estate. The Michigan Territory, open to white settlers without condition, allowed people of African descent to settle there only if they posted a $500 bond to guarantee their self-support and good behavior. In the late 1840s and early 1850s, Illinois, Indiana, and Iowa all passed laws intended to prevent free Black settlement.[19] Sometimes these laws referred in exclusionary terms to "negroes" and "mulattoes"; at other times, they specified that rights belonged to persons accounted "white."

In the Southern states that pioneered the policy of removal, the laws extending over Native residents were unapologetically inegalitarian. In Georgia and Alabama, Native people who remained resident after removal came under the jurisdiction of courts and tax authorities; creditors could now sue individual Native people for debt. But in neither state did non-whites, including Native people, have the right of testimony against white people. This meant that Native people could not challenge white people's claims against them, which made their property rights and persons vulnerable to every imaginable abuse from squatters, purchasers, lessors, or speculators. Despite this discriminatory denial of rights, state laws simultaneously made Native residents responsible for fulfilling obligations of militia and road service.[20] Incorporation was a form of subjection.

It was only a few years after their deportation to the "Neutral Ground" across the Mississippi River that the Ho-Chunk too faced the threat of state jurisdiction. Policy makers and settlers had set their eyes on Ho-Chunk land as part of the new state of Iowa, and they were determined to clear the area of its Native inhabitants. Federal officials brought Ho-Chunk leaders to Washington in 1846—the first time since the disastrous 1837 negotiations—to explain that the Ho-Chunk people could not stay where they were. Once the Neutral Ground became part of Iowa, officials warned, that state would extend its laws over Ho-Chunk lands and lives, and after that, "your Great Father will not have it in his power to protect you." Like Cherokees in Georgia or Choctaws in Mississippi, they would be at the jurisdictional mercy of settler society. If they refused, or if they continued to cross the Mississippi back into Wisconsin, they risked something worse than law: "The militia has to be called out, and troubles come heavily upon you."[21]

Against the threats of subordination and violence, Ho-Chunk leaders challenged the government's claim to have already settled the matter. "The Great Spirit placed the Winnebago in a large fine country," Little Hill explained; "we much fear we have offended the Great Spirit in giving up as much of the good country he gave us as we have already given to our Great Father, and now, we do not wish to ... part with any more." The Neutral Ground, adjacent to and closely resembling parts of their homeland, was in effect an extension of that gift of the Great Spirit. They also reiterated their rejection of the 1837 treaty. "We did not cede away the country where we now live," one explained. "It was ours—we did not give up our title, or sell to our Great Father any right to it." U.S. negotiators brushed their objections aside, but down to the moment of signing the Treaty of 1846, the Ho-Chunk delegates remained vigilant. "We hope the paper which we now sign will not be changed like the last one was," admonished Little De Korrie.[22]

They did not go quietly. In 1848 U.S. troops began rounding up Ho-Chunk bands for a march to the land the government had assigned them at the headwaters of the Mississippi River, at a place called Long Prairie. Coming Thunder and other leaders tried a variety of tactics to delay or halt this deportation. At several moments, Ho-Chunk fighters dressed for war. Before the march began, one group rode furiously around the agency house in the Neutral Ground. Later, a larger party charged toward U.S. troops who had been sent to keep the people moving up the Mississippi River. Meanwhile, Coming Thunder conducted secret diplomacy with his cousin, the Mdewakanton Dakota leader Wapasha. As Coming Thunder and his brother Short Wing Winneshiek told the story for decades to come, he purchased land from Wapasha for a new Ho-Chunk home—a substantial swath on the west bank of the Mississippi near today's Winona, Minnesota, just across the Mississippi River from their ancestral homeland. These efforts failed in the face of U.S. infantry and cannon. Officials imprisoned Coming Thunder at Fort Snelling until he agreed to stop impeding the removal. By late summer 1848, about 1,500 Ho-Chunk people found themselves in the unfamiliar woods and prairies of their new home.[23]

Even as the United States declared victory, however, the Ho-Chunk pursued their most familiar strategy: they slipped out from under American eyes and returned to the landscapes they cherished. During the march, and especially during the Ho-Chunk fighters' military maneuvers (which may have been intended as distractions), hundreds of people fled for destinations near and far. Over the next few years, Ho-Chunk bands could be found living among Sauk, Meskwaki, Potawatomi, Otoe, Iowa, and Omaha communities in Iowa and the Minnesota Territory and as far away as the Great Nemaha Agency, across the Missouri River in Indian Territory.[24] Many more Ho-Chunk returned to Wisconsin as part-time or permanent inhabitants. By the time the party of deported Ho-Chunks reached Long Prairie, they numbered fewer than a thousand, far less than half the total population.[25]

If the only choice was between dispossession and incorporation under discriminatory state laws, that would have been bad enough, but looming over

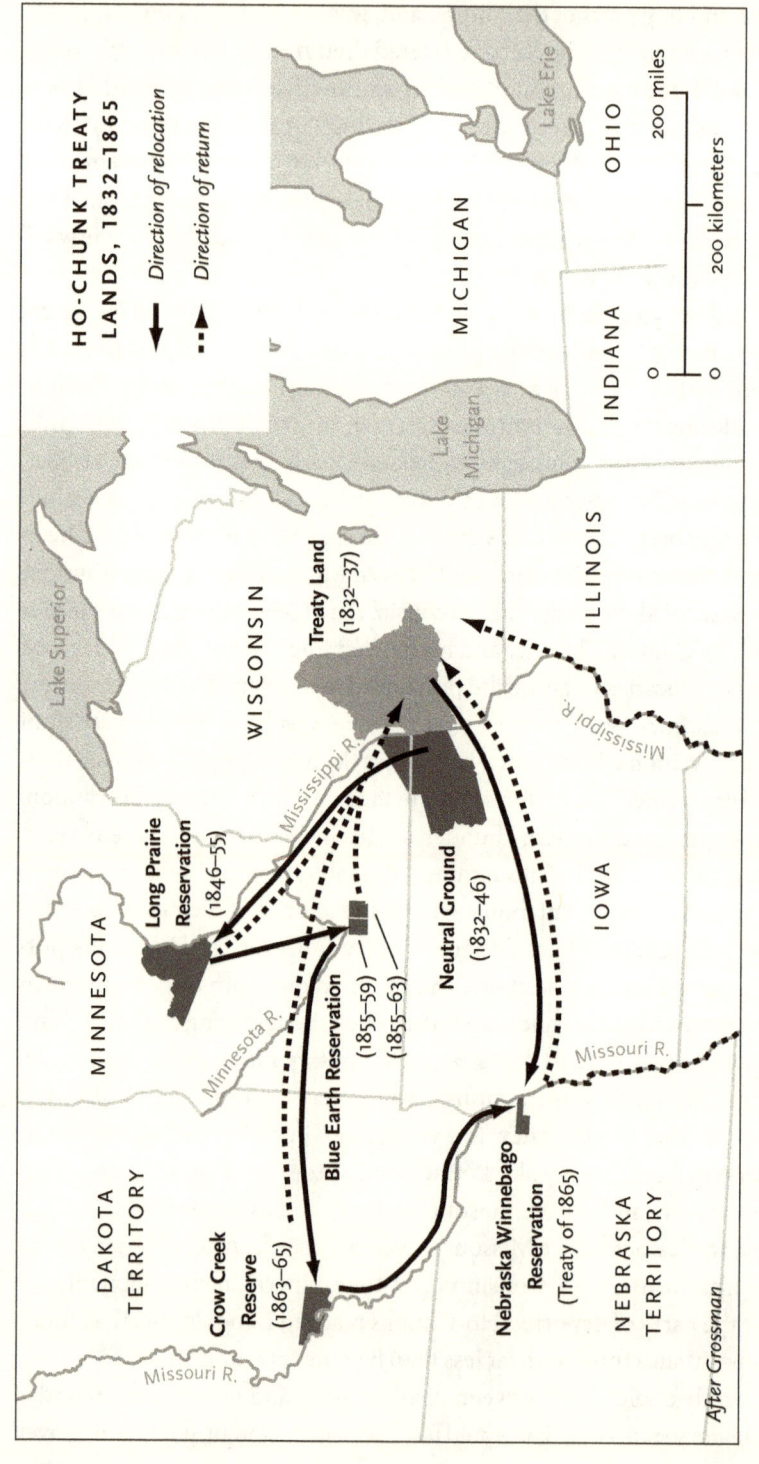

Map. 2.1

every option was the murderously worse possibility of finding oneself wholly outside the law and at the mercy of settler society. In the Oregon Territory, the settler conquest of the Willamette Valley during the mid-1840s killed most of the region's Kalapuya, Molala, Clackamas, and Chinook people and relegated many of the rest to seasonal wage labor or worse.[26] California's horror soon unfolded on an even wider scale. "We desire only a white population," declared a settler newspaper in 1848; "even the Indians amongst us, as far as we have seen, are more of a nuisance than a benefit to the country; we would like to get rid of them."[27] Over the next two decades, a flood of immigrants from all over the world devastated California's Native communities. In the early 1850s U.S. envoys and Native communities negotiated treaties that might have provided some protection against this onslaught, but eighteen of those treaties languished in the Senate, which not only failed to ratify them but kept their existence a secret. The consequences were shattering. Before the gold rush, approximately 150,000 Native people lived in California. By 1865, fewer than 34,000 remained. Historian Benjamin Madley has shown that the campaign against California's Indians in these decades—well-organized campaigns of murder of 10,000 or more by the California Volunteers, subsidized with federal dollars—meets modern definitions of genocide.[28]

These brutal continental contexts of exile, subordination, and extermination help explain why some Native people pursued various forms of incorporation that recognized at least some rights: any tool that might help Native communities avoid these horrors was worth considering. Thousands of Choctaws, for example, remained on allotments and other lands within Mississippi. There they retained their language and identity for generations to come, carving out a community life despite their inferior legal status.[29] Landownership under the terms of state incorporation might have been a frail reed, but it did offer some people an alternative to deportation in the 1830s through the 1850s. For some Native people, this was the least bad option available.

The history of Native persistence and incorporation in the Northwest differed in important ways from the situation faced by Indigenous people in the South. In the South, statesmen and powerful economic interests focused relentlessly on the large-scale cultivation of cotton, sugar, and other crops by enslaved labor. Nothing was more important to this system of production than maintaining control over the lives and labors of enslaved people, who constituted a majority of the population in the plantation belt and a substantial minority elsewhere. This political order could not tolerate zones beyond its authority where fugitives could find respite or where populations who were unconcerned with the fate of slavery could grow.

In the Northwest, by contrast, settlers pursued a variety of economic activities, some demanding Native people's expulsion but others relying on their presence. This allowed larger groups of Native people to remain in the areas not (yet) taken up by settler farming or extractive industries. The long history of trade and interaction in the Great Lakes also left a legacy of incorporation. Native people who appeared to embody aspects of American "civilization"— both Native nations migrating from the east and the region's own populations of mixed descent—could sometimes lay claim not only to the bare right to remain but to a degree of equality under state law.[30] From at least the early 1830s, some Native communities in the Northwest sought to avoid expulsion by representing themselves as Christian, orderly, property-owning, and in other respects "civilized." A group of Catholic Potawatomis successfully made this claim in the negotiations around the 1833 Treaty of Chicago. They have ever since been known after their leader, Leopold Pokagon, as Pokégnek Bodéwadmik (the Pokagon Band of Potawatomi Indians). But the Pokagon people's acceptance as residents of Michigan was not citizenship: their permission to stay was contingent on their move to lands farther north on the territory's lower peninsula.[31]

The story of Native U.S. citizenship in the Northwest began with two groups of "New York Indians," the Brothertown and Stockbridge-Munsee peoples. Both groups had adopted Christianity a century earlier in their New England homelands, and both had experienced generations of conquest and expulsion despite their adoption of some of the forms of American life. In the eighteenth century, settlers had pressed them westward into New York; in the early nineteenth century they were driven west again, this time to the far shore of Lake Michigan. These two nations, along with a party of Oneida people also displaced from New York State, settled in what is now northeastern Wisconsin in the 1820s and early 1830s. There, they lived in close and sometimes uncomfortable relation with Menominee, Ho-Chunk, and other Indigenous residents, some of whom regarded them as settlers and interlopers.[32]

In their efforts to establish a durable claim to their new homes, some leaders of these nations aligned themselves with the United States, its settlers, and its practices. In the 1827 "Winnebago War," for example, some Stockbridge and Oneida formed a "New York Indian Militia" to serve with the U.S. forces. But as settlers poured into the Wisconsin Territory in the 1830s, they again feared for their future. In the 1830s, the Brothertowns sought to forestall calls for their deportation by asking to become U.S. citizens and therefore legitimate permanent residents of the Wisconsin Territory. Brothertown leader Thomas Commuck articulated this in the language of "civilization" and race that he hoped settler authorities would approve of: he argued that his people could easily be incorporated into the settler order; "having, all their ways, manner of living, appearance in dress, and speech (not having spoken or known anything of their own tongue for one hundred years)," he explained, they had "become perfectly assimilated to their white brethren."[33] In 1839, with the assent of territorial officials, the Brothertown people became U.S. citizens by an act of Congress.

The Stockbridge-Munsee people soon followed. Wisconsin's territorial governor, James Doty, endorsed their bid for citizenship in 1843 in language similar to Commuck's description of his own people. "Their advances in civilization have gradually influenced them to abandon the hunter life," he explained, and "to adopt fixed places of abode, acquire individual property, cultivate the earth, and assume most of those habits and customs, amongst themselves, which go to distinguish the savage and nomadic life from that of educated and civilized man."[34] In an 1843 act, Congress also recognized the Stockbridge-Munsee people as U.S. citizens, divided their common land into family parcels, extended the jurisdiction of the United States and the Wisconsin Territory over them, and abrogated "their rights as a tribe or nation."[35]

Here, citizenship came at the cost of remaining an independent people in the eyes of the United States. This painful bargain reflected some leaders' assessment of the dangers confronting them, which were in the end not so different from those facing the Cherokee and others in the Southeast. Thomas Commuck himself described citizenship as a last-ditch strategy: "Having no laws which they could enforce, for the protection of their lives and property ... they concluded to petition Congress for citizenship."[36] The Brothertown and Stockbridge-Munsee understood U.S. citizenship first and foremost as a defense against state and individual encroachments.[37]

Other groups in the Northwest were coming to similar conclusions. In the same year that the United States recognized the Stockbridge-Munsee as citizens, the Little Traverse Odawa asked the Michigan legislature to help them secure that status. Soon after, when Michigan's 1850 constitution granted the vote to male "inhabitants of Indian descent" who were "native to the United States and not a member of a tribe," Andrew Blackbird and other English-speaking Odawa representatives petitioned the state government to recognize them as "common citizens of the state of Michigan, to have all the rights and privileges of American citizenship"—chiefly, to be safe in their property and immune to removal. The legislature agreed, petitioning the U.S.

Congress to enable the "civil, well disposed, peaceable, and orderly" Odawa and Ojibwe among them to "remain in Michigan to become civilized and share with us in our social, political, and religious privileges."[38]

Although these Native communities sought citizenship as a bulwark against deportation and the outright theft of their lands, citizenship also led to significant land loss. In the Stockbridge-Munsee case, the transformation of their commonly held land into private parcels, combined with the end of their treaty relationship with the United States, meant that they could be taxed, foreclosed on, and sued by Americans. At the same time, as historian David Silverman shows, the U.S. government refused to pay the Stockbridge the money to which they were entitled "because it held that, as Indians, they would squander these funds." Impoverished people sometimes had no choice but to sell their now-private holdings to white settlers. The consequences, there and elsewhere, were predictable: in Michigan, within twenty years of the beginning of allotments, less than a tenth of all allotted lands remained in Native people's possession.[39] Across the region, allotment was followed sooner or later by significant alienation of land to settlers.

The costs of citizenship proved to be so high that, in very short order, both the Brothertown and Stockbridge people sought to roll it back. A majority of the Stockbridge-Munsee people rebelled against a citizenship that left them, in the words of anti-citizenship leader John W. Quinney, "a weak and dependent band, half '*citizens*,' and half '*Indians*.'"[40] In 1846, the anti-citizenship forces won a partial reversal of the 1843 act and regained federal recognition as a Native nation. By the 1850s, many Brothertown people reached the same dispiriting conclusion about citizenship and allotment, but their efforts to reverse the law making them citizens were not successful. Odawa and Ojibwe people in the region, paying attention to these dynamics, also began to seek collective or individual title to land without U.S. citizenship.[41]

But these experiments with Native incorporation as citizens left durable traces. As the states and territories of the Northwest wrote or rewrote constitutions during the 1840s and 1850s, a new language emerged to define the parameters of civic inclusion: whether people were "civilized" or evidenced "the habits and customs of civilization." Wisconsin's 1848 constitution enfranchised "civilized persons of Indian descent not members of any tribe," and similar language shortly followed in the constitutions of Michigan and the Minnesota Territory.[42] Minnesota's adoption of similar constitutional language followed the petitions of the Hazelton community, a Christian group of Dakotas, who at that state's first constitutional convention sought to be recognized as state citizens on the basis of their adoption of a wide range of

"American" practices and customs: republican government, education, labor, literacy in English, and "the dress and habits of civilized men."[43]

The imprecise criterion "civilized" allowed settler communities great latitude in determining which Native people belonged within the civic body. In particular, by including only those who were "not members of any tribe," these provisions mainly embraced people of mixed descent, often members of long-standing trading families. These provisions sometimes made an explicit distinction between mixed-descent people, whom lawmakers assumed could function well in American contexts, and Native people of unmixed descent, whose "civilization" required further scrutiny. Minnesota, for example, enfranchised Native men of mixed descent who "adopted the habits and customs of civilization," but it required men of unmixed Native descent to provide an additional certificate from a district court attesting to their fitness for citizenship.[44]

The constitutional recognition of some Native people as part of a state's civic body, subject to its laws, remained an important way of getting control of their land. Nowhere was this clearer than in Wisconsin's 1848 constitution, which civilly enfranchised all Native people whom Congress had at any time declared citizens. This provision responded to the recent reversal of Stockbridge-Munsee U.S. citizenship, which cast doubt over many land sales and over the ability of settlers to bring their claims to those lands to court. By declaring anyone who had ever been a U.S. citizen subject to state law, Wisconsin's constitution effectively circumvented the Stockbridge-Munsee people's reacquisition of federal recognition and returned legal disputes over earlier sales of Stockbridge-Munsee lands to the jurisdiction of the state courts. The point, historian James Oberly explains, was to ensure that these Indians could sue, be sued, and be held responsible for contracts they undertook—that is, that they could not reassert collective title over land they had sold or lost while they were U.S. citizens.[45]

Native citizenship in the Northwest could also have concrete political effects. Between the late 1840s and the early 1860s, historian Jameson Sweet has demonstrated, men of mixed ancestry who met the criteria for enfranchisement in the constitutions of Wisconsin and Minnesota voted in state and territorial elections. At least five men of Native descent, three of them Brothertown, sat in the Wisconsin legislature, and at least nine were elected to the Minnesota legislature.[46] "Local whites conflated whiteness with citizenship and the concept of being 'civilized,'" Sweet argues, "and politicians exploited the loyalty of mixed-ancestry Indians to the Democratic Party." The result was that these groups were able to exert political force.[47]

On the other side of the nation's partisan divide, however, the "civilization" that enfranchised these men could seem fraudulent. In 1857, Amos Coggswell, a Republican delegate to the Minnesota Territory's constitutional convention, complained about the "grand frauds" Democrats perpetrated at the ballot box under the standard of "civilization," of "putting a coat upon one Indian, and when he has voted, stripping it off and putting it on another, and thus running them up to the poll by hundreds."[48] Six months later, when Minnesota's petition for statehood reached Congress, U.S. senator Henry Wilson—a radical Republican from Massachusetts and staunch advocate of equal rights for African Americans—elaborated on this story to reach a partisan conclusion: "There was near by the place of voting a large collection of Indians, in their native habits and costumes." A Democratic operative "robed" a few of them in "articles of apparel that civilized men wear," marched them to the polls, then returned and repeated the operation until "a very large Indian vote was taken." These votes, asserted Wilson, made up the margin of victory by which the Democrats had won the territorial election.[49] This story continued to circulate a half century as a tale of "half-breed" men arriving in a "swarm," with a single pair of pants among them: "One would don the trousers and go out and vote, and, soon coming back, passed the garment to the next man, while he resumed the breech clout [sic] and blanket."[50]

Fractional truth or partisan fiction, the parable of the pants expressed a deeper perplexity for American officials: how to determine when people had crossed the line between "Indian" and something else—"civilized," or "citizen," or close enough to count.[51] During the 1850s, the stakes of this question became ever greater. In 1849, federal oversight of Indian Affairs moved from the War Department to the new Department of the Interior, whose officials began to focus more stringently on "civilization" as a positive good and a practical necessity. Many officials believed that if U.S. policy failed to draw Native people to lives as individual property owners, they either would be exterminated (as was taking place on the West Coast) or would simply die out under the corrosive forces of white settlement.

As an alternative, U.S. officials imagined the post-removal Indian future as a slow but steady march toward their own idealized vision of themselves—an ideal captured by the word "citizen." Officials imagined a long process—"a work of time," the commissioner of Indian Affairs wrote in 1851. It would begin in pupilage and compulsion, with Indians "compelled by sheer necessity to resort to agricultural labor or starve," but it would lead finally to Native people's "incorporation into the great body of our citizen population."[52] This was the policy that, a decade later, brought Coming Thunder's confrontation with the Americans.

The Ho-Chunk people living under the eyes of Indian agents west of the Mississippi River understood what the policy of "civilization" intended, but they regarded it as misguided. Throughout the years on the Neutral Ground and well into their time in Minnesota in the late 1840s and 1850s, they sometimes ignored federal plans, sometimes protested them, and sometimes made use of their resources without embracing their underlying intentions. But they could not miss the government's ambitions to take control of their resources, redirect their activities, and remake them in the image of American "civilization."

The federal government most clearly explained the components of "civilization" in the provisions it inserted into its treaties with the Ho-Chunk. These provided funds for teachers, farmers, and blacksmiths and spoke with remarkable specificity about the hope to teach Ho-Chunk children "reading, writing, arithmetic, gardening, agriculture, carding, spinning, weaving, and sewing." American plans particularly emphasized teaching the Ho-Chunk "agriculture," ignoring the obvious fact, constantly noted in official reports, that they were ardent cultivators of corn.[53] Treaties and exchanges between agents, superintendents, and other officials clarified what made a household "civilized," including a new gendered division of labor that moved men into the fields and women out of them; and attention to culturally specific forms of women's home production—carding, spinning, weaving, and sewing—revealed these officials' apparent unawareness that women already bore responsibility for a family's clothing.[54]

From the beginning, most Ho-Chunks regarded the agency schools with skepticism or outright hostility. Band leaders petitioning the government in 1835 dismissed the project; "we are not capable of profiting by it," said Big Mouth, "and do not wish it."[55] When the first school opened in the Neutral Ground, Agent David Lowry groused that "the whole tribe declared in opposition to it, refusing to send a single child."[56] Those who did ultimately enroll their children did not seem to have done so out of a desire for cultural transformation, Lowry acknowledged, but because "they can thereby get their children clothed and fed."[57] In 1845, twenty-seven leaders including Coming Thunder protested the use of their annuity money on plans of education that, in their view, corrupted their children. "We do not wish to be compelled to have our children taught different from what we ourselves believe to be right," they told their interpreters.⁵⁸ Agents optimistically described Ho-Chunks who took up residence near their agencies as the "school band," but this expressed a wish more than a reality.⁵⁹ The largest part of the "school band," led by Little Hill, apparently included many settled farming households who sent most of their children to school. But most other bands who took up what agents recognized as "agriculture" shunned the school. One American observer claimed in 1851 that more than half of Coming Thunder's band had become American-style farmers, yet he reported that only three of the group's children attended the school.⁶⁰

Nowhere was the collective lack of interest in the school clearer than in the failure of English-language education. English was a new and unfamiliar language in the treaty era. Indeed, well into the 1830s negotiations between the Ho-Chunk and the United States had to be conducted with two translators—one from Ho-Chunk to French and another from French to English.⁶¹ Over the next decades, a small number of families, mainly of mixed Ho-Chunk and European descent, sent their children to school regularly. Some became conversant in English, and a few became skilled interpreters. But even in the 1840s, the regional superintendent of Indian Affairs claimed that "there are not now in the tribe ten Indians who can read, write, and speak the English language."⁶²

The "civilization" that agents most desired was the adoption of American habits of settlement and agriculture, and here the Ho-Chunk generally refused to comply. Agents developed elaborate plans for their settlement at Long Prairie, depicting neat wooden houses and carefully demarcated fields clustered around the agency house.⁶³ But while some bands initially located themselves near the agency, most did not. Instead, they sought out the landscapes and resources that would allow them to recreate their seasonal itinerary. A majority of the Ho-Chunk people at Long Prairie encamped themselves miles away from the agency on the banks of the Mississippi River, which continued to serve them both as a resource and as a highway to more familiar environments, including Wisconsin. Within a few years, in fact, most of the Ho-Chunk nominally living at Long Prairie spent much of the year entirely outside the reservation. Even the families of the "school band" moved their settlements seasonally, as far as fifty miles away during the winter hunt.⁶⁴ A dispirited agent counted only 1,480 people at Long Prairie, and he admitted that even these mostly spent the winter months on land south of the reservation. In 1853 a government surveyor met Coming Thunder himself, the U.S.-recognized "principal chief," far outside the reservation with a large hunting party.⁶⁵

Faced with the Ho-Chunk people's refusal to remain where they had been placed, the government bent. Officials knew that any attempt to restrain

Ho-Chunk migrations with soldiers would be both expensive and counterproductive; Ho-Chunk residents knew the country better than their pursuers and would "break and scatter" if confronted with troops.[66] And as it was, they were well beyond the oversight and control of their nominal authorities. "Unless they are satisfied with a new country, their tribe will be broken in fragments and they become mere wanderers and vagabonds," explained a U.S. official. "This we suppose the govt will seek earnestly to avoid."[67] So within five years of the Ho-Chunk people's arrival at Long Prairie, the U.S. and the Ho-Chunk began negotiating to exchange that tract for lands where the Ho-Chunk would be satisfied to remain.[68] In the end, after years of negotiation and a failed treaty in 1853, the Ho-Chunk traded Long Prairie for 200,000 acres on the Blue Earth River in south-central Minnesota—a region whose topography, climate, and resources closely resembled their homeland.[69] They seemed to have won a great victory over the inconstant Goliath.

But the Treaty of 1855 placed the Ho-Chunk squarely in the path of that decade's policy locomotive. The man with whom they negotiated this treaty, Commissioner of Indian Affairs George Washington Manypenny, sought to transform Indian policy by setting Native nations on a swift and managed course toward allotment, incorporation, and cultural transformation. He was convinced that Native people needed to be permanently settled, not constantly removed; that annuities should not be paid in cash, which encouraged Native autonomy and debt, but in goods and stock that would encourage Native people to adopt sedentary lifestyles; and, above all, that Native people's land should be allotted as individual landholdings. All of this, he believed, should be overseen from Washington, with the places of resettlement, the pace of allotment, and even the particular goods distributed determined by the government. Manypenny concluded more than fifty treaties between 1853 and 1857, and most reflected variations on these themes.[70]

Manypenny and other federal officials represented the transformation of tribal people into allotted citizens as both progressive and essential, but it was also a means to another end. Historian Joshua Catalano concludes that one of Manypenny's main objectives was "to secure a solid legal footing for future American encroachment."[71] Allotment and citizenship helped accomplish that objective by diminishing or eliminating the territorial and political obstacles represented by Native people's collective landownership and sovereignty.

The Treaty of 1855 won the Ho-Chunk a new home at Blue Earth, but it also marked a profound shift in the exercise of federal power over Ho-Chunk resources. Manypenny explained this to the Ho-Chunk negotiators in blunt and uncompromising language: the cost of their new home would be submission to his vision of "civilization." "If we exchange countries," he lectured, "you will have to quit gambling, quit drinking, and get your women to live in houses like white people while the men do the work. I will insist upon this being a part of your bargain."[72] He achieved this in a provision that gave federal officials the power to spend much of the tribe's annuity, with the goal of their "advancement in civilization."[73]

Control over annuities allowed agents to pursue a long-sought goal: replacing Ho-Chunk practices of leadership and governance with forms that Americans could better understand and control. Officials had long resented the fact that the Ho-Chunk organized themselves in autonomous bands, not as a unitary "tribe" with a single "chief." "They have no principal chief or influential man among them," officials complained. "Each separate village or lodge has, however, one man whom they call chief, who does not pretend to exercise any authority or influence beyond the few families who reside with him."[74] Authority in Ho-Chunk society flowed upward as much as downward, and leaders relied both on personal authority and on the maintenance of consensus. From American perspectives, this seemed a very weak form of leadership. As early as 1840, the U.S. agent described them as "in a very disorganized state, without government, among themselves."[75] "Being much divided," another official concluded, they "are unable to act collectively."[76]

Officials showed no sign at all that they understood Ho-Chunk clan organization, including the distinctions among Thunder, Eagle, Bear, Water Spirit, and the eight other clans that apportioned social and political responsibilities across the nation. Paying as little attention as they did to Ho-Chunk marriage and kinship, they would not have noticed the prohibition on marrying within a clan. Caring as little as they did about who signed treaties, they ignored the protests of the 1837 delegation that they were mainly not Huuc (Bear) clan and therefore not empowered to negotiate about matters of land.

American officials yearned for a clearer line of authority and hoped to "establish in the hands of one or two chiefs a portion of influence over the nation."[77] U.S. officials sometimes named a particular band leader the "principal chief" of the nation, a status they assigned to Coming Thunder in the 1840s. Petitions from the 1840s identify Coming Thunder as "principal chief," and once in the 1850s even as "president" of the tribe.[78] Yet he was simultaneously the leader of the resistant diplomacy that led to the clash with U.S. troops during the removal of 1848, which culminated in his arrest and imprisonment at Fort Snelling. Despite this, he remained "principal chief" in American eyes for another decade, through the years at Long Prairie and the first four years at Blue Earth.

Authorities used their control of the distribution of annuity payments to reward or punish particular band leaders. At Long Prairie, Jonathan Fletcher refused to give provisions to band leaders he deemed "intemperate" or otherwise unacceptable. He insisted his efforts were nothing but "a judicious interference ... in the tribal arrangements of the Indians" and that he did not "make or break" chiefs. But he simply "refused to transact business" with one man and put another "in charge of the band."[79] The Treaty of 1855 allowed Fletcher to insert himself even further into Ho-Chunk life. To reduce the power and status of band leaders, he distributed provisions directly to the heads of families, and he asked the regional superintendent to withhold part of the salaries of band leaders whom Fletcher believed sanctioned violence or improper activity.[80]

Ho-Chunk leaders furiously protested these intrusions. In a petition to President Franklin Pierce, they charged Fletcher with causing "distress, misery, suffering, and starvation" and denounced his peremptory removal of a half-dozen band leaders. To be a band leader was "a right and an honor which have been conferred upon me by my Nation," Little Hill explained.[81] But Fletcher continued to assert control over leadership. He disparaged another band leader, Little Priest, as a "a lawless and reckless character" and sought to strip him of his "chieftainship."[82] Within a few years, however, Little Priest was "elevated" again. Perhaps these roles were not as fully within American power to give or withhold as Fletcher claimed.

The Ho-Chunk at Blue Earth also faced renewed threats from settlers. During the late 1850s, the bountiful woods, streams, and meadows around Blue Earth drew an ever-increasing flood of white settlers, and the American grid again began to close in on Ho-Chunk sovereignty. Relations with the growing settler population in the region were sour from the beginning: Ho-Chunks and settlers each suspected the other of stealing resources and goods, settlers around Blue Earth began petitioning to have the Ho-Chunk expelled, and interactions could quickly turn violent.[83] Fletcher tried to adjudicate disputes, but it was a rough justice that satisfied neither aggrieved Ho-Chunks nor their new neighbors.[84]

Agents and the settler state worked to bring the Ho-Chunk under American jurisdiction. By 1856, Fletcher achieved a long-standing wish, compelling Ho-Chunk leaders to adopt "a code of laws ... for the protection of their persons and property, and for the punishment of crimes."[85] Meanwhile, settlers and their governments took aim at Ho-Chunk autonomy. Minnesota's very first state legislative session in 1858 targeted Ho-Chunk and Dakota movement beyond the borders of their lands: it made Native people subject to state law for crimes they committed off their reserves; more, it required them to obtain "passports" from military or Indian officials in order to travel beyond those reserves and empowered sheriffs and other local officials to remove them by force if necessary.[86] The imposition of state authority over their individual lives and collective self-government, part of the threat that had driven them from the Neutral Ground a decade earlier, had followed them to their new home.

In 1858, Regional Superintendent of Indian Affairs William Cullen envisioned allotment as a path to racial uplift for the Ho-Chunk, Dakota, and Ojibwe people in his charge. Property ownership would speed the work of their "civilization." It would "individualize and bring to them the comforts and permanence of civilized life, and preserve them in their property and rights" and would ease their "gradual incorporation into the habits and systems of government of those who hold to them now the position of a dominant race." Their growing commitment to individual rights, private property, and republican self-government would "eventually entitle them to the rights and privileges of a condition of actual citizenship."[87] How long that road would be and how fast a people could move along it remained uncertain, and Cullen's "eventually" and "actual" highlighted a deep and continuing hesitation about incorporation of Native people as citizens.

The vision of that "dominant race" incorporating Native Americans ("eventually") as citizens could not take place in a policy vacuum: it inevitably became entangled with the parallel but fundamentally unlike question of the status of free African Americans. Although the two questions emerged from distant quarters of American life, and with vastly different implications in national politics, lawmakers and jurists understood that they could not raise one question of citizenship without dealing with the other. In the abstract, the issue might seem simple: either the United States was a white republic, in which neither Native people nor African Americans could be coequal members, or it was not. But in practice the questions of Native and African American citizenship arose from disparate historical dynamics, and they were not susceptible to the same resolution. In the mid-1850s, just as Manypenny promulgated his treaties of allotment, civilization, and citizenship, and Cullen imagined the Ho-Chunk in "a condition of actual citizenship," two much more famous American officials were forced to deal with questions of Native citizenship in the context of a bitter national struggle over African American citizenship.

The first of these cases was rooted in the complex social world of the Native Northwest, and it posed thorny questions about the relationship among allotment, race, and citizenship. In 1856, Attorney General of the United States Caleb Cushing was asked to decide whether an Ojibwe man of mixed descent, a person entitled to an allotment under the 1854 Treaty with the Chippewas of Lake Superior, could use the Pre-emption Act of 1841 to take that allotment on land that he had already occupied and improved. This man, though Cushing did not refer to him by name, was Vincent Roy, an interpreter and trader whom anthropologist Larry Nesper has carefully situated in a complex Ojibwe and American world. The terms of the 1841 law extended the right of preemption to U.S. citizens and to eligible aliens who had declared their intention to naturalize. Did Roy meet those criteria?[88]

As Cushing pondered this matter, he knew that the stakes surrounding questions of non-white people's national citizenship were unusually high. At that exact moment, the Supreme Court was considering the case of *Dred Scott v. Sandford*, in which an enslaved Black man claimed freedom on the basis of his long residence in Illinois and the Wisconsin Territory, both of whose laws forbade slavery. Scott's suit hinged in part on a question of citizenship: if he were not a U.S. citizen, he would lack standing in federal court. If the court ruled that Dred Scott had standing to sue for his freedom in federal court, and especially if it ruled in favor of his freedom, slavery would be significantly weakened. On the other hand, to the extent the court ruled against Scott's claims, it would limit abolitionists' ability to challenge slavery in legislatures and courts.

Cushing's ruling on Roy's claim, which came before the Supreme Court issued its ruling in *Dred Scott*, was careful not to get out ahead of whatever the Supreme Court might say. He explicitly refused to consider what he called the "serious question of the constitutional *status*, relatively to the question of citizenship, of the African race in the United States." But he was unequivocal about the particular question before him. As a Native person, Cushing ruled, Roy was both jurisdictionally and racially ineligible to preempt land. First, the man was not a natural-born citizen. Echoing the Supreme Court's ruling that declared Native sovereignties "domestic dependent nations," Cushing argued that Native people were "in our allegiance" as "domestic subjects of this Government," "denizens," or "domestic aliens." But their nations, however "dependent," were sovereignties, and that meant that their members stood outside U.S. jurisdiction. Whether Roy was considered a citizen of his state was irrelevant: Wisconsin, Michigan, or Minnesota might recognize him as a citizen or voter, but the possession of state citizenship did not by itself convey U.S. citizenship.[89] Finally, since Roy was of Native descent—and therefore not a "free white person"—he was not eligible to naturalize as a citizen, and he could therefore not claim preemption rights on the basis of the intent to naturalize.

Cushing's opinion in Roy's case anticipated many of *Dred Scott*'s rulings about the racial limits of citizenship and the irrelevance of state citizenship to U.S. citizenship. In a vote of 7–2, the Supreme Court held that by virtue of his status as "a negro," the enslaved man Dred Scott could not be a U.S. citizen, and that African Americans by definition lacked standing to sue in federal court. It ruled, further, that Congress lacked the power to bar slavery from federal territories, as it had done in the Missouri Compromise, and that residence in a free state or territory did not liberate a person from slavery. It was a mighty blow against the vision of a "free soil" republic and to the fast-growing Northern political movement built upon it, the Republican Party.[90]

Chief Justice Taney was a former slaveholder from Maryland and Attorney General Cushing the scion of an old Massachusetts family, but as conservative Democrats, nationalists, and anti-abolitionists they shared the conviction that African Americans had no place in the nation's civic life. Although the *Dred Scott* decision was deeply unpopular in Cushing's home state, he applauded it and gave public speeches defending the decision and its author. In one of these, Cushing even extended Taney's dictum that at the founding "the black man had no rights which the white man was bound to respect." At the moment that Americans declared independence and established a constitution, Cushing declared, "The men of European race,—the white men as distinguished from the red men and the black men,—constituted the political society, of which they alone were coequal members,—while the Indians and Africans were not citizens, but subjects."[91]

Cushing spoke in bluntly white nationalist terms, but he knew, just as Taney did, that the question of Native citizenship could not be so simply settled. In fact, Taney was at pains in *Dred Scott* to distinguish the intrinsic ineligibility of African Americans from the situation of Native Americans, who he wrote first entered into relation with the United States as "free and independent people."[92] Cushing's 1856 opinion similarly revealed a tolerance for ambiguity about Native citizenship that was absent from his post–*Dred Scott* defense of Taney. After concluding that Roy was ineligible to preempt land, Cushing conceded that when such people took up allotments, it implied that they "intended thereafter to quit the tribe, with its community of rights, and become citizens."[93] This might seem to make Roy a citizen-in-waiting, analogous to an eligible alien who had declared his intent to naturalize. However, Cushing cautioned, Roy took up his allotment under the terms of a treaty, and the United States made treaties with "Indians." Holding land under the terms of a treaty meant that Roy "had not yet passed the line between the aboriginal and *the civilized or citizen* status."[94] Nevertheless, the implication was plain: Native people, unlike African Americans, were not inherently ineligible. They might under some circumstances become citizens of the United States.

Approached purely through the lens of the nation's racial hierarchy, the distinction that Cushing and Taney made is hard to interpret. A common view of the Jacksonian Democratic Party—the party to which both Taney and Cushing belonged—depicts it as the party of the white republic, equally and unequivocally hostile to the aspirations of African Americans and Native Americans. Cushing even offered up that blunt version in his partisan speech. But when it came to lawmaking, more precision was required. Cushing and Taney both promoted racist visions of the United States, but the Democratic Party they served needed different things from the nation's populations of Native and African-descended people.

Cushing's and Taney's racism, like their party's, turned out to be purposeful, strategic, and variegated. From the standpoint of Democratic politicians, the most important task of the 1850s was to prevent questions about slavery from tearing their party apart, and this meant securing settler access to western lands on terms that alienated neither the Northern nor the Southern wings of their party. They understood that the voting population of the non-slave states was larger and faster-growing than that of the slave states; even the three-fifths compromise, which bolstered slave-state representation by counting a fraction of the enslaved population, could not make up for this. They understood, too, that a large and growing proportion of Northern voters worried about the expansion of slavery and were being rapidly recruited into a regional party that opposed it. The latest version of that party had emerged in 1854 as the Republican Party, based almost entirely in non-slave states, and from a Democratic perspective it had performed terrifyingly well in the presidential election of 1856. Democrats had to counter the Republicans' vision of restricting western settlement to non-slaveholders, or they would alienate their Southern base, but they could not take the hard line that many Southern slaveholders demanded. Only if they retained substantial support in non-slave as well as slave states could they control Congress and the presidency.

Dred Scott, and *Dred Scott*, suggested a white supremacist way forward for Democrats. First, African American claims to equality, including equal citizenship, offered Democrats a potent wedge issue. Not only did the interracial abolition movement demand the immediate end of slavery, but some of its leaders and adherents also challenged racial prohibitions on voting; racial discrimination in hotels, restaurants, and railroad cars; and prohibitions on racial intermarriage. At the same time, many white Northern voters—even those who had grown hostile to slaveholders and the institution of slavery—found the idea of nonracial equality in daily life unsettling, absurd, or revolting. Democrats' best hope for undercutting Republican appeals was to tie the party, relentlessly and usually falsely, to racial equality—to dub them the "Black Republicans." Whether one was a rigid white supremacist ideologue or a pragmatic politician trying to maintain a Democratic Party majority in the slave and non-slave states, unequivocal opposition to Black citizenship was an indispensable political tactic. Second, Democrats hoped that the Supreme Court's ruling in *Dred Scott* that Congress had no power to bar slavery from the territories would cut off the Republicans' platform at the knees and remove that question from the center of national political debate.[95]

But the question of Native American citizenship required subtler and more complex management than the question of Black people's status. From the Democratic Party's beginnings, it had championed the nation's expansion across the West and the displacement of Native people before it. The Indian Removal Act was essential to Jacksonian policy in the 1830s, and the same ideas animated the party's leaders a generation later. But managing Indian removal, as we have seen, was a different kind of problem than managing the status of African Americans. Citizenship, like removal and warfare, was one of the tools available for solving that problem. Historian Frederick Hoxie argues that Taney's apparent concession to the possibility of Native citizenship was in keeping with Jacksonian Democratic practice: making Native people into citizens was one way, sometimes an important way, to dispossess them of their land. Cushing's flat exclusion of "the red men and the black men" would not serve this end.[96]

Out in Minnesota, William Cullen wrote as if he understood these dynamics intimately. His high-sounding phrases about the future of the Ho-Chunk people, the "comforts and permanence of civilized life," and a future "condition of actual citizenship" were not rooted in philosophical meditations or Christian benevolence but in the demands of white settlers on the borders of the Blue Earth reservation. As he explained in his official report, "White settlers in the immediate vicinity ... desire to possess the fertile lands."[97] They had petitioned and protested against the establishment of the reserve in 1855, and since then they had sought to steal it; in 1858, Blue Earth County even drew township boundaries that marked out the Ho-Chunk people's Blue Earth treaty land as if they were part of the United States' public lands.[98] Cullen's vision of Ho-Chunk cultural transformation flowed from his need to appease these settlers. "I cannot suggest any practical method of divesting [the Ho-Chunk] of these areas," he mused, "unless it be by the individual farming system, which gradually destroys their present banded system, and creates in each individual member of the tribe an interest in the soil, which must result in materially advancing their progress toward civilization."[99] Civilization and citizenship served the greater good, less of racial uplift than of advancing settler claims.

The Ho-Chunk were not alone in facing the crushing pressure of settler encroachment, the speed with which officials bent before it, and the thin reed of hope represented by allotment and citizenship. In the same years, the late 1850s, those pressures transformed the federal government's own "Indian Territory," a vast trans-Mississippi domain including what are today the states of Oklahoma, Kansas, and Nebraska. For decades, the federal government had treated this as the destination for Native people displaced from east of the Mississippi River—"exiles and pioneers," in historian John Bowes's words.[100]

Like all other territories possessed by Native peoples, even those guaranteed "forever" by treaties with the United States, these trans-Mississippi lands were viewed by authorities and settlers as only provisionally Indian. For years, settlers and railroad corporations had pushed to claim those lands and turn them into territories of the United States. That movement had been held up not by scruples over Native people's sovereignty but by the national struggle over whether those territories would or would not be open to slavery. Senate Democrats, led by Illinois's Stephen Douglas, finally broke the deadlock in 1854 with the Kansas-Nebraska Act, which organized those territories under a principle dubbed "popular sovereignty": Congress would neither legalize nor bar slavery from territories organized in that region; instead, the settlers themselves would decide in democratic elections whether their territorial constitutions would permit slavery. Opponents, notably, dubbed this "squatter sovereignty."[101]

That legislative compromise drew competing invasions of settlers into the territory—one proslavery, one antislavery, each seeking to determine by force of numbers, or simply by force, whether slavery would take root. Students of U.S. history generally think of the ensuing guerrilla war between these groups as one of the sparks that ignited the Civil War. But viewed from Indian Country, the war over Kansas was simply a naked act of conquest: the United States passed the Kansas-Nebraska Act, "opening" the territory to settlement "when not one square foot of it was legally available for public ownership."[102]

The arrival of pro- and antislavery colonists in the mid-1850s portended disaster for the Native exiles and emigrants in eastern Kansas. Even as white settlers murdered one another over the future of slavery, they agreed on one thing: all that Indian land was going to waste. Commissioner of Indian Affairs Manypenny, who had his own ideas about how to order the transfer of land from Native nations to the United States, decried the "disorderly and lawless conduct" of white immigrants to the territory. "While they have quarreled about the African," he protested, they "have united upon the soil of Kansas in wrong-doing toward the Indians."[103] Settlers squatted on Native lands, plundered timber and game, and confronted those nations with an array of bad choices: fight back and face overwhelming federal force, or make the best of a bad situation. For some, that "best" seemed to be a version of the strategy undertaken over the preceding decades in the western Great Lakes. A variety of Native peoples began to consider new treaties that included allotments and citizenship, hoping that these might protect them from invasion, plunder, and expulsion.[104]

The Wyandots, who were on the verge of being overrun by squatters, were the first to take this route. Their 1855 treaty with the United States declared them "sufficiently advanced in civilization" to become "citizens of the United States, to all intents and purposes."[105] It dissolved the tribe, divided the people's common lands into family allotments, and sold what remained. As in previous cases, the best bad choice remained terrible. Within fifteen years, squatters, laws, and taxes cost the Wyandots almost all of their Kansas lands.[106]

Struggles over the fate of Kansas shaped national politics throughout the late 1850s, but that debate mainly took the conquest of the region for granted. The most famous debates about Kansas, the celebrated 1858 contests between Illinois U.S. Senate candidates Abraham Lincoln and Stephen Douglas, did not mention Native people at all. Lincoln was a Republican, and his position was that the West should be "free soil" from the start; Douglas, the Democrat, promoted "popular sovereignty." At one of their debates, in the northern Illinois town of Freeport, Douglas represented territorial conquest as axiomatic: "To increase, to multiply, to expand, is the law of this nation's existence," he declared. Lincoln did not dispute this. He merely wanted that expansion to be premised on the exclusion of slavery from the new territories.[107]

The settler statesmen Lincoln and Douglas made their speeches that day on the banks of the Pecatonica River, on land that the United States had recognized as part of the Ho-Chunk homeland in 1829. Freeport, the town in which they spoke, dated its founding to 1827, two years before legal settlement was possible for Americans. Born as a squatter town, Freeport had supplanted a

Ho-Chunk village—in fact, the village in which Coming Thunder Winneshiek came of age, the one he had probably last seen in 1827 as a prisoner of Henry Dodge. A few traces of that settlement survived in 1858: in Taylor's Driving Park, a settler historian wrote, the rows of the Ho-Chunk cornfields could still be seen. But their lodges had been replaced by the yards of the Central and Northwestern Railway, and the freight house of the Illinois Central stood atop their graves.[108]

By the late 1850s, at least some Ho-Chunk leaders reached the conclusion that their best hope of avoiding complete dispossession was to take ownership of the land on the terms—allotment and citizenship—that Americans recognized.[109] The question had become urgent. On one front, settler vigilantes in the town of Mankato, just outside the Blue Earth reservation, held public meetings and organized "home guard" companies to demand the Ho-Chunks' expulsion. The threat of violence was explicit.[110] On another, the annuities negotiated in the treaties of 1829 and 1832 were about to expire. It was under these precarious circumstances—one might even call them "blended grounds of conquest & contract"—that federal officials pressed the Ho-Chunk to accept mandatory allotment and give up a significant fraction of the land they had negotiated for just a few years before.[111]

Ho-Chunk delegates understood that their bargaining position was poor. They came to Washington to ask that "their great father . . . invest them with the indissoluble right to remain upon the land of their choice . . . without molestation or fear of being driven thence by their remorseless neighbor, the white man."[112] The delegation understood that to guarantee their right to remain at Blue Earth and set their finances in order, they would have to sell lands and accept allotment. They sought the best deal available under the circumstances: a new round of annuity payments to replace those about to expire, to help them establish households on their allotted acres. "You want us, Father, to act like white men, and we want to tell you that it requires a great deal of money to do so," Baptiste Lasallier explained.[113]

The 1859 treaty pursued the goal of allotment in the most radical way. It envisioned the sale of the western half of the reservation and the abolition of Ho-Chunk tenure in common on the rest. It proposed to assign the remaining lands to individual families in eighty-acre, individually owned allotments—what was called "ownership in severalty." These allotments were to be assigned in as contiguous a fashion as possible. The unallotted areas in between those parcels would remain tribal property for the moment, and the whole area together bounded as "the Winnebago reservation." That tribal domain would

Figure 2.2. John St. Cyr, photographed in Washington, D.C., in 1875. The son of a Ho-Chunk woman and a mixed-descent man, St. Cyr moved between Ho-Chunk and Euro-American worlds. At various times a farmer, an interpreter, a U.S. soldier, and an allotted landowner, he became a U.S. citizen in 1870 but continued to live and work with Ho-Chunk people in Nebraska, Minnesota, and Wisconsin. (Princeton University Library Digital PUL)

remain under the supervision of the United States, and "no white person" except government employees could enter it without permission of the tribe's agent. The acres assigned to individuals could not be taxed or sold to persons outside the tribe. This seemed to promise both territorial integrity and safety from taxation and alienation of land. But half of the Ho-Chunks' Blue Earth domain disappeared at a stroke.

For the minority of Ho-Chunk people at Blue Earth who had already taken up elements of American-style residence and farming, the Treaty of 1859 promised a path to security and independence. This group of about sixty families of mixed descent included John M. St. Cyr.[114] Born in Wisconsin about 1841 to a Ho-Chunk mother and a father of mixed French and Ho-Chunk descent, St. Cyr grew up as his family moved from the Neutral Ground to Long Prairie and then to Blue Earth. John was one of the few Ho-Chunk youth of his generation to attend the agency school consistently, and he became fluent and literate in English. He also worked on his father's Blue Earth farm of four improved acres and $400 worth of livestock, the largest Ho-Chunk holding on the Blue Earth lands. From his family's perspective, a deal that secured both a common reservation and individual landholdings was as strong a barrier as they could imagine against the demands of settlers.

Yet there was less security than met the eye. The sale of the entire western half of the Blue Earth lands was only the beginning. The treaty allowed a year after its ratification for the Ho-Chunk diaspora to come home to Blue Earth and claim allotments from the remaining tribal domain. Once that time expired, unassigned lands from the eastern half could also be sold to settlers. Soon there might be no Ho-Chunk tribal land at all. Whether St. Cyr, Baptiste Lasallier, and their compatriots knew it or not, they were entering a vortex they would not easily be able to control.

Meanwhile, most residents at Blue Earth continued to pursue a seasonal round and to live in bands knit together by kinship and affinity, not in the settler homesteads of official fantasy. "In the spring they go to their sugar camps to make sugar," an agency employee observed. "When summer comes it brings them back to the prairies to plant and raise corn; in autumn they seek the vicinity of rivers and lakes to hunt and trap; in winter they take up their abode in the forest.... They keep continually changing their location with every change of the season."[115] And where they did live on allotments taken under the treaty, they did not conform to American expectations, "in some cases there being from three to ten cabins or lodges on the same eighty acres."[116]

Coming Thunder Winneshiek identified much more closely with these Ho-Chunk people, the majority of the nation, than with St. Cyr and other settled, English-speaking farmers of mixed descent. He was still "principal chief" in the late 1850s, a sign of the respect and legitimacy he had in his people's eyes as much as or more than a sign of American officials' confidence in him. So it worried officials in 1858 when he opposed sending a delegation to Washington to negotiate a new treaty. Agent Charles Mix tried to go around him by holding a council without him. Coming Thunder responded by walking to the center of the council as it met. "I ... asked Agent what he had been doing & what he was trying to send certain chiefs to Washington City for? to sell our land? He did not answer. I told him that there was no use, for we did not want to sell our land."[117]

Coming Thunder remained a potent adversary after the treaty was signed. Mix tried to extract his retroactive consent to the treaty by withholding the payment due him as a band leader. When that did not work, he tried to bribe him with a presidential peace medal. Coming Thunder felt insulted. The peace medal had once represented a respectful nation-to-nation relationship, but now it seemed more like a badge of submission. He refused. Mix's superior, Superintendent William Cullen, reported to Washington that he then struck Coming Thunder from the roll of "chiefs." This was essential in this case, he explained, "in order to maintain that respect which is necessary for the maintenance of subordination."[118]

Coming Thunder and other Ho-Chunk people could not miss the sharp, new insistence on American authority and Ho-Chunk obedience. Cullen proudly pointed to what he saw as the success of this policy. Little Priest, whom the agent had imprisoned in the reservation jail and stripped of his office not long before, had "entirely reformed and conducted himself with propriety ... exhibiting contrition for the past." Cullen therefore "restored him again to the chieftainship of his band." In his mind, the long-standing forms of Ho-Chunk leadership were about to be a thing of the past. Ho-Chunk "political office" was the agent's to control.[119]

The Native citizenship that American authorities such as Cullen envisioned in the late 1850s was neither the confident claim of a white settler nor the aspirational demand of a Black activist. Rather, it was a relation of wardship, tutelage, and parental duty. The "Great Father" loomed, in loco parentis, over whole nations whose fitness for incorporation remained in doubt. This was efficiently expressed in the bald terms of the 1859 treaty, which granted the president the power to alter any provision of any former treaty "to whatever extent he may judge to be necessary and expedient for their welfare and best interest."[120] One could almost hear the echoes of Cullen's reflection that

Ho-Chunk progress toward civilization would "eventually" bring the people "the rights and privileges of a condition of actual citizenship."[121]

As Coming Thunder looked around Blue Earth in the last days of 1859, he saw Ho-Chunk dignity and self-determination under siege. The agent who had "control over our affairs," he complained to the commissioner of Indian Affairs, neglected his duties, sold them liquor, and provided "cheap flimsy clothing, made to suit white men & not Indians." Elsewhere at Blue Earth, John St. Cyr and others seemed comfortable in "citizens dress," but from Coming Thunder's perspective, "white men's clothes" were part of the colonial cultural transformation that was wreaking havoc in the life of his people.[122]

In a letter to the commissioner of Indian Affairs, Coming Thunder tried to capture how profoundly American "civilization" had disordered his society. His brutal account of a world gone wrong identified American ways, from liquor to clothing, as the source of violence that destroyed lives, households, and an entire society.

> Some 40-odd days ago one of our men, who had got some white men's clothes from the Agent went to Mankato with his wife & got drunk, & on their [way] home he attacked his wife without any cause, & having on heavy boots, kicked her to death, and the Agent did not have him arrested. . . . 3 days after he had committed the murder another Indian brother of the murdered woman, went & killed the aforesaid murderer who was trying to act white man. So you can see what effects result from trying to make white men out of Indians, by putting white men's clothes on them, & then allowing them to get whiskey & get drunk.

If the man had worn traditional Ho-Chunk deerskin moccasins, he likely would not have killed his wife. If there were no liquor—if Americans enforced their own prohibitions on the sale of alcohol—if there were no town of Mankato—he would not have become drunk. Yet the Americans would not accept responsibility for the disorder they sowed. Agent Mix did not have the killer arrested, so a revenge killing followed. The tragedy lay in the particulars, but those particulars pointed to a profound and negative transformation—"trying to act white man," Coming Thunder bitterly called it—that the requirements of the Treaty of 1859 would only accelerate.[123]

This was why Coming Thunder Winneshiek mobilized his compatriots to oppose the census and the survey in the summer of 1861. What he saw from his vantage point at Blue Earth was an American net closing around his people's lands, reshaping their relations to one another, to the land, to their ways of governing. He saw a nation about to break apart under the strain.

What Coming Thunder could not see in the summer of 1861 was that the nation confronting him, the United States, was at a breaking point of its own—that it had, in fact, already fractured and gone to war with itself. Even as he sparred with census takers and surveyors, armies on a scale the continent had never seen were mobilizing for battle. The militia captain whose army had invaded his land thirty years before, the politician who gave speeches over the ruins of his childhood village, was now president of the United States, struggling to suppress a slaveholders' rebellion against the election that had put him in power. Most of the military struggle between the United States and its rebel Southern provinces would take place far from Blue Earth and the Ho-Chunk homeland. But just as the conquest of Native lands had reverberated through the struggle over the future of slavery, the shockwaves created by that clash of armies and ideas would return to reshape the politics of Indian Country, and to upend Coming Thunder's world once more.

CITIZENS, WARDS, AND OUTLAWS

In August 1863 Roaring Thunder stood in the executive chamber of the Wisconsin capitol, preparing to make his case. Some twenty-five years before, he had defied settler authorities to their faces, rejecting their treaties as fraudulent and dismissing their demands that his people leave the state. But these were different days. The brief and bloody war between the United States and the eastern Dakota bands in Minnesota, almost twelve months before, had set off a settler panic and widespread violence against Native communities. On the day after Christmas, federal authorities had hanged thirty-eight Dakota men who had been sentenced to death in hasty and one-sided military tribunals. In the months that followed, officials banished Native people from Minnesota by the thousands, including nearly the entire Ho-Chunk community at Blue Earth. In Wisconsin, threats of vigilante violence against Native people, including the Ho-Chunk, continued to pour into the governor's office in Madison. The questions that Wisconsin officials had posed to Roaring Thunder over the past several weeks made it clear that they were terrified of having to fight another campaign against insurgent Native nations at the same time they waged their war against the rebel slaveholders.[1]

So Roaring Thunder worked to keep the peace. Earlier in the year he had prevailed upon a settler to translate and write a message to the governor, Edward Salomon. Later, he sent Salomon a calumet, a pipe representing the Wisconsin Ho-Chunk bands' desire for amicable relations. But in July soldiers had found him and locked him up for two weeks. Now the governor had summoned him to Teejop, which he called Madison, to a vast stone building on the isthmus between the lakes.

Governor Salomon was not sure what to make of the longtime resister standing before him. Was he, as some reports suggested, the agent of a pan-Indian alliance that hoped to take advantage of the Confederate rebellion to strike at settler society? Was he even, as one report implied, a "secessionist"? What did he know about the U.S.-Dakota War? Were Dakota fugitives from that war living among his people in Wisconsin? In the wake of the killing of a Wisconsin settler woman by a Ho-Chunk man, could he promise peace? What, really, did Roaring Thunder and his people want?

The waters around Roaring Thunder and his people were deep and fast-moving. They had already swept away the reservation at Blue Earth: Coming Thunder and his compatriots were exiles again, and many of them at that very moment were suffering and dying in a camp in the Dakota Territory. How much more vulnerable were Roaring Thunder and his people, who did not even have a treaty relationship standing between them and exile? At the same time, Roaring Thunder must have believed that coexistence remained possible. As he prepared his words, he had decades of experience in settler Wisconsin to draw upon and explain. He may also have known that, even in war-torn Minnesota, some Ho-Chunk had found a way to remain despite demands for their expulsion. There were many truths he could speak in this moment. Perhaps there was one that would work.

In the years that followed, Ho-Chunk people in Wisconsin and across their diaspora forged three distinct paths. Those in Wisconsin's Ho-Chunk bands continued to adapt their lives to the margins and interstices of the settler grid. They were sometimes feared, sometimes welcomed, but always outlaws—"wandering vagabonds," Americans called them—and never sure when another campaign to banish them would arise. A second group, those exiled from Minnesota to Crow Creek, continued the tradition of geographical self-determination. They fled the western camp they had been deposited upon and sought respite with their relations in the Nebraska Territory. They soon persuaded the federal government to let them remain there, but—as with the Treaties of 1855 and 1859—the price was an ever-more-constricting form of wardship. Finally, a small group from Blue Earth, mainly families of mixed descent who had already taken up allotments, worked their knowledge and relationships into a new status: by the end of the decade, they made themselves into landowning citizens of the United States.

Figure 3.1. Roaring Thunder (Wakajaxetega), whom Americans called "Dandy," photographed during the visit to Madison in 1863 when he conferred with Governor Edward Salomon. (Wisconsin Historical Society, WHI-61426)

These three disparate outcomes reflected long-standing dynamics in Ho-Chunk and Native life, but they also unfolded in relation to the rapidly evolving meaning of citizenship in the post–Civil War United States. In the aftermath of Confederate defeat and slave emancipation, the United States grappled with twin questions of consolidating its authority: over the people and land of the former slave states, and over the people and territories, now definitively "free soil," of the West. These questions converged in the U.S. Congress as the war's victors considered laws, amendments, policies, and treaties that they hoped would clarify crucial questions of rights, membership, and jurisdiction. Some of these questions were explicitly labeled "Indian Affairs." But the status and future of Native Americans also played a role in debates focused explicitly on Reconstruction and the status of African Americans, especially Congress's 1866 debates about the definition of national citizenship. These conversations, and their outcomes, revealed the dynamics at the core of the midcentury conquest and the history of Native citizenship. The consequences of these debates would shape Ho-Chunk life, and Native life generally, for decades to come.

The U.S.-Dakota War had its origins in the U.S. invasion of the Dakota homeland and the forcible transformation of most of that domain into "Minnesota." First the United States imposed treaties on the eastern Dakota bands that relegated them to territories too small to support them, promising annual payments of cash and goods in exchange. But as the Civil War began, the United States failed to make those payments, and in 1862 Dakotas began to starve. In mid-August, Dakota fighters went to war, killing hundreds of settlers and putting thousands to flight. For a few weeks they controlled the territory. But the U.S. military soon arrived in Minnesota in force. Soldiers imprisoned thousands of Dakotas, both fighters and noncombatants, in concentration camps, and they pursued many more across the Great Plains in what came to be called "the punitive campaigns."[2] The military then subjected hundreds of Dakota prisoners to military tribunals. These hasty and vengeful proceedings were trials only in name, but they resulted in more than 300 sentences of death, which were forwarded to President Lincoln for review. He approved a smaller number of executions, and on the day after Christmas 1862, authorities hanged thirty-eight Dakota men at a mass gallows in the center of Mankato, Minnesota, on the edge of the Blue Earth reservation.[3]

The war put the Ho-Chunk at Blue Earth in an impossible position. Dakota leaders understood that their only hope for a lasting victory was to recruit a broader Native coalition, and they made overtures to Ho-Chunk leaders in the days before the war began. There were some reasons to imagine this might succeed: Dakotas and Ho-Chunks had been neighbors long enough to marry one another; their languages were related; and both peoples had experienced enormous dislocation and suffering in their encounter with the United States and its settlers. But the two nations were not in the same circumstances in the summer of 1862. Despite the hardships and conflicts of recent years, the Ho-Chunk were situated on lands they desired and had chosen, and they were surrounded by white neighbors whom they could not afford to antagonize. The Dakota situation was far more dire. So Dakota overtures for military support appear mainly to have failed, and some Ho-Chunks even seem to have made efforts to warn white settlers of impending attacks.[4]

Nonetheless, U.S. tribunals finally charged fifteen Ho-Chunk men with participating in the war against the settlers. Based on the testimony of multiple witnesses, a tribunal initially sentenced Little Priest and another man to death. But as the prosecutions proceeded, the army's chief witness, a Ho-Chunk man whom surviving sources call O-ton-ka, came to seem less and less credible. Little Priest's sentence was overturned, and nearly all the rest were acquitted. Only one captive, a young man called Monekasdayhekah in the trial record but identified elsewhere as Maznopinka, stood convicted and under sentence of death for participating in two attacks on settlers. Maznopinka's final fate is unclear: his trial took place after the initial list of Dakota convictions was sent to Washington, so his case seems not to have been reviewed by President Lincoln. He was not among those executed on December 26, 1862, for his name is found on a later list of prisoners "condemned to be hung." There does not appear to be a record of his subsequent execution or of his death while in captivity, and a family account suggests that he may have survived.[5]

Forces who for years had sought expulsion of the Ho-Chunk took advantage of the settler hysteria of late 1862 and 1863. Some settlers had been organizing since the late 1850s, holding public meetings and organizing "home guard" vigilante companies that threatened violence against Native people. Countervailing forces also existed: the Ho-Chunk at Blue Earth participated in a wide range of economic interactions with the settlers around them, including purchasing local farmers' goods with their annuity money. But in late 1862 a Mankato editor dismissed such arguments: "Winnebago gold, piled high, cannot offset the atrocities of the past two months.... Our rich and fertile prairies must either be the abode of thrift, industry, and wealth, or the hunting ground of a barbarous and worthless race." These forces now mobilized popular hostility into violence against Dakota captives, leading to serious confrontations with the federal forces guarding them.[6]

Inevitably, settler vigilantism also took aim at the Ho-Chunk. Leading men in Mankato founded a secret society, the Knights of the Forest, to consolidate their efforts to drive the Ho-Chunk from Blue Earth. Members of that organization later claimed to have lain in wait outside the borders of the reservation and to have killed Ho-Chunk people who crossed the line. These claims cannot be proved or disproved, but they are within the range of vigilante authority often asserted by settler citizens during real or imagined crises.[7]

Settler threats and demands persuaded the government to abandon its treaty commitments to the Ho-Chunk, to expel them from Minnesota, and to reduce them to something like wards. In December 1862, settler representatives in Congress introduced a bill stripping the Ho-Chunk of their common lands and banishing them to Crow Creek, a barren camp far to the west on the Missouri River. The bill took full advantage of the terms of the 1859 treaty, which allowed the president to alter terms as he saw fit. In particular, it transformed the distribution of annuities, allowing "reasonable discrimination ... in favor of the chiefs who shall be found faithful to the Government of the United States, and efficient in maintaining its authority and the peace of the Indians." And, despite the Ho-Chunk people's treaty relation with the United States, the bill also extended American legal jurisdiction over them; the Ho-Chunk would now be "subject to the laws of the United States, and to the criminal laws of the State or Territory in which they may happen to reside." Finally, even though they were now under American law, the bill emphatically excluded them from citizenship: "They shall be deemed incapable of making any valid civil contract with any person other than a member of their tribe." The bill reached President Lincoln's desk by early March 1863, and his signature authorized the expulsion of the Ho-Chunk from Minnesota.[8]

Pro-expulsion forces in Mankato reveled in this law's unprecedentedly blunt dismissal of Native sovereignty. "The Indians pretend," sneered the *Mankato Record*, "that ... they did not understand [previous] provisions obviating the necessity of further treaties and placing the nation under the control of the President and Congress."[9] But this, the paper asserted, was the plain meaning of the 1859 treaty's Article IV, which gave those officials "full power to modify or change any of the provisions of former treaties."[10] This treaty was "the best ever made," said the *Record*, "as it treats them simply as wards of the Government, which they are in fact, and not as an independent nation."[11] If this was not a fully accurate assessment, it did capture the accelerating federal assault on Ho-Chunk sovereignty.

As expulsion bore down on the Ho-Chunk, Coming Thunder sought to delay or redirect it. As most of the Ho-Chunk assembled at Mankato in early May, Coming Thunder was not among them. He and a large group, perhaps 700 people, took shelter at a remote lake just north of the reservation. But when the U.S. officer brought a small detachment to demand that he comply with the removal order, he apparently did.[12] Soon the people in Coming Thunder's party were boarding boats and wagons for Fort Snelling, the first leg of a brutal journey that would take them down the Mississippi River and then up the Missouri River to Crow Creek in the Dakota Territory, 300 miles west of their most recent home.

Coming Thunder remonstrated with officials, enumerating the broken promises and hardships inflicted by the United States. To the officer sent to bring his party in, he exhibited "an autograph letter from General Jackson, as President of the United States, certifying to the old Chief's [his father's] bravery and fidelity to the whites, and he begged to be permitted to end his few remaining days amid the graves of his children and relatives."[13] A few days later, while the refugees waited for a steamboat to transport them from St. Paul, he called on General Henry Sibley, a former fur trader and regional politician whom the Ho-Chunk had known for decades.[14] He again protested his people's exile to new lands, "far from the graves of their fathers; and among a strange, and perhaps hostile, collection of various bands of Indians."[15]

To the last, Coming Thunder asked that they be allowed to go home. Fifteen years earlier, during the deportation to Long Prairie, he had tried to thwart the removal by obtaining land on the west bank of the Mississippi River from his cousin the Dakota leader Wapasha. Coming Thunder now explained to General Sibley that he had sent a paper granting that land "to their Great Father, who approved it, but the paper was never returned to Winneshiek." He understood that this territory now lay within the boundaries of the state of Minnesota and that he therefore could not expect to obtain it. Rather, he asked to exchange Wapasha's grant for an equal area "on the Chippewa River in Wisconsin, and he and his band be allowed to reside there."[16]

Instead, soldiers deported 2,000 Ho-Chunk people to poorly provisioned Crow Creek.[17] The expulsion killed hundreds, some in internment camps, some en route, and some of hunger and disease after arriving at the new settlement. Two generations later, one of Coming Thunder's descendants remembered the horror of the deportation. The survivors, John Blackhawk told a settler historian, "went through those terrible days and shudder at the thought of them, when they were the helpless prey of the ruffian soldiers. Women and girls raped, men murdered, and subject to every insult and indignity that brutal men could invent ... for no crime whatever except that they had been unfortunate enough to be born Indians."[18]

Even before the Ho-Chunk were boarded onto the steamboats, settlers asserted their prerogative to squat and claim. By May, more than 150 claims had been taken on the former reservation and "white men, in large numbers," had moved onto the reservation "with a view to pre-empt." In Oak Grove Township, east of the agency building, there were two or three settler families by mid-May, but two months later there were forty—"a good class of people," reported a Mankato newspaper, "mostly from Wisconsin and Illinois, and just the kind of citizens we like to have among us."[19]

Those citizens moved onto the Blue Earth lands with all the confidence that the history of conquest could provide. Coming Thunder had implored General Sibley to let him remain "amid the graves of his children and relatives," but that was not to be his fate, or theirs. Frank Kennedy occupied a Ho-Chunk homesite with a cemetery, the graves covered with wooden houses and surrounded by painted pickets. "Soon after the Indians left the fences were appropriated by one of the settlers to fence his garden," Kennedy recalled. A few years later, Kennedy's hired man desecrated a grave, finding the remains of a man "with a rusty gun barrel, a tomahawk, a pipe and other things."[20]

The settlers who replaced the Ho-Chunk refashioned their dwellings for their own purposes. George Covel was a little boy in the summer of 1863 when his parents took possession of Little Priest's village site. Settlers had already stripped the large council house of its boards, but Little Priest's bark-covered lodge and several others were intact. Covel's family lived in the lodge that summer and afterward used it as a summer kitchen.[21] The Atcherson family moved onto the lands of Little Hill's large band, where they found the band's council lodge, a round, roofed structure more than sixty feet in diameter. The Atchersons occupied the lodge for the next year while they built their log house on the ground Little Hill had expected his family to occupy forever.[22]

The lands that had already been allotted to some Ho-Chunk families at Blue Earth suffered the same fate. Most of these lands were taken in trust by the government to be sold by sealed bid.[23] But the voice of squatter prerogative, the *Mankato Record,* warned that these lands would be "occupied by settlers by the day of sale" and that "associations for mutual protection and resistance" would ensure that squatters already moving onto Blue Earth, not far-off speculators, secured those lands.[24] "The houses of the half-breeds," the newspaper confirmed a year later, "are generally occupied by white families."[25]

The settlers' awareness of a distinction between people of mixed descent and the rest of the Ho-Chunk population reflected the long history of such people as intermediaries and interpreters and the fact that they were more likely to speak English and to dress in the American fashion. For some of these families, this distinction seemed to offer a means to remain at Blue Earth, and perhaps even on their allotted lands.[26] Minnesota's 1857 constitution granted the right of suffrage both to "persons of mixed white and Indian blood, who have adopted the customs and habits of civilization," and to Native people of unmixed descent "who have adopted the language, customs and habits of civilization" and who demonstrated to a district court judge that they were "capable of enjoying the rights of citizenship within the State."[27] Reading this backwards, it seemed clear that meriting the right to vote in one of these ways conveyed or implied citizenship, and with it the right of residence.

As authorities put the expulsion act into motion in the spring of 1863, Ho-Chunk people who recognized themselves in those provisions of the Minnesota Constitution moved swiftly. At the beginning of May, about forty Ho-Chunk residents of the Blue Earth lands presented themselves to the state district judge at the Waseca County courthouse, just east of Blue Earth, in a bid to prove to him that they merited that citizenship. A white man, Marcus Moore, accompanied them as an intermediary. The *Mankato Record* was sure that they hoped to gain the right to remain on the lands already allotted to them. But this plan foundered on the rocky shore of settler hostility. The Waseca County judge refused their petitions. Local settlers then summoned the U.S. officer stationed at the Blue Earth agency, and soldiers came to arrest Moore at his home. There they found forty Ho-Chunk people, "with their poneys and goods," preparing to make an escape eastward. The soldiers turned them back toward Mankato, hoping to ensure that they would be deported with the rest.[28]

Yet the settler veto of their bid for citizenship was not the last word. A number of Ho-Chunk residents—most or all apparently people of mixed descent, very frequently bearing French-derived surnames—were able to remain in Minnesota through the expulsion of May 1863, or to quickly return. Over the next few years, white squatters on the Blue Earth lands complained that "several of the Half Breeds and others of said tribe are returning and claiming their allotments, where actual settlers have settled and are opening farms"—in other words, where squatters had taken possession of those lands. The petitioners urged that these lands "be immediately brought to market" so that they could preempt them and "prevent the return of said Indians to said lands."[29] Local officials asked the commissioner of Indian Affairs what to do about the land claims of "those parties who are remaining here," people who "have continued to cultivate and improve [the land] since it was allotted to them" and "do not wish to follow the tribe."[30]

Citizens, Wards, and Outlaws

These mixed-ancestry people, their families, and compatriots fought to remain with languages and actions that they hoped would signal a full embrace of American "civilization." Twenty-three landholders of mixed descent engaged a lawyer, Francis Beveridge, to press their claims under the terms of the 1859 treaty. Beveridge asserted that his clients "have long since adopted the habits and customs of civilized life" and that "being anxious to retain their civilization, and through fear of relapsing into barbarism, they declined to remove with the Winnebago."[31] The Treaty of 1859 did not speak directly of citizenship, let alone promise it to those who took up allotments. But its language of allotment as a means of cultivating "settled habits of industry and enterprise" and its assignment of those lands to individuals and their heirs in perpetuity certainly suggested that allottees thereby became legitimate residents.[32]

"Civilization" was one route to civic inclusion and a right to remain for these non-white residents of the United States, but the Civil War provided another avenue: military service. At the precise moment that Beveridge's clients made their bid to remain on their Minnesota allotments, thousands of free African American men from across the non-slave states were forging their own path to recognition and inclusion by donning the blue uniform of the United States. Their military service began as a tentative experiment, but it quickly became a kind of cultural revolution. The common and long-standing view of African Americans as anti-citizens stemmed in part from white people's fear that they were essentially savage and violent—a danger to U.S. communities and a force to be guarded against, not potential guardians themselves. This view explained why, even after enlisting Black men as soldiers, the government refused to allow them to command Black regiments, or even at first to serve as officers at all. But Frederick Douglass expressed a common view among Black activists and their white allies when he saw military service, even on unequal terms, as a strategic opening. "Once let the black man get upon his person the brass letters *U.S.*," Douglass wrote, "let him get an eagle on his button, and musket on his shoulder, and bullets in his pocket, and there is no power on the earth ... which can deny that he has earned the right to citizenship in the United States." In Douglass's hopeful view, that citizenship included a panoply of rights and privileges heretofore denied most African Americans, including a permanent and dignified place in American civic life. Many heeded his call. In July 1863 the thousand Black soldiers of the Fifty-Fourth Massachusetts defied their anti-citizenship on the sands of Charleston Harbor, failing to take Battery Wagner from the rebels but demonstrating that they would fight and die under the nation's flag. Nearly

200,000 more African Americans would follow their example over the next two years, moving Douglass's prophecy ever closer to realization.[33]

During the same summer that the Fifty-Fourth marched into battle, men from Blue Earth also put on blue uniforms in an effort to establish their bona fides as Americans who should be able to settle and reside where they wished. Twenty-four men of Ho-Chunk descent enlisted for three-year stints in Minnesota regiments. John St. Cyr and a younger brother were among those who joined Company E of the Second Minnesota Cavalry in December 1863, while another group joined the Second Minnesota Infantry.[34] Their purposes were clear: the common demand of these soldiers, their wives, and women who had received allotments but whose husbands were now at Crow Creek was that they be entitled to retain their allotments and remain in Minnesota. And it appeared to work. In July 1863, the commissioner of Indian Affairs confirmed that they were entitled to retain their claims.[35]

By late 1863, the disparate fates of the Ho-Chunk who had lived at Blue Earth captured two possible futures for Native people. Thousands were banished to Crow Creek because federal officials scurried to comply with settlers' demands and threats, never mind that this expulsion made a mockery of several treaties and the federal government's entire program of allotment and "civilization." By contrast, those Ho-Chunks who could credibly claim to represent "civilization"—in their landownership, in their apparent embrace of other American "habits and customs," and finally in military service—managed to carve out a space of welcome for themselves in the wartime settler order.

Back across the Mississippi River in Wisconsin, a third Ho-Chunk path continued to unfold. By the 1860s the thousand or more Ho-Chunk people living within the boundaries of the state had reconfigured their seasonal itinerary to deal with the growth of American settlements. Their villages now mainly lay in the wide area between the Wisconsin and Black Rivers, on the north-northwest periphery of settler society. This region offered bountiful resources: in the summer and fall, berries that were in great demand from traders; in the winter, ample hunting. Their relative remoteness from the unfolding American grid also meant in many places they could safely plant acres of potatoes and corn. Their seasonal round included wider travels as well through Iowa, Minnesota, and southern Wisconsin, and they maintained amicable relations with some settlers in those places.[36]

Even in Teejop, now the settlers' capital, Ho-Chunk people continually returned to fish, trade, trap, and live for months at a time. Hundreds returned annually to the northwest shore of Wąąkšikhomįkra, where White Crow's village had once stood. They built ciiporoke covered in rush matting or birch bark and piloted dugout canoes on the region's lakes.[37] Elsewhere on the outskirts of the city of Madison, dozens of Ho-Chunk people spent spring and fall months making maple sugar and hunting and trapping muskrats, which they traded with downtown storekeepers.[38]

Despite this tradition of coexistence, the news from Minnesota in 1862–63 gave the Wisconsin Ho-Chunk every reason to fear a similar panic and purge. Settlers and officials seemed primed to read their activity as seditious. An agent in Green Bay "discovered," apparently through hearsay, that Roaring Thunder had tried to incite the Menominee to join in "hostile operations at some future time."[39] During the U.S.-Dakota War, Governor Salomon of Wisconsin distributed arms to the state's western settlements, "assuring the alarmed settlers."[40] Then in July 1863, while U.S. forces pursued Dakota bands across the northern plains and tensions remained high in the western Great Lakes, a Ho-Chunk man in western Wisconsin killed the wife of a white liquor dealer.

The killing unleashed a wave of white vigilantism. Settlers lashed out indiscriminately against Ho-Chunk people, replaying the kind of conflict that had been taking place since at least the 1820s.[41] Settlers threatened to wage "a war of extermination against them" unless they were removed from the state. Pro-expulsion forces even printed a blank petition form for use by local communities that warned that unless the government removed the Ho-Chunk from western Wisconsin, "we shall be compelled, in self defense, to exterminate them." It was in this context that settler authorities near New Lisbon took Roaring Thunder and other men prisoner, ostensibly "for their own protection against the excited white settlers."[42]

Governor Salomon did not want another war. His job, as he understood it, was to reassure settlers "so far as any apprehension from the Indians is concerned." The capture of Roaring Thunder offered an opportunity to provide that reassurance. He had already sent agents to confer "with their controlling chiefs" to "quiet the present difficulty." Now he had the most famous Ho-Chunk leader in the state standing before him.[43]

Roaring Thunder understood how badly things could go if settler authorities decided he was a danger to their order. This was why he had written to the governor and sent him a calumet in 1862.[44] Now, in his conversations with authorities at New Lisbon and then with Governor Salomon in Madison, he tried to change the terms of the conversation—to persuade his interrogators that his people sought peaceful exchange, not anticolonial war, and to redirect the expulsionist movement before it swept him and his people away to Crow Creek, or worse.

Roaring Thunder's message was simple: the Ho-Chunk required peaceful relations with settlers to sustain their reconfigured way of life. Living on the periphery of American settlement—not too close, but not too far—was essential to their changed circumstances. They had to live far enough from intensive settlement and agriculture not to run afoul of landowners' prerogatives; as early as 1866, settlers in western Wisconsin objected to the Ho-Chunk people's use of unimproved grassland to feed their horses.[45] But at the same time, they had to market their berries, maple sugar, and horses, which meant "constantly trading and mingling with the whites."[46] When the officer at New Lisbon warned Roaring Thunder that his people must stay away from outlying settlements, and to trade only at stores, he demurred. "What will Indian do, when hungry, who lives far from stores? They must sell deer, fish, &c., to get bread."[47]

Roaring Thunder repeated this message of peaceful coexistence in his conversation with the governor. Shaking the white man's hand and offering him his calumet, he told Salomon that he and his people "want to walk in a straight way and have no trouble." He came as a leader—"I am ruler of them," the interpreter reported—but he was no more able to control the conduct of individual Ho-Chunk people than Salomon could oversee the actions of individual settlers; "when they start to pick berries, they do not all go together but go where they have a mind to." Yes, some obtained liquor from white men and committed crimes. The murder of the settler's wife followed from the illegal liquor trade, but that was an aberration, the act of a particularly troublesome man, "most of the time half crazy," a "bad Indian."[48]

Like Coming Thunder, a few years before and a few hundred miles away, Roaring Thunder laid the blame for these conflicts on the American conquest, not on the Ho-Chunk character. He "had seen better days than now, when the old nation was here," he said. "If you had seen me in my younger days, and should come now to my wigwam," he told the governor, "it would hurt your feelings." But the poverty of the present made it all the more important to keep the peace. "He only wanted to make money out of his berries, and if he quarreled with the whites, they would not buy his berries," he explained. "To be poor is bad enough," Roaring Thunder concluded, "without fighting."[49]

Roaring Thunder's account mingled protests of harmlessness with descriptions of survivance. His description of his people's poverty, their desire for peace, and their decentralized political order implicitly reassured officials that they could pose no military threat to settler society. At the same time, in detailing a world of semiautonomous bands working a seasonal itinerary, Roaring Thunder told a story about the kinds of sovereignty Ho-Chunk people still sought to exercise: not sovereignty over territory, which would set them in dangerous conflict with the Americans, but over food and movement. That sovereignty was precarious and contingent, but it represented his people's distance, in values and daily life, from the settler society around them. As Roaring Thunder explained to the officer at New Lisbon, the Ho-Chunk had not assembled there to challenge settlers' claims but to pick whortleberries for trade. When the whortleberries were gone, they would go too. This simple declaration was a synecdoche for an entire way of life.[50]

Governor Salomon and other American officials may not have fully understood Roaring Thunder's account, but they made a temporary peace with it. Salomon remained confused about why the Ho-Chunk were still there at all: with their title extinguished by the treaties of the 1830s, he wondered why "they are allowed to wander at will over the wide region lying between the Wisconsin, Mississippi, and St. Croix rivers." But when John Pope, the general in charge of the war against the Dakota, offered to engineer their expulsion, the complexities became clearer. The Office of Indian Affairs told Pope it had neither personnel nor funds to offer in support of a removal, and it warned him that if he acted against the Ho-Chunk, "they will be on your hands."[51]

Beyond the question of resources, federal officials worried that the use of military force would scatter the Ho-Chunk instead of collecting them. The long-term policy goal remained the expulsion of the Ho-Chunk bands from Wisconsin to a reservation farther west, but that would require close knowledge of their whereabouts and activities. So in 1864 the Office of Indian Affairs created an unusual new position—an agent to the "stray bands" of Ho-Chunk and Potawatomi in Wisconsin.[52] The derisive term "stray bands" was a poor description of the lives that Wisconsin's persistent Ho-Chunk people had forged, but it represented the Office of Indian Affairs' acknowledgment that the government had thus far not managed to contain or control Roaring Thunder and his people.

By the time the special agent to the "stray bands" made his first report in the fall of 1866, a revolution was unfolding in American life. More than a year before, the United States had defeated the armies of the rebellion. By the end of 1865, the constitutional amendment abolishing slavery, passed by Congress the previous winter, was ratified as the Thirteenth Amendment. African American soldiers made up a substantial fraction of the U.S. military force occupying the former slave states. And across those states, freedpeople tested the meanings of their new status in their ability to move freely, assert themselves in ways large and small, and rebuild families and communities torn apart by slavery. Everywhere, one could hear what the abolitionist and U.S. military officer Thomas Wentworth Higginson called "the choked voice of a race at last unloosed."[53] Reconstruction had begun.

But Reconstruction faced fierce and violent opposition. Lincoln's successor in the White House, Andrew Johnson, was as committed to white rule as any pre–Civil War Democrat, and he had restored representative governments in the former slave states on the same white-only basis as before the war. During the winter of 1865–66, just as the Thirteenth Amendment achieved ratification, state legislatures across the South began to pass overtly discriminatory laws, known as "Black Codes," whose overriding purpose was to confine freedpeople to low-wage agricultural work for white landowners. Some barred Black people from living in town or from renting land; others established differential punishments for Black and white people. Meanwhile, white vigilantism against African Americans' assertions of autonomy took new forms: in Tennessee, a group of white men established a club they called the "Ku Klux Klan." From Johnson's White House to rural strongholds of white Southern resistance, a campaign emerged to secure a very different reconstruction—the reestablishment of the rule of the region's white property holders.[54]

Republicans, who had just concluded a war against the slaveholders' rebellion, moved quickly to beat back the "Black Codes." As historian Kate Masur shows, many of them had long championed free Black people's equal rights at the state level. During the Civil War, many of them had fought to secure equal status for Black soldiers and sailors. So they were well prepared to combat assaults by state legislatures on the rights and freedoms of newly freed people. Their answer was a national civil rights bill that transformed what had mainly been the state-granted entitlements of white citizens into a new set of nationally guaranteed civil rights. The bill sought to establish that all citizens, "of every race and color," shared common rights "of persons and property." They could make contracts; sue and be sued; give evidence; own, rent, lease, and inherit property; and demand the same legal protection for themselves and their property "as is enjoyed by white citizens." Most of the bill as it finally became law, and most of the debate about it, concerned how aggrieved citizens and their national government could "vindicate" these rights through legal proceedings.[55]

Nothing in this bill seemed to concern Native people—neither exiles like the refugees in Nebraska, nor allotted landowners such as those in Minnesota, nor "stray bands." When U.S. senator from Illinois Lyman Trumbull brought the civil rights bill to the floor of the Senate in January 1866, he fully expected debate to revolve around the status of African Americans and the changing power relations between the federal and state governments. But it turned out he was only partly correct. In seeking to codify fundamental matters—who belonged to the nation, what rights accompanied that belonging, and how the nation would guarantee and enforce those rights—the Republicans' bill raised questions about Native people's lives and status that they had not anticipated.

An essential starting point for establishing national civil rights was reversing the *Dred Scott* ruling that African Americans could not be citizens, so early in the process Trumbull proposed an affirmative and inclusive definition. His formula combined well-accepted parameters of allegiance and birth: the citizenry should embrace "all persons born in the United States, and not subject to any foreign power." With that, he thought, the important work of including African Americans in the nation's civic body would be accomplished, and the exclusionary verdict of *Dred Scott* once and for all reversed. African Americans, guaranteed "the full and equal benefit of all laws ... as is enjoyed by white citizens," would no longer be legally regarded or treated as Roger Taney's "degraded class."[56]

When Trumbull proposed nonracial citizenship, he no doubt expected the explosive objections of his more strenuously anti-Black colleagues.[57] But he was not prepared for the very first objection to his citizenship language: wouldn't it "naturalize all the Indians of the United States"? What he at first assumed was a quibble turned out to be much more than that. Over the ensuing days of debate, senators from all corners of the chamber jumped in with related questions and objections: What about those "wild and savage" Native people whose governments had been smashed or dissolved and who were therefore no longer "subject to any foreign power"? What about those who lived close to U.S. settlement, in circumstances that resembled U.S. ways of life, but who remained in a treaty relationship with the United States? What about those made citizens by state law? As senators proposed language that would include or exclude particular categories of Native people, their colleagues interjected, pointing out unintended and often undesirable consequences of those formulations. Trumbull grew frustrated and "wish[ed] this whole Indian question was out of the way." "It is not the great object of the bill," he complained.[58]

In one sense, Trumbull was right. The 1866 congressional debate over Native citizenship did not arise because of pressing questions about the status of Native people or the terms of their inclusion or exclusion. The premise of the civil rights bill was that African Americans, as a previously enslaved or subordinated population, required a new status, newly enumerated rights, and new means of enforcing those rights in order to escape continuing subordination. But the framers of the postwar Constitution were determined to prevent racial hierarchy in *any* form from shaping civic and political life. In the laws and amendments that were their founding documents, they expressed their rejection of slavery and its consequences in universal terms—not the abolition of "African slavery" but of "slavery or involuntary servitude"; not a prohibition on denying the vote to Black men but to persons "on the basis of race, color, or previous condition of servitude." Rights of contract, movement, standing, and enforcement had previously been matters of state law and white racial entitlements, even if some states extended some of these rights to other groups. The civil rights bill was part of the new formulation. It sought to establish a new root principle of national, nonracial rights, privileges, and immunities, secured by federal enforcement.

The problem of determining how, whether, and when Native people fit into the civic, legal, and political order was not new. State governments had been wrestling with this question for forty years as they asserted jurisdiction over Native people within their borders. Georgia and other Southern states had extended jurisdiction while subjecting Native people to nakedly discriminatory laws. Wisconsin and other northwestern states had initially claimed jurisdiction over only small groups of Native people who met certain criteria. Minnesota had recently extended its criminal law over Native people, regardless of their treaty relation to the United States. But the civil rights bill, as national legislation, was new terrain.

The establishment of a uniform, national, nonracial definition of rights and citizenship forced Congress to state explicitly the relationship of Native people and Native nations to the United States, and that summoned to the floor of the Senate a fundamental tension that lay at the heart of Indian policy. On the one hand, the Constitution, treaties, and generations of federal laws held that the United States was the sole authority in diplomacy with Native nations and that those nations' people stood in a relationship to the United States that was different from that of subjects of (for example) European nations. Unlike European immigrants, Native people who claimed allegiance to their own nations did not count as U.S. residents, no matter where they had been born or where they actually lived. They were not presumed to be potential members of the state or national civic body but of their own sovereignties. On the other hand, the trend of U.S. policy since the Washington administration had been to degrade and diminish the national independence of those sovereignties. This was, first and foremost, because the overriding goal of U.S. Indian policy was to take Native nations' land.

The question of Native people's status took on a new urgency in the postwar era because the Civil War ended the long deadlock over the terms of U.S. expansion into the West. In 1862, many legislators had seized the opportunity provided by the departure of slave-state representatives to pass a bold program of "free soil" expansion into the West. The Pacific Railroad Act funded a vast project to knit the far West to the Mississippi Valley. The Morrill Act devoted a portion of the nation's public lands to funding state institutions of higher education. Most importantly, the Homestead Act granted up to 160 acres of the public lands to any loyal citizen, declarant alien, or veteran of the U.S. Army or Navy for nothing more than a ten-dollar filing fee, so long as they actually settled and improved the land. Slaveholding representatives had thwarted these policies for years, fearing that they would allow the tides of immigration, which sharply favored non-slave states, to shift the nation's balance of population and power even more decisively toward "free soil." But their day was done.[59]

The senators and representatives of 1866 assumed that a central mission of the victorious U.S. government was to facilitate further western settlement and that that settlement would sooner or later sweep most Native people before it. If the hundreds of thousands of Indigenous people living between the Mississippi and the Pacific wanted to survive that onslaught, the legislators believed, they would have to adapt to life within the borders of the United States. The starting point of the legislative debate, whether or not its participants said so explicitly, was the assumption that the U.S. conquest of any Native people's territory that it (or its settlers) wanted was more or less inevitable. It can be discomfiting to state the facts this bluntly, because so many people have learned to view the consequences of the U.S. victory over the rebellion only through the lens of slave emancipation and Southern Reconstruction. Conquest and dispossession are not comfortable companions to this story. But however we name it, the post-emancipation United States was an avowedly settler-colonial state.[60]

In 1866, conquest was already taking form in the assertion of U.S. jurisdiction over Native sovereignties. Congress ruled in 1862 that Native nations taking up arms on the side of the rebellion, as leaders of the Cherokee, Creek, and other nations in Indian Territory had, thereby abandoned their treaty relationship with the United States. In 1865, U.S. senator James Harlan of Iowa proposed a consolidated territorial government for Indian Territory, subordinating individual Native governments to a confederation framework put in place by the United States. By 1866, now serving as secretary of the Interior, Harlan imposed treaties on the Cherokee and other nations whose citizens had held African American slaves, forcing them to grant land or extend citizenship to their freedpeople. From the perspective of formerly enslaved people, these federal fiats promised freedom and a measure of equality, but they also formed part of a consolidation of federal authority over Indian Country and an abandonment of the idea that treaties were in any sense consensual contracts.[61]

The conquest of Native people's lands would unfold on the terms set by the war's antislavery victors, but they pursued that conquest mindful of the ways it could go wrong. The memory of horrific massacres of Native people by U.S. soldiers at Bear River and Sand Creek lingered in congressmen's imaginations. Peace had not yet been reached with Dakota combatants. What would soon be called Red Cloud's War was already underway on the northern plains. The prospect of a long, bloody, and expensive conflict was all too real, posing dangers both to white settlement and to Americans' desire to view themselves as a Christian people. But if congressmen imagined endless war with dismay, they were equally wary of the blanket incorporation of Native people, especially under the new constitutional basis of nonracial equality. This explained the shocked question that set off the 1866 debate, about whether Trumbull's language effectively naturalized all Native people.

As they argued about the relationship of Native Americans to the United States, many congressmen revealed that they knew little or nothing about Indian Country. The evolving policies of "civilization," allotment, and citizenship did not make up a well-defined and well-understood program over which policy makers deliberated and which they consciously embraced. Rather, those policies, developed piecemeal in laws and treaties under a succession of administrators, had been applied in a wide range of ways across a million square miles of North America. For example, later investigators would estimate that there were 12,000 citizen Indians by 1866. But not even this basic level of information structured the conversation about Native incorporation during the early months of 1866.[62]

The lawmakers' 1866 debate over the terms of Native people's incorporation also revealed the diversity of local histories of colonialism and demonstrated that what suited one regime of conquest, settlement, and incorporation might not suit another. Senators from the upper Midwest, the central and northern plains, and the far West dominated these conversations. They brought to bear their own particular, often idiosyncratic, perspectives on Indians and their future relation to the United States, insisting that whatever general rule the country adopted must suit their specific needs. When it came to who was or should be a citizen and what that should mean, it turned out that Trumbull's "Indian question" was not one but many.

The senators debated Native American citizenship in relation to two familiar keywords: "jurisdiction" (whether Native people were subject to U.S. authority or to that of their own nations) and "civilization" (whether lawmakers thought they had sufficiently adopted American arrangements of property, family, subsistence, and comportment to constitute members of settler communities). Senator Trumbull initially imagined that, with the proper wording, these criteria could be easily applied. He assumed the great mass of Native people to be both "savage" and "foreign"—in his words, "wild Indians who do not recognize the Government of the United States at all."[63] But it should be simple, he thought, to make room within the citizenry for those few who were "separated from their tribes and incorporated in your community."[64] Yet as the debate proceeded, it became clear that the concepts of jurisdiction and civilization could not, separately or in tandem, produce consensus about who was or should be included. Jurisdiction and civilization, it turned out, were not straightforward categories at all but shorthand for settler-colonial processes and imperatives, which were in turn both local and ongoing. Neither term could be discussed without drawing in the myriad and divergent histories of settlers and settler states and their complicated legacies of cultural intermixture and interaction with Native communities.

Given the history of allotment in relation to citizenship, especially in the treaties of the Manypenny era, it is not surprising that one of the first proposed amendments to Trumbull's definition was that Indians should be deemed citizens of the United States if they held "land in severalty by allotment."[65] But the source of this proposal exposed the more pragmatic, indeed mercenary, motivations that underlay the policy in the first place. The man moving this amendment was Kansas Republican James Lane, a shameless speculator in Native land. And Lane's object in proposing this amendment was to steal the Potawatomi people's land.

Despite an 1861 treaty that had sought to steer the Potawatomi in Kansas toward allotment, that nation had managed to retain a good deal of its land on terms that left the land neither taxable nor salable. During the Civil War, Lane and his colleague Samuel Pomeroy secured congressional approval for presidential authority to extinguish all Native title in Kansas; nevertheless, the Potawatomi and other nations persisted.[66] Lane saw the 1866 debate over national citizenship as a way to break this logjam. Adding the phrase "and Indians holding land in severalty by allotment" to the citizenship criteria in the civil rights bill would cut the Gordian knot of treaties, federal supremacy, and Indian title. Native people who had taken up allotments would automatically become citizens, subject to state laws regarding the sale and taxation of property. The treaty's restriction on sales would evaporate. Lane and the rest of the Kansas delegation thought it "wise policy that they [Native people] may have the privilege of holding these allotments and selling them. That is the object."[67] But when he explained his "object" as granting Native people "the privilege of holding these allotments and selling them," he knew that they already had the right to hold allotments. What he was after was the selling.[68] The unilateral imposition of U.S. citizenship would facilitate that.[69]

But to incorporate Native people as citizens on the simple basis of having taken allotments ran up against other regional histories. In particular, Lane's proposal foundered on its potential consequences for what remained of Indian Territory, to the south of Kansas. Trumbull pointed out that a universal equation of allotment with citizenship could make citizens of those who held lands allotted under the authority of the Cherokee nation, or anywhere else "outside of the organized jurisdiction of the United States in the Indian country."[70] What would it mean for citizenship to follow allotment automatically?[71]

Trumbull's proposal to define citizens as people "not subject to any foreign power" generated another set of objections, some of them rooted in the genocidal conquest of the far West. Murderous campaigns that began during the early years of the gold rush continued in the far West as the 1866 debate unfolded. Barely two weeks after Trumbull offered his citizenship language, for example, scores of U.S. cavalrymen and vigilantes chased a band of Northern Paiutes across the California-Oregon border, surrounded the party, and over the next six hours killed between 80 and 125 people.[72] Violence on this scale destabilized Native societies and produced floods of refugees. Their circumstances created new uncertainties about jurisdiction—about who was still "subject" to a foreign power and who was for all practical purposes subject only to the United States.

In the 1866 Senate debate, California's John Conness explicitly worried about the status of Native people whose "tribal authority" he believed to have been destroyed by conquest. He described California's reservations as refugee camps into which survivors of extermination campaigns were herded and held by force. From his perspective, their governments had been shattered and their reservations were wholly under the authority of U.S. agents and soldiers. He saw neither any pretense of a policy of "civilization" nor anything resembling "tribal authority."[73] His Oregon colleague George Williams painted a similar portrait of utter Native subjection to U.S. power: "The Government of the

United States feeds, clothes, and takes care of these Indians, and treats them as wards, treats them as incapable of self-government; and they are governed by such rules and regulations as are prescribed by the Government from time to time, and as the necessities of the case seem to require."[74] Trumbull's language excluding Native people as subjects of a foreign power would not cover these people; neither would additional proposed language excluding those under "tribal authority."[75] If these remained the only exclusions, all of the people whom Conness and Williams described would be fully incorporated into the United States. Yet in Williams's view, "they are no more qualified to become citizens than when they existed as original tribes."[76]

These descriptions of wardship and internment confused some of the westerners' Senate colleagues. The broad-brush American description of all Native groups as "tribes" and all leaders as "chiefs" led many lawmakers to assume that Native jurisdictions were all clearly bounded political communities with equally clear, singular, and authoritative political leadership. They could not imagine collectivities without "tribal organization." But in countless ways, Native polities did not conform to American ideas of hierarchy, leadership, or decision-making. Since whether Native people were or were not subject to "tribal authority" was the entire conceit that underlay the treaties and state and federal enactments that provided a path to citizenship, some found it shocking to consider that the most basic terms that Americans used to talk about Indians' political and social organization might fail upon close inspection.

Others knew better, and they warned their colleagues to heed what Williams and Conness were saying. "Tribe" was a "loose and ill-defined thing," explained Alexander Ramsey, U.S. senator from Minnesota. A standard based on "tribal authority" might incorporate people who were neither "civilized" nor subject to U.S. jurisdiction in any sense that he recognized. But Ramsey's own concerns were rooted in a different history, and he wanted amended language to reflect that difference. His proposal was to allow each state to use its own parameters for Native citizenship; he suggested excluding "Indians not admitted to citizenship by the laws of any of the states."[77] This acknowledged his own and other states' paths to citizenship for "civilized" Indians who submitted themselves to their jurisdiction, although Ramsey doubted that such people existed.[78]

Ramsey was thinking his way through a different history of conquest, especially the U.S.-Dakota War, the ensuing expulsion of the Dakota and Ho-Chunk from his state, and their continuing return. By 1866, as we will see, the U.S. position was that the Ho-Chunk formally belonged in an exile reservation community in the Nebraska Territory. Shortly after the conclusion of the debate on the civil rights bill, the Senate would ratify the treaty that formally exchanged Crow Creek for these lands.[79] But Ramsey was thinking of another group: the many Ho-Chunk people who for decades had refused to stay where the government wanted them, and who even now maintained lives along the lakes and rivers of Wisconsin, Iowa, and Minnesota. Like a generation of officials before him, Ramsey depicted Ho-Chunk self-determination and seasonal itineraries as evidence that they were a "vagabond" and "wandering" people. He called them "outlaws," "refugees from all tribal authority, ... recogniz[ing] no such authority."[80]

Ramsey's derisive language was not just invective but a warning to his colleagues about the peril of definitions. From his point of view, Ho-Chunk people's unpoliced "wandering" meant that they were no longer under "tribal authority" nor subject to any "foreign power." If that was the case, then Trumbull's proposed language effectively made citizens out of them. And if they were citizens of the United States and of Minnesota, it followed that Ramsey's Minnesota constituents lacked the authority to expel them. Whether Minnesota settlers liked it or not, they would have a formal right to settle and remain in the state. As a representative of settler interests, Ramsey could not allow that to happen.

Trumbull finally acknowledged the variety of competing settler claims, grumbling about "how difficult it is to accommodate the different interests that are represented here." Lane's crass gambit promised unforeseeable complications. Conness's description of California was worrying, and Ramsey made similarly trenchant points about the troubling looseness of "tribal authority." But Ramsey proffered a definition of citizenship that returned authority to the states, when what the moment required was a uniform national standard. To put an end to debate, Trumbull proposed that the Senate return to the Constitution's familiar language and exclude from citizenship "Indians not taxed."[81] Surely that would at least answer Ramsey's objections.

The history of "Indians not taxed" stretched back to the Constitution, but even there it remained curiously undefined. Where definitions did exist, they were unhelpful: the instructions given to census enumerators in 1860, for example, provided that "Indians *not taxed* are not to be enumerated" but that "the families of Indians who have renounced tribal rule, and who under State or Territorial laws exercise the rights of citizens, are to be enumerated."[82] But what precisely did it mean to "renounce tribal rule"? And what sense would it make, while Congress was establishing federal supremacy over rights and citizenship, to revert to whatever rules states or territories might enact?

Moreover, even this rule might produce more confusion—what about those who renounced tribal rule but lacked state or territorial citizenship rights, or vice-versa?

But Trumbull knew what he was doing. He had deduced that the definition of national citizenship could not be too precise, lest it restrict local settler communities' ability to define their own parameters for Native inclusion or exclusion. He admitted that "Indians not taxed" was not really a property qualification; instead, it was meant to be a proxy for Native people's acceptance of U.S. jurisdiction and their embrace of its civilization. "Not taxed," he explained, meant "considered virtually as foreigners." "Taxed," by contrast, meant those Natives who had "separated from [their] tribes, and come within the jurisdiction of the United States so as to be counted."[83] And that standard, he later clarified, embraced only "a class of persons; that is, civilized Indians."[84] Oregon's George Williams, no doubt much relieved, expanded Trumbull's meaning further: taxation or its absence "is the most certain way of defining the distinction between wild, savage, and untamed Indians, and those who associate with white people, own property, and exercise the privileges that generally attend a citizen in the community."[85] From this point of view, an "Indian taxed" was not defined literally by the fact of tax assessment or payment. Rather, that status denoted Native people who were accepted as neighbors by local settlers, at least to the degree that they were willing to tolerate their presence and take in their tax moneys. In this way, the exclusion of "Indians not taxed" captured the demands for a formula that embraced only Native people who were deemed both civilized and materially enmeshed in settler society.

With this addition, the citizenship clause was complete. Its final version read, "All persons born in the United States and not subject to any foreign power, excluding Indians not taxed, are hereby declared to be citizens of the United States." The civil rights bill containing this language was passed by Congress, vetoed by Andrew Johnson, and passed immediately over his veto. It became law on April 9, 1866.[86]

Yet within weeks congressional Republicans had a change of heart. As they began writing citizenship into the draft Fourteenth Amendment, the useful imprecision of "Indians not taxed" started to seem risky. The purpose of creating national citizenship, after all, was to establish national rights that could be federally enforced against state action. Yet the federal government was not the only entity with the power to tax. If courts took the language of "Indians not taxed" literally, cities or states might be able to include or exclude Native people as citizens simply by the way they exercised their own taxing power. The Colorado Territory, for example, could tax property held by Native people and by that means make them citizens of the United States.⁸⁷ "Indians not taxed" began to portend an outright contradiction of the federal supremacy that was central to the Civil Rights Act, the Fourteenth Amendment, and, at least in theory, Indian policy.

To remedy this, the Fourteenth Amendment's drafters settled on alternative language that underscored the supremacy of the federal government: "All persons born or naturalized in the United States and subject to the jurisdiction thereof are citizens of the United States and of the States wherein they reside."⁸⁸ They understood this to exclude Indians under tribal authority and children born to the families of diplomats, but to include everyone else born or naturalized on U.S. territory.

"Jurisdiction" served some of the same deliberately imprecise functions as "taxed." On the one hand, it allowed the United States to define most of Indian Country as outside the scope of the amendment, thereby excluding the great majority of Native people from the start. As Trumbull put it, the United States had within its territorial limits "a large region of country, unorganized, over which we do not pretend to exercise any civil or criminal jurisdiction, where wild tribes of Indian roam at pleasure, subject to their own laws and regulations, and we do not pretend to interfere with them. They would not be embraced by this provision." The exclusion from citizenship of Native people in the unorganized territories claimed by the United States had always been assumed, and Trumbull assured his colleagues that it remained so.⁸⁹

But jurisdiction was not as straightforward a criterion as it seemed. Consider how Jacob Howard, managing the amendment's passage through the Senate, described the exclusion of Native people from citizenship. "Indians born within the limits of the United States, and who maintain their tribal relations, are not, in the sense of the amendment, born subject to the jurisdiction of the United States," he said. "They are regarded, and always have been in our legislation and jurisprudence, as being *quasi* foreign nations." Not actually foreign; note that they were, in his view, "born within the limits of the United States." But they were foreign enough to be excluded when that was desirable.⁹⁰

Yet to describe Native polities as "quasi foreign nations" and their sovereignty as limited raised further questions about the extent of U.S. jurisdiction and the limits of Indian foreignness. Native nations, Howard explained, had a "national character." The United States treated with them as "sovereign powers." But as the Supreme Court had put it three decades before, "The Indians are our wards." So Howard described Native sovereignty in terms of the limits the country was entitled to set upon it: "They have a national independence. They have an absolute right to the occupancy of the soil upon which they reside; and the only ground of claim which the United States has ever put forth to the proprietorship of the soil of an Indian territory is ... the right ... to be the first purchaser from the Indian tribes." But that "only ground of claim" was in practice almost infinitely expansive. Read through the actual history of the United States since 1830, Howard's account of jurisdiction confirmed a fundamental principle that was rarely articulated so baldly: that the United States asserted the right to tell Native sovereignties when their sovereignty was at an end.[91]

By some lights, this assumed right was itself a kind of jurisdiction. That was how Wisconsin's Senator James Doolittle saw it, at least. He had spent the preceding year traveling the West and taking testimony on the "Indian Question," and he knew more than most of his colleagues did about the diversity and complexity of Native life at the border of U.S. settlement.[92] He emphatically did not want to incorporate Native people: "They are, in my judgment, utterly unfit to be citizens of the United States," he said. But he was equally certain that Howard's language of "subject to the jurisdiction" did just that. The United States claimed the sole right to treat with Native nations, he reasoned; it subdued them with armies and laws, and it seemed certain to continue on that course. In that sense, then, would not all Native people between southern California and northern Minnesota, at least in the future imagined by lawmakers, be "subject to the jurisdiction" of the United States, and therefore citizens? Doolittle's assessment was that Native sovereignty was a fiction, that Native people were "completely our subjects, completely in our power." It was in that sense that "we hold them as wards." As people fundamentally "subject to the jurisdiction" of the United States, they would therefore be made citizens by the Fourteenth Amendment.[93]

Doolittle therefore warned his colleagues not to adopt the standard of "jurisdiction" and to hold instead to the looser "Indians not taxed" language of the Civil Rights Act. Over time, he said, "Indians not taxed" had "come to have a meaning that is understood as descriptive of a certain class of Indians that may be enumerated ... as part of the citizens of the United States."[94] The passive voice did not disguise who was "understanding" and "enumerating." Like the rest, he wanted a standard that limited citizenship to those whom a community of settlers or a state was willing to accept. But Doolittle's counsel went unheeded. He was a supporter of Andrew Johnson, and in Republican eyes he was therefore an apostate. They rejected his amendment.

But the extension of U.S. jurisdiction over the next five years underscored Doolittle's argument about who was subject to it. During the second half of the 1860s, the United States embarked on what appeared to be two distinct military and bureaucratic projects. One, a fitful and under-supported effort to defend the civil and political rights of Black and white Southern Republicans and transform the region into a bastion of free labor, encompassed the Fifteenth Amendment, which led in turn to the establishment of the Department of Justice and a series of Enforcement Acts designed in part to protect Black and white Republican voters in the former slave states.[95] The other, the project unfolding in Indian Country, continued and extended the work of "civilization," allotment, and citizenship once championed by men like Commissioner George Manypenny. It sought to abolish Native sovereignty, reduce Native nations to reservation communities, and reshape Native people's lives along American lines.[96]

The projects of Reconstruction and "civilization" initially shared some important features. Many white proponents of a future without racial hierarchy assumed that non-white people would require a period of paternal oversight and tutelage. This idea had coursed through American social thought and policy for generations, not just in the policy of "civilization" but also in the "apprenticeship" of people born to enslaved parents under Northern states' policies of gradual emancipation. And just as a generation of Indian Office administrators imagined the remaking of Native people as landowning citizens, the Republicans of the 1860s longed to see the revolution of slave emancipation followed by the transformation of nearly 4 million freedpeople into model free-labor actors. During and just after the war, Northern emissaries to the South strove to make former slaves understand what freedom should mean in their domestic and economic lives in terms that echoed Indian policy: "civilization and Christianity," "order, industry, economy, and self-reliance." On former plantation lands occupied by Union soldiers, Northern capitalists and philanthropists sought to control the movements, labors, and education of people recently freed from slavery in ways similar to what U.S. Indian Agent Jonathan Fletcher or Superintendent William Cullen imagined in Minnesota.[97]

In the postwar era, however, these parallel projects quickly diverged. It was precisely this kind of authority, asserted by former slaveholders under the Black Codes, that inspired the Civil Rights Act of 1866. The new order of equal standing before the law, equal rights of property and contract, and equal rights of mobility and residence made it all but impossible to establish such paternalist oversight. As much as "benevolent" whites might want to exert control over how Black people lived, worked, socialized, and migrated, they could not do so after 1866. But Indian policy, even policy that spoke of "citizenship," continued to embrace that paternalist program without apology. Oversight over how Native people lived and used their resources was exactly what George Manypenny demanded in his treaty with the Ho-Chunk in 1855. It was what William Cullen envisioned when he imagined how the Ho-Chunk people's "gradual incorporation into the habits and systems of government of those who hold to them now the position of a dominant race" would "eventually entitle them to the rights and privileges of a condition of actual citizenship."[98]

Since at least the 1830s, the Supreme Court had described Native people as "wards," a word that echoed through the decades and all through the 1866 debate. Most Americans viewed Native people as only potentially or provisionally capable of taking proper places in the U.S. order; most were thought to require an extended, possibly indefinite, apprenticeship in American ways. This thinking lay beneath the very first objection to Trumbull's citizenship language: the civil rights bill surely could not mean to incorporate Native people, Senator James Guthrie said, for they were "mere dependents on the government."[99] Over the next years, federal policy did not abandon the language of "citizenship" for the imagined future of Native people. But the path to that status and the way Native people would be guided along it took on an ever-more paternalistic cast. Superintendent Cullen's "eventually" in 1858 was echoed in Ulysses S. Grant's inaugural address in 1869, in which he looked forward to an Indian policy that would lead to their "civilization and ultimate citizenship." When an "ultimate citizenship" would "eventually" unfold remained an open question.[100]

As Congress debated civil rights, the exiles from Blue Earth struggled for bare survival. Amid grievous loss and physical hardship, Coming Thunder and others led an exodus from Crow Creek in canoes crafted from cottonwood trees. Evading the small detachment of troops stationed with them, they paddled back down the Missouri, finding shelter with the Iowa and Omaha peoples.[101] Agents pleaded for troops to restrain the Ho-Chunk or return them to Crow Creek, but it was 1864: with the U.S. Army enduring some of its worst days against rebel forces, the government paid little attention.[102] By late 1864, more than a thousand Ho-Chunks were living with the Omaha, including the bands led by Coming Thunder, his brother Short Wing, and Little Priest.[103] In 1865 the federal government acknowledged these facts on the ground. It conducted a new treaty with the Ho-Chunk, along with the purchase of land from the Omaha, to create a new homeland for them along the Missouri River in the Nebraska Territory.[104]

Coming Thunder protested their circumstances directly to President Lincoln in 1864. They knew where the blame resided: with the government that dispossessed them, allowed them to be defrauded by agents and traders, and appointed bad or incompetent men to lead them. Their protest noted the pressing hardship of inadequate blankets and clothing. But they pointed to a deeper problem of leadership. The agent appointed by the government would not even tell them how many people were on his roll, making it impossible for them to calculate whether they were receiving the goods and amounts they had been promised. Their "chiefs" were of no use, since they had been appointed by the government and were afraid of being "broken and punished by the agent," as Coming Thunder himself had been a few years before. From top to bottom, the people placed in charge—chiefs, agent, or interpreter—"refuse to look after our interests and protect us from wrong and injustice."[105] But the dislocations and devastation of the early 1860s left the Ho-Chunk in a poor position to resist the postwar government's demands. When the treaty establishing their new homeland was finally ratified in 1866, the Ho-Chunk had not received annuity goods or money for nearly three years. The government was able to use their poverty to extract new concessions: a new census, a new push for allotment, and new intrusions into their practices of government, justice, spiritual life, and even dress.

Longtime band leaders such as Coming Thunder were not the only ones who saw a crisis of leadership and governance in the late 1860s. Ho-Chunk men who had worn the blue uniform of the United States, many of them not formerly leaders, emerged to play central roles in the struggle with American colonialism on the Nebraska reservation. Most of these soldiers, recruited in Nebraska during the dire early months of 1865, had served with the Omaha Scouts, a cavalry company of Native Americans who helped prosecute the "punitive expeditions" against the Dakota.[106] Among the eighty or so men who enlisted in these western campaigns during the middle months of 1865 was Little Priest, who rose to the rank of sergeant.[107] Some young veterans, as we have seen, served earlier and longer; they were among the small group of Ho-Chunks, mainly of mixed descent, who remained in Minnesota or returned to it shortly after the expulsion of the rest of the tribe and who enlisted in Minnesota regiments.[108]

In the late 1860s, an aspiring group of "braves and young men," with John St. Cyr at their head, made a bid to take charge of Ho-Chunk affairs in the name of "civilization." Within a year of his arrival in Nebraska, St. Cyr and other young men, many of them veterans, began demanding a more powerful role in the nation's affairs and a change in the tribal leadership—perhaps even for St. Cyr himself to be made "head chief."[109] As he put it, "A large portion of the tribe are desirous of advancing in civilization as rapidly as possible & desire, men for their chief & leading men who will most aid them in this matter."[110] St. Cyr had a rare combination of skills and experiences, including literacy and familiarity with American institutions, most recently through life as an American officer. As one petition stated, "Having been a great part of his life among the whites [he] possesses more knowledge of the way in which we should act to secure for us peace and harmony with our white brothers."[111]

St. Cyr cuts a singular figure in this history, and his course during the 1860s and 1870s defies easy categorization. The bilingual son of a mixed-descent bilingual trader, born in the Neutral Ground, he had spent most of his childhood in the Ho-Chunk exile community. He was one of the few children to attend the early reservation schools with consistency, and later he often served as an interpreter. He was among the allotted Ho-Chunk who successfully asserted a right to remain in Minnesota in 1863, and he almost immediately thereafter enlisted in a Minnesota regiment. But despite his postwar status as a veteran and landowner in Minnesota, he relocated to the postwar reservation in Nebraska and sought to play a pivotal role in its political life. And this was not the last move he would make.

St. Cyr and the other "young men" of the late 1860s claimed to want allotment and civilization, but their movement did not seek to dismantle tribal authority and replace it with U.S. citizenship. Instead, St. Cyr seems to have been demanding a new kind of citizenship within the Ho-Chunk world and to control affairs on the reservation. The "braves and young men" even tried to assert majoritarian control over the petition process itself, in 1868 claiming to have "made a law among ourselves that the chiefs should not sign any petitions unless the tribe [w]as talked to about it."[112]

One result of this movement was a written legal code, adopted by a tribal council in July 1868, that employed the forms and language of American government to codify and consolidate tribal authority. Using terms that U.S. officials would understand, the code vested "executive and judicial power" in fourteen "Chiefs" and established a police force and rules governing crimes against persons and property as well as laws regarding debt, civic order, and school attendance. This document acknowledged the authority of the U.S. Indian agent over the tribe's annuities, giving him the power of appointing the police force, but it placed judgments of guilt, innocence, and punishment entirely in Ho-Chunk hands. Trials for theft of property—whether from "a white man, Indian, or from the United States"—were to take place before the chiefs.[113]

What the "young men" sought dovetailed in important ways with currents of reform then reshaping the nation's Indian policy. In 1867 Congress established an Indian Peace Commission to persuade Native nations to accept permanent reservations in exchange for permanent peace. Lawmakers described this as "the hitherto untried policy... of endeavoring to conquer by kindness," but it was in many ways a familiar form of conquest, in which reservation life would be the site of a renewed policy of "civilization." The government would rationalize, reform, and improve its tutelage by establishing more uniform policies, replacing corrupt reservation agents with the representatives of Christian denominations, and taking full control of annuity disbursements. Native people would learn to speak English, abandon their languages and national identifications, and be severed from relations with other Native groups. The result, reformers hoped, would be an end to military conflict, an end to tribal government, and the gradual merging of Native people into American life.[114] In 1869 President Grant began affirming elements of this "Peace Policy." In his inaugural address he declared that he would favor any Indian policy "which tends to their civilization and ultimate citizenship," and the policies he and Congress pursued over the next few years affirmed the spirit of the Peace Commission's recommendations. Quaker, Baptist, Catholic, Congregational and other church missionary groups nominated agents to oversee reservations and the implementation of "civilization" policies.[115]

Under this policy, the Ho-Chunk reservation fell under the supervision of Howard White, a Quaker agent who just happened to be the son of the regional superintendent of Indian Affairs. White and the other Christian reformers whom the United States appointed in this era no longer saw themselves as an earlier generation of agents had, as intermediaries between the two parties to a treaty. They understood themselves instead in terms that George Manypenny and William Cullen would have approved, as the paternal overseers of a civilizing program.

White eagerly sought the transformation of governance among the Ho-Chunk. Identifying with the "young men," he described "a strong party feeling" that separated older leaders who "wish to retain their old customs and traditions" from "the half breeds and most of the young men, who see that the only salvation for the tribe is for it to adopt the ways of the whites, and become civilized." He happily took sides and replaced the old chiefs with "twelve of the most enterprising young men."[116] He followed this with a ratifying vote by the reservation's men. Election of chiefs then became the custom, if not the official policy.[117] White asserted that elections provided the Ho-Chunk with "a republican form of government, and thus pav[ed] the way to citizenship."[118] Official pronouncements from Washington similarly praised the election of leaders because it would "weaken the old tribal relation, with all its superstitious ideas and customs, ... prepare the people for self-government ... [and] pave the way for the Indians to become citizens."[119] White took credit, but given the years of agitation and growing political sophistication that preceded this transition, it seems plausible that St. Cyr's "young men" were driving this process as much as the agent was. John St. Cyr did not become a "chief," as he wanted, but after the Quakers' arrival he did become chief of police under the recently adopted legal code.[120]

Allotment, a keystone in the renewed "civilization" policy, remained deeply controversial on the new reservation. Agents continued to imagine that allotment would "tend to civilize them more than any one act ... as it would break up their banding together" and deter them from engaging in non-acquisitive pursuits.[121] They asserted that the Ho-Chunk people wanted nothing more than to become American-style farmers and that they would succeed in it. But in the next breath, officials acknowledged the coercive implications of their prescription: "The only way to make Indians self sustaining is as soon as possible to throw them on their own *individual* resources, by so doing, the idle and worthless ones are compelled to labor or suffer, and the more industrious ones derive the exclusive benefit of their own exertions."[122] On the eve of the allotment of the Nebraska lands in 1869, the agency physician bluntly reported a "talk" he had with some Ho-Chunks "about the land." "I think they all know now what is required of them, and will try and do it," wrote Dr. Joseph Paxson. "Not from choice, but because they see that the land will be divided whether they want it done or not."[123] By the end of 1870, it was done.[124]

The "young men" also aligned themselves with other intrusions into Ho-Chunk community life that far outstripped whatever mandate they had. This was particularly true about the ceremonies associated with the Medicine Lodge, an important Ho-Chunk religious institution. The activities of the Medicine Lodge fascinated and troubled outsiders. Paxson, the reservation physician, attended again and again, but he fretted over its unapologetically Ho-Chunk character. "I do not think it is best for the Indian to encourage such things," he wrote. In 1870, after five young men were charged with the murder of a white farmer, officials blamed Medicine Lodge leaders—"devoted to their superstitious rites, opposed to civilization, and utterly inefficient for any useful purpose"—for impeding the investigation.[125] The aspiring "braves and young men" saw an opening. In council, "the young men made all kinds of fine promises" about what they would do if the agent deposed the chiefs and installed them, including abandoning the Medicine Lodge. But by then, after a year on the reservation, even Paxson could see that this was a foolish promise. "I fear that if they attempt that thing they will get in any amount of trouble."[126]

Remaking the Ho-Chunk people's spiritual and communal life turned out to be much harder than the apostles of "civilization" claimed, which may explain why authorities soon became preoccupied with changes they could more easily demand, encourage, and measure. The Office of Indian Affairs told agents to enumerate the signs of Indian "civilization": how many schools and pupils attending them; how many churches and church members; how many acres cultivated and bushels produced. At the bottom of this was the same long-standing preoccupation with the "progress" a given people were making toward "civilization," the necessary predicate for citizenship.

Nowhere was the imagined relationship between "civilization" and citizenship clearer than in a new emphasis on Anglo-American styles of clothing. Officials sometimes called this "the dress of the whites." But more often, and in the statistical tables that accompanied their regular reports to Washington, they named it simply "citizens' dress" or "citizens' clothing."[127] To reformers, "citizens' dress" offered a compact and efficient marker of Native people's willingness to dissolve their tribal ties and become liberal individuals who could legitimately take up the mantle of "citizen."[128]

Ho-Chunk people's adoption of American styles of clothing flattered the prejudices and ambitions of officials. It offered an apparently unambiguous victory over "savagery," one that they could see and celebrate. Once the first shipment of "citizens' clothing" from Quaker patrons arrived at the Ho-Chunk reservation in 1869, Dr. Joseph Paxson found the rapid transformations thrilling. "The change was wonderful—from a dirty little Indian, wrapped in a blanket—came a neat well formed pleasant looking little Indian boy."[129] Dress quickly came to signify acquiescence to the new order of things: a year later, a superintendent bragged about the high caliber of the new "chiefs" he had appointed, "all working men of good character, who dress like white men."[130]

In fact, the politics of dress in the Ho-Chunk world of the 1870s both reflected and shaped the larger contest between Indians and colonial authorities, a contest that was not simply defined by the alternatives of assimilation and resistance. Across the Ho-Chunk diaspora, as in many parts of Indian Country, people neither fully acknowledged nor directly contested U.S. hegemony. Instead, through decades of losses and dispossessions, they forged an alternative order that took account of what officials wanted without either embracing or directly attacking it. They might sometimes wear civilization's clothing, but not always as a sign of their incorporation in the American order.[131]

While officials used clothing as an index of the tractability, progress, or worthiness of the people they hoped to "civilize," Ho-Chunk and other Native people often took on "citizens' clothing" expediently, to improve their position relative to settlers, employers, agents, missionaries, and lawmakers. Clothing was as easily shed as donned. An 1869 Quaker delegation noted that Ho-Chunk men put on citizens' clothing in some circumstances, but that same delegation carefully described men wearing breechcloths, blankets, leggings, and moccasins, the latter two often "finely worked and beaded."[132] In these contexts, dressing as a "citizen" could seem to be a self-conscious performance for the benefit of agents, missionaries, and employers.

The performance of "citizens' dress" refracted through the very different gendered prescriptions for men's and women's "civilization." The adoption of "citizens' dress" helped men gain work as agricultural laborers, an increasingly common dimension of subsistence as the territory around plains reservations filled up with white settlers. This was the economic reality behind the Indian Office's statistical category "male Indians engaged in manual labor in civilized pursuits." An 1869 Quaker delegation to the Nebraska reservation noted that "these Indians are mostly willing to work for wages, and when they ask for work, they come, 'dressed like white men,' knowing the Agent will not employ them when 'dressed in blankets.'"[133] Elsewhere, some agents were said to treat "farmer Indians" who wore citizens' clothing better than those who did not.[134]

Men were supposed to adopt citizens' dress for the labor market, but they were not expected to produce that clothing. Women, by contrast, were not supposed to enter the wage-labor market but were supposed to learn to produce citizens' clothing, embracing their proper productive roles in the settler order. So as the Quakers began their work, the agent "ordered a suit of clothes for each man," but bought or requested donations of cloth so that Native women could be instructed in cutting and sewing clothes.[135]

But while citizens' clothing might provide Ho-Chunk men access to wage work, it conferred no similar benefits on women. So perhaps it is not surprising that by 1872 the agent saw a pattern emerging: "The men have nearly all adopted the dress of the whites," but he could only "anticipat[e] . . . that the women will do the same so soon as they shall come to live in houses."[136] The one official enumeration that broke down "citizens' dress" among the Ho-Chunk by gender, in 1878, revealed a stark division: the agent reported that while 694 men had adopted "citizens' dress," only one woman had done so.[137]

Perhaps here, as in other modern colonial contexts, women's exclusion from the world of wage work and its requirements left them the primary (though not sole) bearers of Indigenous forms of dress.[138]

If Ho-Chunk responses to "citizens' dress" revealed skepticism about the program of "civilization and ultimate citizenship," the unfolding of that program during the 1870s gave the people ample reason to be suspicious. What was emerging on the Ho-Chunk reservation, and on so many others, was not a pathway to citizenship but an intrusive and paternalist wardship. In 1873, for example, officials presented the Ho-Chunk as being "on the high road to civilization." But either progress was not all it was cracked up to be, or the road was lengthening even as the Ho-Chunk moved along it. The same officials concluded that the tribe should "remain as wards of the Government until further advanced in civilization."[139] This was a refrain that would become familiar to colonized people the world over: they might be praised for their steps toward the light of civilization and incorporation as equals, but they would never quite be ready for equality.[140]

Even as the main landmarks of the "high road to civilization" turned out to be constricting and authoritarian forms of wardship, some Ho-Chunk people cleared a different path. Those who had already taken allotments in Minnesota, served in the Minnesota regiments, and remained in the state past the deportation of 1863 were able to escape the net.[141] They soon went much further, pressing their case that they should be allowed to make good on the promises of the treaties of the 1850s.[142] They sought to reside peacefully on their allotted acres and to claim the status of citizen, hoping to achieve a status that would permanently protect them from being rounded up as "wanderers," "vagrants," and "Indians."

As this group of about 160 people sought U.S. citizenship, they knew the formulas that would ring persuasively in officials' ears. "They wish to merge themselves into the civilized community with which they are surrounded, and to abandon entirely and forever their savage habits and relations," their lawyer told Secretary of the Interior James Harlan. They wished to hold their lands in fee simple, like other settlers. "Most of them," Beveridge even claimed, "are already citizens of the state of Minnesota, and all of them by the laws of the state may become such." In exchange for their new allegiance, they asked for their prorated individual shares of the large annuity fund that the federal government still owed to the Ho-Chunk as a nation.[143]

Settlers remained divided about this group. Some leaders viewed the Ho-Chunk claims as outrageous and unacceptable to the new owners of the

Blue Earth lands. Minnesota Republican congressman William Windom warned against allowing any of the Ho-Chunk to return to lands already occupied by settlers, since "the prejudice of the people in that part of my district against Indians is very bitter, and not without cause."[144] But in this era of reform and the "Peace Policy" they also found allies. Ho-Chunk petitions reminded legislators of a grotesque injustice that was in their power to redress: the cost of the expulsion to Crow Creek had been charged against the Ho-Chunk tribal fund.[145] Officials confirmed Ho-Chunk allotment claims and even canceled some white settlers' claims when those interfered with allotments that had already been made.[146] Most importantly, Congress began to consider the broader question of the Ho-Chunk people's status. By April 1866, at the very moment that national citizenship became law in the Civil Rights Act, Congress considered legislation that would allow them to prove they had "adopted the habits of civilized life and are able to support themselves and their families," dissolve their formal relationship to the Ho-Chunk, and "become citizens of the United States."[147]

In 1870 they won. In a late series of amendments to an appropriation act for Indian Affairs, midwestern senators crafted special language for these allotted Ho-Chunk people. The legislators' statutory text allowed this group to remain in Minnesota on their assigned lands, or on newly selected ones if those had already been claimed; they could then hold those lands without the right to sell them further, and they would continue to receive their annuities according to treaty. But those who desired to become U.S. citizens could make the required attestations of allegiance, civilization, and self-support. If their petition to do so were accepted in federal court, they could then ask the secretary of the Interior to grant them a prorated share of their tribal funds and fee-simple patent to their lands, which would allow them to sell them at will. They would then "cease to be members of said tribe" and would be subject to the same taxation as other citizens.[148] This conferral of national citizenship was not grandly framed in a treaty or constitutional amendment. It consisted, in total, of sections 9 and 10 of an appropriation bill for Indian Affairs. But over the next two years, about 160 people took up citizenship under its terms.[149]

The process of making Ho-Chunk people into U.S. citizens began at the federal courthouse in St. Paul in October 1870, when fifty-four Ho-Chunks appeared before U.S. district judge Rensselaer Nelson to submit to the naturalization examination described in the statute. Fifty-one passed Judge Nelson's examination that day, though three did not, for reasons unspecified in the newspaper coverage.[150] Although this process was called "naturalization,"

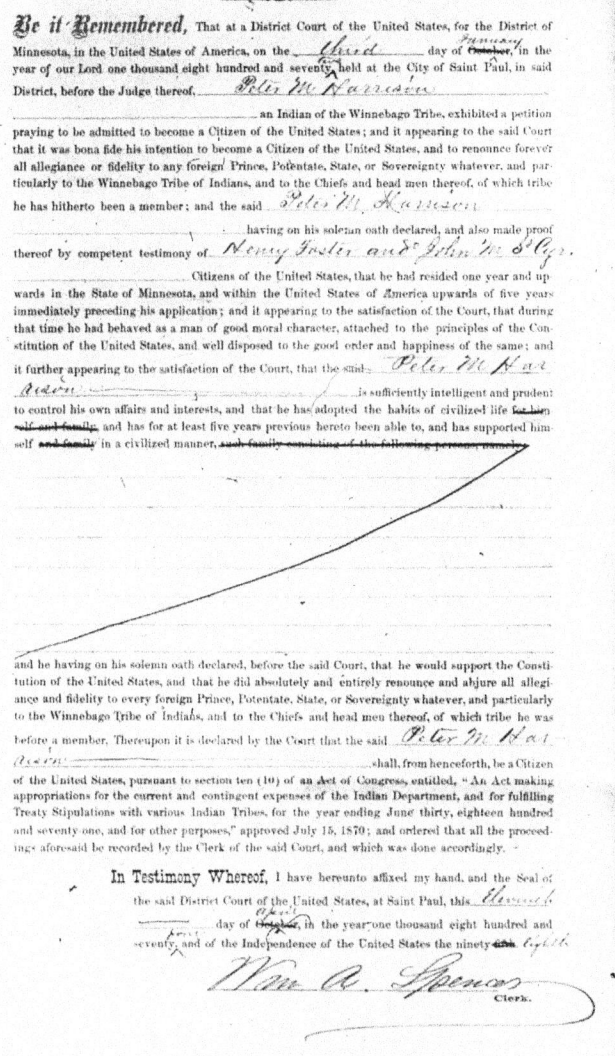

Figure 3.2. Certificate of Naturalization as a U.S. citizen for the mixed-descent Ho-Chunk man Peter M. Harrison, received in the federal courthouse in St. Paul in 1872. Note that John St. Cyr, who became a naturalized citizen in the same way two years before, served as a citizen witness to Harrison's fitness for that status. (*LROIA*, Winnebago Agency, Roll 943)

the fifty-one were not naturalized as individuals, as European immigrants would have been, but under the names of twelve heads of household, who made the required attestations of "civilization" and self-support on behalf of their dependents.[151] Those naturalized on this first day, including John St. Cyr and Baptiste Lasallier, soon received patents for the lands formerly allotted to them, making their landownership the same as that of non-Native people.[152] A second set of naturalizations brought the total number of people to 154.[153] This time, John M. St. Cyr was one of the citizen witnesses attesting to the morality, prudence, intelligence, and civilization of the petitioners.[154] A series of special agents traveled to Blue Earth to ascertain the eligibility of the claimants, deliver annuity payments, and finally make the distributions from the tribal fund to those who had naturalized as citizens.[155]

For a brief period in the early 1870s, it seemed that this might become a more generally available pathway to national citizenship. The General Land Office, which oversaw the sale of public lands, suggested a version of this policy, coupling land acquisition and citizenship, for Native people generally. In early 1870, the land office ruled that those who chose to dissolve their tribal relations could enter lands under the Homestead Act of 1862, on the same basis as other settlers.[156] The department even helpfully provided model forms for the dissolution of tribal identity.[157] These forms became the basis for new bureaucratic instruments, including "citizenship certificates" devised by local Indian agents.[158] But unlike the special legislation won by the Ho-Chunk in 1870, these policies required Native people who wished to become citizens under the terms of the Fourteenth Amendment to surrender not only their cultural and political self-definition but also their rights to treaty funds.

The naturalized Ho-Chunk citizens could seem to represent the triumph of a generation of Indian policy. Agents crowed that the new citizens "are fully competent to take upon themselves the duty of Citizenship. Many of them engaged in farming, having farms well supplied with stock, agricultural implements, etc., and they are devoting themselves also to the education of their children."[159] Yet not everyone who naturalized had this trajectory in mind or sought to impart this lesson. Less than a year into the law's operation, the agent in Nebraska complained that several newly naturalized Ho-Chunks had just arrived from Minnesota and showed no sign of settling down as American homesteaders. To his dismay, their report that they had each received their individual shares of the tribal fund—more than $800 a person—inspired some of the people of mixed descent on the reservation to seek to do the same.[160] A federal policy aimed at a small number of Minnesota residents was echoing across the Ho-Chunk diaspora in Nebraska, not entirely in the way that policy makers intended. Soon these people and their stories would reach Wisconsin as well.

The new regime of national citizenship and equal rights, including extensions of national citizenship to Native people, confused even learned lawmakers. In 1870, a newly seated Republican U.S. senator asked his colleagues for clarification: Had the Fourteenth Amendment in fact made citizens out of all Indians? Incredibly, his colleagues didn't seem to know, so they commissioned the Senate Judiciary Committee to issue a report. Had he still been in the Senate, James Doolittle would surely have smirked.

That Senate report reached a foregone conclusion: Native Americans were not, as a rule, citizens. As nations, they retained "their respective nationalities, their right to govern themselves," and "other attribute[s] of a separate political community." The report did seek, however ineffectively, to clarify the meaning of "jurisdiction" of the Fourteenth Amendment. In an economical recapitulation of the 1866 debate's vagueness, it affirmed that when Native people were "merged in the mass of our people," they "become equally subject to the jurisdiction of the United States." But the Senate's 1870 report on citizenship contemplated one other group: it concluded with warning not to engage in treaty-making with Indians who were "scattered." This was an offhand observation in a brief final paragraph. It concerned the status of a very small minority of the Native American population. But it recalled Alexander Ramsey's objections from four years before. In what way could scattered remnants of a tribe fit within the well-developed framework of civilization first, citizenship after? Could defiance of both tribal and treaty authority be rewarded, paradoxically, with U.S. citizenship?

On the question of such "scattered" nations the report was silent.[161] But there could be no more important question for the future of the Ho-Chunk people in Wisconsin. Roaring Thunder had died in 1869, but in the decade that followed, his people stood at a crossroads. Their relations in Nebraska faced an emboldened Indian Office, which ever more confidently treated them as wards of the United States. But the precedent set by the Blue Earth allottees during that same period suggested that American commitments to expulsion and dispossession need not be irreversible and that their history of treaty-making provided resources that under certain circumstances could be taken up to their advantage. Their own history of resistance to removal and enmeshment with settler communities in Wisconsin put them precisely where James Doolittle had feared: so far outside "tribal government" that they could claim the status of citizen on their own terms and for their own purposes. In very short order, that is exactly what they did.

4

TO REMAIN UPON THE LAND

In the early morning hours of December 20, 1873, more than eighty Ho-Chunk people were celebrating an annual feast in a camp on the Baraboo River when two dozen soldiers of the Twentieth U.S. Infantry surrounded their lodge. The government agents leading the soldiers had chosen this group as the first target of their campaign of expulsion because the leader of the band, Big Hawk, was "one of the most obstinate against the removal." They hoped, by making an example of him, to break Ho-Chunk resistance before it took deep root.[1] Through an interpreter, the commander told these Ho-Chunks that they were to accompany the soldiers to a nearby railroad line, from which they would be sent to the reservation in Nebraska. Big Hawk refused, demanding to speak with his attorney, Henry Lee, who lived in nearby Portage. Soldiers trained their weapons on Big Hawk, seized him, and placed him in handcuffs. Soon nearly the entire group was being marched several miles through the woods to the depot.[2]

Three days later, these Ho-Chunks arrived on the Nebraska banks of the Missouri River, where they would freeze and go hungry. This horror unfolded again and again over the next months. More than 800 Ho-Chunk people were forced from their homes, shipped across the Mississippi Valley in winter without their belongings, and deposited on a Nebraska reservation that was unprepared for their arrival. The deportation tore families and bands apart. Children and adults died of hunger, cold, and disease. In their absence, settlers plundered their lodges and horses. Like the deportation to Crow Creek a decade before, the experience lives in the memory of Ho-Chunk people as a cataclysmic event that ended many lives and reshaped many more.

But over the same heartbreaking months that settler demands for their expulsion came to fruition, the Ho-Chunk brought to bear countervailing histories that had been developing over the entire course of their encounter with American power. First, the Ho-Chunk understood that the invaders were not all of one mind. They might be collectively committed to taking whatever Ho-Chunk land they wanted, but they remained divided over whether there could be a place for Ho-Chunk people on that conquered ground. Through relations of trade or the purchase of real estate, Ho-Chunk people had sometimes gained a measure of acceptance within or alongside settler communities. Second, they saw that the invaders' government was partly in earnest when it spoke of "civilizing" and incorporating them but that its agents did not know precisely what "civilization" was, how to measure it, or how much of it was enough. The precise relationship between land, citizenship, and other markers of "civilization" remained unclear, but the power of the relationship was obvious. Some of their relations in Minnesota had satisfied those criteria, thereby gaining the right to remain where they wished and the control of their shares of the tribal fund. Perhaps they could achieve something similar.

As 1873 turned to 1874, these histories refracted through the bitter partisan struggle underway in Washington and the South over the enforcement of citizenship rights for African Americans. For reasons having nothing to do with the justice of their cause, the Ho-Chunk had a powerful ally in the U.S. Senate. Allen Thurman, an avowed white supremacist, nevertheless saw the effort to expel the Ho-Chunk from Wisconsin as an opening through which he might lay bare Republican hypocrisy about equality and cast doubt on the entire enterprise of equal citizenship. Thurman embarrassed his Senate rivals into a crucial concession: a promise not to use force to remove the Ho-Chunk from Wisconsin.

The Ho-Chunk in Wisconsin were no more interested in Reconstruction than they were in "civilization," but both of those forces played crucial roles in the unfolding struggle between 1873 and 1875. Nearly fifty years lay between Coming Thunder's seizure by vigilante squatters and Big Hawk's arrest by soldiers, and in that time the landscapes of both the Ho-Chunk homeland and the United States had undergone revolutionary changes. But across this era, one force remained as potent as the posses of armed white men: Ho-Chunk people's determination not to leave their homeland. In the end, they defeated the government's effort to expel them, overrode the settler veto, secured the aid of the federal government, and established their collective right to remain in Wisconsin.

As the 1870s began, the Ho-Chunk in Wisconsin felt pressure from all directions. Settlers bought up much of western Wisconsin, including the marshes where Ho-Chunk people had been picking cranberries for the market. As this resource became unavailable, game also became scarce. Meanwhile, settlers moving into the region characterized the Ho-Chunk as a danger to their property. Polk County petitioners portrayed "roving idle Indians who infest the houses, localities, and premises of white settlers" as "a material obstacle to the settlement" of the region. They began demanding that the legislature see to the final removal of the Ho-Chunk from the state.[3] In 1870 the commissioner of Indian Affairs recommended that Congress appropriate tens of thousands of dollars to transport 1,500 Ho-Chunks and Potawatomis from Wisconsin to the western reservations where treaties said they belonged.[4] In 1872, when the bill authorizing funds to expel the Ho-Chunk from Wisconsin came to the floor of the U.S. Senate, Wisconsin's Timothy Howe described the "fragmentary bands" as a "disturbing element." "The people of Wisconsin," he explained, "do not like such neighbors."[5]

By the time Congress set its removal plan into motion, Ho-Chunk leaders and their settler allies had developed a counterstrategy based on the acquisition of land. By 1870, according to the government agent, "quite a number" had followed the example of Blue Wing and Yellow Thunder and gained ownership of at least a few acres of land, while others rented from white settlers.[6] These lands became permanent homes for some Ho-Chunks and seasonal homes for others, safe havens within the ever-expanding settler society around them.[7] The precedent of allotments and citizenship for the Ho-Chunk at Blue Earth offered encouragement, though it also contained a worrying note, as it seemed to apply primarily to people of mixed descent. But there were other models. In the early postwar years, some Sauks and Meskwakis had taken up residence in Iowa and purchased land from white settlers. In 1867, Congress authorized them to settle there permanently, despite an earlier treaty that demanded their removal, while also allowing them to continue to receive their share of the tribal funds. Several hundred Ho-Chunk people lived near or among these returnees, and they were almost certainly in communication with their relations in Wisconsin.[8]

In early 1873, Ho-Chunk leaders of this countermovement to expulsion took their case for land, and a right to remain in Wisconsin, to Washington. Coming Thunder had died in Nebraska shortly after the establishment of the reservation there, but in the years since, his brother Short Wing Winneshiek had rejoined the Wisconsin Ho-Chunk community. He became part of a delegation of band leaders that included Mary Crane (Hotokawinga) as an interpreter.

Crane was born Odawa in the early days of Michigan statehood and learned to speak English at Albion Seminary's "Indian Department" in the late 1840s. Around that time, she married a Ho-Chunk man, whom she joined in the removal to Long Prairie in 1848. Her husband served in the Omaha Scouts and died in the late 1860s. By the early 1870s, she was apparently part of a Ho-Chunk band on one of the Mississippi River islands just above Winona, Minnesota. She lived in a Ho-Chunk context, but she also understood the power of landownership to guarantee a right to reside and remain: in 1872 she claimed to be part-owner of land originally acquired by her brother in southwestern Michigan, and she seemed confident that she could live there if she chose.[9] Instead, she played an important role as interpreter as the Ho-Chunk fought against their deportation in 1873 and 1874.

Short Wing, Crane, and the other travelers presented themselves in Washington as an official delegation, several of the men outfitting themselves in elaborate regalia to signify their status, achievements, and seriousness of purpose. But they received no encouragement.[10] Senator Howe and Commissioner of Indian Affairs James Cowan each told them that the lands in western Wisconsin on which they currently planted and lived would soon be populated by settlers. The Ho-Chunk people would be better off, these officials said, in Indian Territory.[11] Editors back in Wisconsin took up the refrain: "It is bad for them here now, but they will find it much worse every year they remain here."[12] Reaching back a quarter of a century, Short Wing Winneshiek offered an alternative destination: the land his brother had acquired from Wapasha in the 1840s. The paper describing that sale, Short Wing told the commissioner, "was kept in Washington, where it would not be destroyed." But Cowan said he knew nothing of the matter.[13]

Over the next year, across Wisconsin, Ho-Chunks and their settler allies worked at the openings they perceived: the legitimating force of landownership, the emergent policy of Native naturalization, and the principle of nonracial national citizenship. After a conference with Ho-Chunk band leaders in Prairie du Chien, merchant Horace Beach appealed to his congressman in the language of emancipation and Reconstruction. "I write to you in the cause of humanity," he explained. "You and I were for the abolition of slavery and I believe you are in favor of assisting the poor oppressed & lowly of whatever race recognizing them as the children of our common great father." Applying

Figure 4.1. Hotokawinga (Mary Crane), born Odawa, lived most of her adult life among Ho-Chunk people in Wisconsin and territories across the Mississippi River. She interpreted for Ho-Chunk and English speakers in the course of official delegations and negotiations. (American Indian Classified File, Wisconsin Historical Society, WHI-151455)

those moral and political principles to this case argued for the settlement and "civilization" of the Ho-Chunk, not their expulsion. "What prevents these men," Beach wondered, "under the 14th Amendment becoming citizens & taking homesteads."[14]

A hundred miles north, in Black River Falls, longtime trader Jacob Spaulding also saw individual landownership as the ticket to Ho-Chunk people's permanent residence in Wisconsin. Writing directly to President Grant, Spaulding proposed that Ho-Chunk heads of families be allowed to choose homesteads on vacant state or federal land in northwest Wisconsin. This land was mostly swamp, he explained, good for picking berries and with enough woodland to suit their needs. The Ho-Chunk were already deeply enmeshed in the local economy, he explained, having sold as much as $30,000 worth of huckleberries during the past season, as well as working for wages in the pineries. His Ho-Chunk acquaintances protested the paternalism they experienced on the Nebraska reservation; his plan—"parcels of lands to heads of families, *as citizens and not as a tribe*"—would constitute fair treatment, which was all they or "any good citizen" desired.[15]

Across the state, near Portage, a small group of Ho-Chunk men approached a longtime acquaintance, attorney Henry Lee.[16] They described lives that fit a familiar Ho-Chunk pattern: primary residence in one area with sojourns to other parts of the state, and long-standing relationships of trade, credit, and debt with local whites. Lee informed the Indian Office that "they do not wish to be removed [and] are willing to do anything to be allowed to stay [and] would gladly become citizens if there is any way for them to do so." "Some of them now own real estate," he noted. "Is there any law by which they can become citizens?" He offered to circulate a petition against the removal of these "peaceable and law-abiding inhabitants."[17]

The conversation between the Ho-Chunk men and Lee became the foundation for the petition of Dandy's Band. As we have seen, that petition layered the languages of citizenship, civilization, real estate, and rights atop an implicit affirmation of the petitioners' continuing identity as Ho-Chunk people—an identity confirmed by many features of the petition, not least the fact that nearly all of the petitioners identified themselves in untranslated Ho-Chunk names. But Ho-Chunk people's "local knowledge" of American activities extended beyond the keywords of liberal citizenship. On its final page, the petition asked, with breathtaking specificity, whether they could secure citizenship through the 1870 "act of Congress making appropriations for the current and contingent expenses of the Indian Department and for fulfilling treaty stipulations with various Indian Tribes." This was, in fact, the act whose ninth and tenth sections provided the mixed-descent Minnesota Ho-Chunk with their pathways to homesteads and citizenship.[18]

How exactly all of this language and knowledge came together in the petition remains uncertain. Read by itself—in light of the fact that most Wisconsin Ho-Chunk people were not literate in English and Lee was an attorney—the petition could seem to be Lee's creation, a scattershot amalgam of legalese, political shibboleths, and proposals. But such an interpretation ignores Ho-Chunk people's well-documented engagement, through interpreters, with the treaties, laws, and policies that had so radically reshaped their world over the past half century. It is impossible to read the treaty journals of the 1830s, 1840s, and 1850s, for example, without recognizing that Ho-Chunk leaders were well versed in treaty stipulations and knowledgeable about the course of past negotiations. And when Lee forwarded the petition, it had been only a few months since Short Wing's delegation moved confidently through the marble corridors of the federal government, seeking out political allies and legal avenues that might secure the people's right to remain. Seen through this history, the petition can be understood as a collaborative work whose essential claims, aspirations, and proposals were deeply rooted in Ho-Chunk people's experiences.

The petition's last-ditch offer, should all else fail, was that the Ho-Chunk be moved to the reservation in Nebraska, with "citizenship provided for them as soon as may be."[19] But although officials made efforts in this direction in 1873, they met with resistance from both directions.[20] In July, Charles Hunt, the special commissioner appointed to remove the Ho-Chunk from Wisconsin, managed to bring nearly ninety people to the Nebraska reservation.[21] But there was not enough timber on the reservation to begin with, and those Ho-Chunk already in Nebraska apparently feared that the arrival of a thousand or more new residents would upset their precarious order. The commissioner of Indian Affairs offered a ruling that was both incentive and threat: wherever the Wisconsin bands lived, they would hereafter be entitled to their proportionate share, perhaps 40 percent, of the tribe's annuity payments. The point was to give the Nebraska bands a powerful incentive to keep those resources close to home by accepting their Wisconsin compatriots.[22] But the effort to make Nebraska seem attractive to the Wisconsin bands mostly failed. The hundred or so Wisconsin Ho-Chunks who did move to Nebraska in the fall of 1873 found themselves without adequate supplies or shelter.[23] The shortages were probably a bureaucratic failure, but the new arrivals could not have missed the Nebraska agent's disdain for them. Writing to Washington for supplies, he referred to the Wisconsin arrivals as "a degraded and immoral Indian horde" and hoped the government would prevent his charges "from being demoralized by this accession to their numbers."²⁴

Instead, Ho-Chunk leaders in Wisconsin tugged harder and harder at the one thread that seemed promising: the ownership of land. Even Senator Timothy Howe, an earnest advocate of removal, seemed to think that Ho-Chunk landowners ought to be allowed to remain. Back in February 1873 he told a Wisconsin newspaper that "no Indian will be deprived of his possessions, and if any own lands they will not be driven from them."²⁵ But as word spread that Ho-Chunk people were arriving at the land office with cash in hand, state officials from the governor on down sought to douse this flame of hope. They insisted that the Ho-Chunk lacked any rights in the state, including the right to purchase land. At a meeting near Sparta in June 1873, Governor Cadwallader Washburn told 400 assembled Ho-Chunk people that they could not legitimately own land in the state: "I am informed that some of you think you can avoid going by buying land here. In your present condition you are the wards of the government, and cannot hold lands without its consent."²⁶ But that was not how the law operated, and in July Charles Hunt pleaded with Commissioner of Indian Affairs Edward Smith to have the state's land offices closed to the Ho-Chunk.²⁷

Landownership conveyed so much legitimacy that even Portage's bitterly anti-Ho-Chunk newspaper editor Andrew Jackson Turner—father to young Frederick Jackson Turner—felt compelled to turn its meanings over in his mind. When the longtime landowner Yellow Thunder arrived in a nearby town, Turner reflected, "We do not suppose that anyone claims that he should be removed. He has performed those acts which secure to him citizenship, just as any Indian who wants to become civilized may do, by the government's consent." But Turner cautioned that this embrace of American patterns of life, the performance of those "acts," must be earnest and unstinting; it could not be a fig leaf of a few acres, intended to mask a preconquest mode of life.²⁸ He could not resist a disdainful description of what he called the Ho-Chunk people's "strolling, vagabond life": "a muskrat f[o]r Monday, a turtle for Tuesday, a few berries for Wednesday, begging for Thursday, strapping up their belt for their Friday's meal and going hungry Saturday with the possibilities of a catfish for Sunday."²⁹ This could not go on. "If they will adopt the manners of white men and become citizens, all right, but if they insist on being Indians let them go to an Indian land. This playing Indian in the settlements is what is objected to."³⁰ Turner demanded a bright line between "the manners of white men and citizens" and "Indians." For him and for many others, landownership literally staked a claim on one side—the right side—of that line.

For the foes of Southern Reconstruction, equal rights, and African American citizenship, it was enraging to hear midwestern Republicans—among the chief architects of those policies—reject the Ho-Chunk as unwelcome cultural aliens who should be expelled. Since before the Civil War, conservative Northern and Southern politicians had denounced the idea of equality and ridiculed its proponents. To such men, the revolutionary transformation of U.S. military service, citizenship, and voting rights over the preceding decade constituted a betrayal of the essential nature of the United States as a white man's republic. Although this group made up a minority in the Congress of the early 1870s, its members pressed back against the new order of nonracial citizenship. For example, they had tried to deny the right of Mississippi's Hiram Revels to take his seat in the U.S. Senate on the grounds that as a Black man he was ineligible: at his birth, they argued, the Constitution did not regard him as a citizen, and now, because he was a native-born inhabitant, he could not be naturalized. These conservatives were compelled to accept an order of things that repulsed them because a mutilated Constitution now said so, and they fumed at the thought that their partisan foes would not play by the same rules.

When Senator Timothy Howe referred to the Ho-Chunk in 1872 as a "disturbing element" whom Wisconsin settlers did not want as neighbors, one of those conservatives pounced.[31] Democratic U.S. senator Allen Thurman of Ohio, his sarcasm growing with every phrase, professed shock at this effort to remove "some disagreeable inhabitants" from one state to another. Wisconsin's Republicans demanded that white Southerners accept the citizenship and enfranchisement of millions of former slaves, he noted, but they refused to contemplate the same for even a few thousand Native Americans in their own state. "I think there is enough charity, there is enough benevolence, there is enough Christianity in the State of Wisconsin among the white people of that State," he sneered, "to make them lend a helping hand to these poor red men who are struggling for an existence."[32]

For Thurman, the campaign to expel the Ho-Chunk was incontrovertible evidence that the proponents of equal citizenship did not believe their own words—that their purposes were partisan and their conduct hypocritical. Republicans, he believed, had established the equal citizenship of African Americans, and created the Department of Justice, in order to legitimize partisan "enforcement" acts against their Democratic rivals in the North, manipulate Black voters in the South, and secure control of national politics. Howe's offhand description of the Ho-Chunk as a "disturbing element" offered Thurman an opportunity to reverse the partisan and regional polarity of that struggle: How did Howe and other white Northern Republicans like it, being saddled with a population that was unfit for citizenship but nonetheless formally entitled to it? Thurman's probing of Republican motives and methods was cynical, racist, and self-serving, but it picked at a genuine contradiction between the egalitarian principles Republicans sometimes enforced in the South and their unapologetically settler-colonial practices in the West.

Thurman was an objectively preposterous ally for the Ho-Chunk bands in Wisconsin. As recently as 1870, he had warned his Senate colleagues that if they abandoned the treaty system, they would effectively make citizens of all Native people. That struck him as a gross error, comparable to Reconstruction: the introduction of "another new body of voters into the country, and a body so savage that every year finds us at war with them."[33] Thurman also agreed with his Republican enemies that the overall goal of federal Indian policy was the replacement of Native nations with American settlers, by law or by conquest. To him, this was a matter of natural law and of common sense. "Was there ever anything so absurd on the face of this earth," he asked, "as to claim that two hundred thousand vagabond Indians own half this continent?" No "set of ragged barbarians" should be able to claim a territory "equal to thirty or forty States as their hunting grounds and keep white people out.... Sir," Thurman concluded, "you cannot expect that the white people will agree to any such thing."[34]

Thurman had long insisted that "white people" had the right to defend their racial civilization with vigilante violence against non-white interlopers. Twenty-five years before, in response to the possibility that Kentucky would emancipate its slaves on the condition that they left the state, Thurman—whose state shared a border with Kentucky—declared "that before the people of Ohio will be deluged with a free negro population, be it law or no law, they will repel the intruders even with the sword."[35] Settlers, that is, were not the only white people to claim the right to vigilante violence, and Native Americans were not their only targets. In the early 1870s, similar exterminationist language could be heard from western Wisconsin, where an editor warned that "if those thieving Winnebagoes do not return to their reservation before winter, there will certainly be *heap dead Injun* by next spring."[36] If Thurman had not had a different partisan point to make, he would have sympathized.

Thurman could not undo the changes Reconstruction had wrought, but he could press at his opponents' hypocrisy and try to make them writhe. Republicans wanted both to enforce their own new national order of nonracial equal rights in the South and to retain their exclusionary settler prerogatives in the Midwest. In his view, this was simply tyranny. The Ho-Chunk, he lectured

Howe, "would not remove from Wisconsin to Minnesota... and when the band was removed two or three times in Minnesota, ultimately to its present site, they would not remove." Was it the intention of the Senate architects of Indian policy "to gather up these people who have manifested for so many years their indisposition to leave their homes, and to remove them by force?" Senate Republicans reluctantly promised that the removal of the Ho-Chunk would be only "with their consent," and Iowa's James Harlan promised to add an amendment to that effect to the appropriation bill in 1872.[37]

At the beginning of 1873, as Republicans prepared for the Ho-Chunks' removal from Wisconsin by soldiers, Thurman returned to this topic with a vengeance. The Fourteenth Amendment, he insisted, could not mean different things in different regions. The Ho-Chunk, who had persistently refused to remain in Minnesota and elsewhere, had abandoned their tribal ties. Under the terms of the Fourteenth Amendment, they were subject to the jurisdiction of Wisconsin and the United States. They were citizens. "There are people in Wisconsin who would be very glad to get rid of them," Thurman acknowledged. "They are not comfortable neighbors, and they want to get rid of them." But the citizens of Wisconsin had no such right. Thurman reveled in the irony: Wisconsin's ardent congressional supporters of the Fourteenth Amendment "helped very much to make these people citizens... and she [Wisconsin, through her elected leaders] denounced everybody who did not like that amendment as being an old fogy who was behind the age, a pro-slavery old fogy.... Now, she made these people citizens, and let her keep her citizens." It was too late to remove the Ho-Chunk again; they had already been "constitutionalized."[38]

Wisconsin's Republicans countered by drawing a bright line between the citizenship status of the freedpeople and that of Native Americans. "Not quite constitutionalized, I think," replied Senator Timothy Howe.[39] The Fourteenth Amendment, Howe claimed, "was carefully drawn for the express purpose of excluding all the Indians from citizenship." Further, he argued, the logic of Native sovereignty militated against seeing the "stray bands" as de jure national citizens. If the simple act of leaving the reservation made Native people into citizens, he explained, "American citizenship is gained or lost simply by crossing the boundary between an Indian reservation and the territory adjoining!"[40] He regarded the Ho-Chunk in a very different light. They remained wards of the federal government, ineligible to acquire real estate or to obtain political privileges; these disabilities made a mockery of any notional citizenship the Fourteenth Amendment might have conveyed. "They have no home in Wisconsin," Howe explained, "not a foot of land there, not even the poor right to vote there." It made no sense to leave them "where they have not a right and cannot get a right, to live on pillage and plunder."⁴¹ Stateless, without either individual property or reservations, they possessed neither the rights and responsibilities of citizens nor the clearly subordinate status of wards. That state of affairs could not continue.

Even as Howe matter-of-factly denied that the Ho-Chunk could be citizens, he seemed aware that he was on shaky ground, particularly over the question of the Wisconsin Ho-Chunk being effectively "subject to the jurisdiction" of the United States. He solved this conundrum by keying his argument in the register of humane sentiment. Removing the Ho-Chunk from Wisconsin was the Christian solution to their miserable, marginal state, he claimed, and the Constitution should not stand in the way of that impulse. Thurman's "love for humanity far transcends his love for the Constitution," Howe suggested, poking at Thurman's opposition to the very amendment on which his argument was based. But with his next step the Wisconsin senator's footing failed him: Thurman, he suggested, would "give way to his humanitarian views and 'let the Constitution slide' for the present."⁴²

Howe had stumbled into Thurman's trap. To "let the Constitution slide" confirmed Thurman's charge that Republicans only insisted on nonracial equal citizenship when it served their party's interests. Howe's description of the Ho-Chunk in Wisconsin as people who "have not a right and cannot get a right," not even the right to vote, gave Thurman all the ammunition he needed, and he laid Howe out. The Wisconsin Ho-Chunk were citizens, the Democrat repeated, under the meaning of the Fourteenth Amendment, and "if there are Ku Klux in Wisconsin who will not allow these people to vote, I pray my friend to be after them with the enforcement act, and punish them, and vindicate the right of suffrage, which belongs to all the people without distinction of race, color, or previous condition of servitude. [laughter] Vindicate it up in Wisconsin before you ask the southern people to vindicate it."⁴³ The laughter Thurman provoked heralded victory. He had backed his opponents into a corner of their own making. His closest friend in the Senate, George Edmunds of Vermont, moved an amendment to the relevant appropriation "that no Indian shall be removed under the authority hereby given without his consent." The amendment passed. The terms of the appropriation for the removal now forbade the use of force.⁴⁴

Since any policy that hoped to expel the Ho-Chunk from Wisconsin and keep them expelled would have to rely on military force, the proviso requiring their consent presented an existential challenge to the entire project. Senator Howe seemed to realize the predicament this might create. A few weeks later, when he was accosted by the Ho-Chunk delegation to Washington, Mary Crane told him that "they had been informed that they were to be driven from the state by the guns of soldiers; and if their poor starving women and children were found hid away, they should be taken and put in jail." Howe replied that this was not true but then immediately made his exit. A Wisconsin reporter understood that Howe was dodging; he headlined this section of his account "How they were deceived."[45] But the commissioner of Indian Affairs told the delegation substantially the same thing, denying that any force would be used and arguing that the government sought only their "comfort and independence."[46] The commissioner repeated this in letters to Henry Lee and to Governor Edward Salomon, emphasizing that the legislation authorizing the removal included no provision for the use of force; the Indian Office "does not feel authorized to initiate any steps to remove the Indians referred to, which would require force to carry them out, and that might possibly result in bloodshed."[47] Thurman's anti-Reconstruction gambit had lodged an unexploded shell at the heart of the removal project.

Even before Charles Hunt's soldiers began rounding up and deporting Ho-Chunk bands in December 1873, the concession of "consent" extracted from Senate Republicans threatened to derail the removal. Hunt had started gathering Ho-Chunk people at his property near Sparta that summer, in preparation for deporting them to Nebraska, but once Henry Lee received word from Commissioner of Indian Affairs E. P. Smith that force was not authorized, "nearly all of them left [Hunt] and went about their business."[48] Not surprisingly, the government's tune soon changed, and the secretary of the Interior suggested that the Ho-Chunk would be removed whether they liked it or not.[49] But Commissioner Smith took the matter seriously enough to travel to Wisconsin to parley directly with several hundred Ho-Chunk people that summer. With Mary Crane interpreting, they carefully parsed Smith's translated words. When Smith remarked that "they would be compelled to go if they would not accede quietly," the entire assembly stood and quickly departed.[50] In August, Charles Hunt called a final council, warning a smaller group of Ho-Chunks (again through Crane's translation) that if they did not prepare to leave by the end of the week, he would put in a requisition for troops to compel them.[51] He told the commissioner that it was "absolutely necessary that some display of force be made in order to convince them that the government is determined that they shall comply with its wishes."[52]

Removal officials in Wisconsin walked a tightrope, paying formal respect to the notion that removal was "voluntary" while signaling clearly that it was no such thing. "Their removal was determined upon," Hunt explained, "peac[e]ably, and with their willing assent, if possible," but "they must go." He spoke with perfect indirection. "If they would not go peac[e]ably," he said, "it was decided that proper and necessary measures should be taken to accomplish that object." He shifted the responsibility for whatever violence followed onto the Ho-Chunk themselves: "Those who should stubbornly refuse to go, would have to bear the responsibility, and await the consequences."[53] As the summer of 1873 faded, "consent" no longer seemed to be a prerequisite for removal.

When the roundups began that December, two other long-developing forces reshaped the removal effort: the legitimating power of landownership and the force of settler prerogative. From the very beginning, proof of landownership provided significant protection against expulsion. When Big Hawk's band was captured on December 20, several men escaped and made their way to the Portage home of their lawyer, Henry Lee. Lee hitched a buggy to his horse, grabbed his lawbooks, and rushed to meet the soldiers and their captives. He drafted a writ of habeas corpus but could not find a judge in Portage who would issue the writ before the soldiers began loading the Ho-Chunk band onto railcars. But although Lee's writ was never issued, his protest was not in vain: one of the judges to whom Lee applied warned Charles Hunt that he should not deport people who could prove they were landowners. Hunt therefore released two families who carried deeds with them.[54] Two families totaling eight people was a small number, especially in comparison to the more than seventy from the December deportation who suffered a freezing three-day journey to Nebraska. But a pathway had opened to enable the Ho-Chunk to claim a permanent place in Wisconsin.[55]

At first, removal officials insisted that they alone should judge whether individual Ho-Chunk people had achieved a status that exempted them from deportation. When Hunt seized more than seventy people at a Monroe County camp, he confronted "Yankee Bill," a Ho-Chunk man who claimed not only to have taken up land under the Homestead Act but to have naturalized as a U.S. citizen in 1870. Hunt deported him anyway but provided a certificate saying that if he found himself dissatisfied in Nebraska, Hunt would try to have his case adjudicated by the proper authorities.[56] Similarly, when Captain H. G. Thomas confronted a growing number of Ho-Chunk people holding titles to land—many of them two- or three-acre tracts recently acquired from settler allies—he asserted the right to determine whether these were legitimate landholdings or, in his words, "fraud." He assessed the deed-holder's "civilization" by a variety of signs. When the landowner in question "lived in a house, however humble, in a place at all improved, and raised a crop, etc.," he had proved his fitness to remain: "he carried the evidence of civilization about him" and was entitled to stay in Wisconsin. But "where the owner was a wandering, blanket, Indian, living in a tepe, hunting for a subsistence, ... the mere fact of a 'deed' conveying a few acres of worthless unimproved land, on which it was evident, that no one could get a living, would not convert him into a 'bona fide' citizen."[57]

But from the beginning, local settlers pushed back against officials. They demanded the right to say who among the Ho-Chunk should not be deported—who, that is, was an acceptable neighbor in the eyes of the settler community. The judge who told Hunt to release the two families in December apparently did so on his own authority, based on his own understanding of the essential elements of settler citizenship, and other citizens of Portage soon assumed the same right. The local paper, generally a fierce advocate of the Ho-Chunk people's expulsion, noted that two other Ho-Chunk men, "although they are not legally entitled to remain ... are vouched for by respectable citizens as making some progress in the line of civilization" and therefore could stay if they chose.[58]

By the end of the first week of deportations, Ho-Chunk landownership and settler prerogatives converged to produce a dangerous conflict with federal forces over the family of Blue Wing. At some time before the winter of 1873, Blue Wing sold his land near Reedsburg and purchased forty acres in Monroe County, fifty miles away. But he and many of his family members remained resident for at least part of the year on lands along the Baraboo River, where they maintained their ties to the Reedsburg settler community. On December 27, Hunt's forces arrested nearly forty people, including members of Blue Wing's family. Almost immediately, the band's local ties proved more formidable than federal force.

Settlers' assertions of their prerogatives threatened to destabilize the removal itself. When soldiers began to force the captives onto the cars in Reedsburg, some settlers rebelled. Blue Wing, the local newspaper asserted, was "well known to be a citizen of the United States, and to be entitled to all the rights and immunities of one." Settlers also seem to have known that Blue Wing's daughter and her husband had already been deported along with Big Hawk's band. When they saw more members of Blue Wing's family at the depot, they turned settler institutions of justice to their purposes. At their insistence, a county court commissioner issued a hastily drafted writ of habeas corpus for Blue Wing's wife, four children, and six grandchildren. When the U.S. officer refused the writ, a large group of Reedsburg residents moved to action. "Our people were 'mad,'" the local newspaper explained, "and as the day progressed they got 'madder and madder.'"[59] More than 200 people surrounded the soldiers at the depot, "overpowering the guard by reason of numbers," and led Blue Wing's family members away "amid great confusion and cheering by said mob."[60] In the course of this protest, several other Ho-Chunk people also made their escape.[61]

Captain Thomas presumed the authority to determine whether Ho-Chunk people's land claims conferred the rights of citizens, but he was less sure what to do when white settlers interfered with his military duties. He was an experienced U.S. officer, brevetted a major general during the Civil War, and he was keenly aware that at that very same moment, white landowners across the former slave states were making their own violent challenge to federal authority. Faced with a defiant mob, how far was he to go in asserting federal authority against local resistance? The essential question, he asked his superiors in St. Paul, was "whether I can fire upon them."[62]

Perhaps it was Thomas's alarming inquiry that caused federal officials to beat a retreat. By the first week of January 1874, they understood that they had to contend not only with Ho-Chunk resistance but with settler resistance as well. Two bloody-minded Civil War heroes, Lieutenant General Philip Sheridan and his superior General William Tecumseh Sherman, soon conferred. "There is great trouble and resistance manifested by some of the settlers in the removal of the Winnebago Indians," Sheridan explained. He warned of impending conflict with state civil authorities, such as the commissioner whose writ his troops had ignored, and "with bands of citizens organized in localities to resist the removal of the Indians."[63] The secretary of the Interior repeated Sheridan's warning: as the removal clearly required force to succeed, and as citizens of Wisconsin were "resorting to force as well as judicial proceedings," perhaps it was best to abandon the removal except to the extent that it could be accomplished by persuasion alone.[64]

Here, Reconstruction's searing politics of race, violence, rights, and enforcement came back into play. Thanks to the colloquy between Thurman and Republicans the year before, the forcible deportations by federal soldiers were outside the law. As reports of the removal reached Washington, Senator Thurman demanded to know why the agreement had been violated and how it was that the Ho-Chunk, who "under the fourteenth article of amendments, are citizens of the United States," should be kidnapped in this way. Brandishing a memorial and numerous affidavits from Wisconsin Ho-Chunks and their settler allies, he told the Senate of Big Hawk's arrest and of the hardships wrought upon Ho-Chunk families and landowners, and he demanded action.[65] By the beginning of February, Ho-Chunk and settler witnesses appeared before legislative committees in Wisconsin. They pressed their claims in the language of equal, nonracial rights and the reversal of *Dred Scott*: that "the Indians had rights which we were bound to respect; that they were citizens as much as the negroes; and it was the duty of the state to protect them in their struggle for an existence in this state."[66] The friends and the foes of the *Dred Scott* decision had found an unlikely point of agreement.

Federal troops deported more than 800 people to Nebraska by early 1874, but the renewed insistence on the letter of the law meant that officials had no power to keep them there. Almost immediately, as in the deportation to Crow Creek a decade before, Ho-Chunk individuals, families, and bands made their escape, "daily returning" to Wisconsin and resuming their lives there.[67] The Nebraska reservation agent tried to assert authority over the people who were supposed to be in his charge. "It is against my orders for any Indians to leave the Reservation without a pass," he insisted, but "the Wisconsins pay little heed to this regulation, consequently I am unable to tell when they leave or how many."[68]

Without the ability to call on military force, though, the best that reservation authorities in Nebraska could do was try to keep the Ho-Chunk from crossing the borders of the reservation. For this task, they only could call on the reservation police force, composed of twelve paid Ho-Chunk employees. It may not be a coincidence that by the end of the summer the agent fired half that force "for not attending to duty."[69] By summer it was clear that nearly all of the people deported during the winter had left or planned to leave, and officials in Nebraska confessed they were "powerless to stop them."[70] By early fall the agent estimated that at least two-thirds of the more than 800 deportees had returned to Wisconsin.[71]

As Ho-Chunk people returned, they sought to ensure that they would not be deported again. One party traveled to Teejop to see the governor, the members telling him of their hardships during the deportation and asking for his help in securing the right to remain in Wisconsin.[72] "They express the determination of never going back," explained a western Wisconsin newspaper.[73]

Hostile settlers complained that the returnees took advantage of the forms of "civilization" without embodying their content. "They have been put to a new dodge," complained a Prairie du Chien correspondent in 1874, "and now rig up with any whiteman clothing they can buy, beg, or steal."[74] Farther up the Mississippi River, another correspondent thought he saw the same thing among a group of returnees from Nebraska. "One of the leaders of the returning party shrewdly declared that he was to have them all dress like white folks and then the Government could not take them back."[75] A pro-removal petition from near Portage similarly complained of "wild Indians" who nonetheless claimed to own real estate.[76]

Like generations of settlers before them, the proponents of removal treated Ho-Chunk people's extensive understanding of "family" as a fraud. Each deed possessed by a Ho-Chunk person implicitly allowed an entire family to remain or return, but Hunt doubted Ho-Chunk people's extensive declarations of kinship. When two deeds, drawn up in June 1873, provided forty-one people with claims to immunity from removal, Hunt complained that "they claim all connections as their families." He assumed their intent was to deceive.[77] "Nearly every Indian returning purchases small worthless tracts of land for the purpose of evading removal," he fumed on another occasion.[78] "This is what is being constantly planned," he reported, "one returning & buying a small worthless piece of land & then getting his family back and if not stopped will get the whole tribe back here."[79]

Across the western half of the continent, settlers wrestled in similar ways with the meanings of Native property-ownership. Was it a sign of their commitment to "absorption ... in the general mass of community" and a path out of their separate nationality and discomfiting wardship? That was how the agent to the coastal reservation at Neah Bay, Washington Territory, described it, in keeping with the long-standing and recently accelerated policy of "civilization." But there were signs it might be something else. Just a few hundred miles east, at the Tulalip agency, he observed "Citizen Indians" taking up homesteads not to improve the land or transform themselves but simply to prevent white settlers from taking up the land and expelling them from it. They remained, in his view, "wild and badly disposed" despite their new title and status.[80]

But the linkage between real estate and legitimate residency had grown stronger during the nineteenth century, and all but the most rigid pro-removal officials believed that Ho-Chunk people whose professions of citizenship and civilization were sincere ought to be allowed to remain. Even Hunt himself helped some people identify which sets of official papers—especially deeds and military discharges—could help them establish their right to remain in Wisconsin.[81] "I have not knowingly removed any one against his will who had a shadow of title to any real estate," he wrote to Washington.[82] With this concession, it was clear that the deportation had failed, and why.

Yet so long as another removal remained possible, the Ho-Chunk victory over removal remained provisional. The tools remaining for removal advocates were among the oldest: vagrancy laws and violence. If the Ho-Chunk were "vagabonds," as was often charged, then perhaps authorities could "treat them as vagrants and imprison them," an editor suggested. "This would stop many from returning."[83] Charles Hunt threatened those who had established their ownership of land near Reedsburg and Portage, telling them "that they must stay right there, and do their begging and stealing off the inhabitants of that vicinity, for if they left, they would be seized and shipped immediately."[84] Or they might suffer a worse fate. After hundreds of returning people settled in western Wisconsin that spring and summer, a meeting of aggrieved settlers in Juneau County threatened vigilante action. "We recognize the right of no man or set of men to encourage these roving vagabonds to trespass upon our rights as citizens," their memorial declared. If the Ho-Chunk people were not expelled within thirty days, "we will proceed to *regulate* this matter in the most expeditious manner."[85]

Confronted with such threats, as credible as a half century of settler violence could make them, Ho-Chunk leaders contemplated how they might achieve a more durable place in their homeland. They had learned that in the nexus of citizenship and landownership lay tangible, perhaps even permanent benefits. They had also learned that those things need not mean, as a generation of agents had insisted, the abandonment of their culture and community.

The cultivation of settler allies had established a counterweight to the forces seeking the Ho-Chunk people's deportation, and those allies continued to support them in 1875. At Portage and Black River Falls, their advocates—lawyer Henry Lee, trader Jacob Spaulding—pressed the case that they would do best by obtaining land under one scheme or another. And Ho-Chunk people sought to bolster their position by demonstrating a willingness to take on further "habits and customs of civilization." Members of Blue Wing's family brought their children to the common school at Reedsburg, "claiming educational privileges upon the ground of citizenship."[86] Twenty-five Ho-Chunk men "for the first time exercised freemen's rights" by casting ballots in the November 1875 election at Black River Falls.[87] Settler allies helped ensure that children were admitted to the school, and the state attorney general confirmed the right of people who had abandoned tribal relations to vote.[88]

But to establish themselves as landowning citizens—people entitled to remain, not interlopers or vagabonds—they needed the money to acquire land. In practice, this meant gaining access to their shares of the tribal fund, a demand that Short Wing, Black Hawk, and John St. Cyr pressed during a trip to Washington in early 1875.[89] Some Wisconsin legislators proposed that the Ho-Chunk be welcomed as "freeholders and citizens," or that the state's congressional delegation be directed to "secure such a law relating to the Winnebago Indians as now relates to the Winnebagoes in Minnesota"—a federal

Figure 4.2. *Left to right:* Black Hawk, John St. Cyr, and Short Wing Winneshiek, photographed during a trip to Washington, D.C., in 1875.
(Ayer Photographs Box 52 AP 1622, The Newberry Library, Chicago)

law that both permitted their naturalization and secured their rights to their tribal fund.[90] Henry Lee traveled to Washington carrying the draft of a bill that would do just that.[91]

Lee's efforts seem to have led to a crucial breakthrough: the so-called Indian Homestead Act of 1875. On March 3, 1875, Congress passed an appropriation act for Indian Affairs that included a provision making Native Americans who abandoned tribal ties eligible to take up land under the Homestead Act of 1862, or to perfect claims they had previously made under its provisions. It also required any Native people acquiring such land to abandon their tribal relations—that is, to submit themselves unconditionally, as individuals, to state and U.S. law—but it allowed them to retain their right to annuities and tribal funds.[92] Henry Lee claimed then and later that the "Indian Homestead Act" was his creation, a claim that is hard to prove or dispute: no congressional debate took place over these provisions, and the records of the Senate Committee on Indian Affairs contain no discussion of them.[93] But if this was not Lee's work, the coincidence of timing and language is extraordinary.

The Indian Homestead Act conferred essential rights. It confirmed that Ho-Chunk people could enter homestead tracts in Wisconsin and that the lands they had entered over the past years could remain theirs. It confirmed their right to remain while underscoring that this did not mean losing access to the tribal fund. Over the next year, scores of Ho-Chunk household heads traveled to the U.S. land office in Lacrosse, Wisconsin, to enter homesteads under its terms, many of them clustered around Black River Falls and to the east in Marathon County.[94]

Yet the Indian Homestead Act did not quite incorporate such Native people as citizens. Unlike the 1870 law for the Minnesota Ho-Chunk, the new law did not include a second provision for formal detribalization and naturalization. It did not use the word "citizen." And despite the use of "homestead" in its name, wardship persisted under its terms. Even though Native people taking advantage of the law were understood to have "abandoned" their "tribal relations," the fact that they were now subject to American law did not entitle them to hold their homestead lands in the same way that non-Native homesteaders did. Their lands could not be sold, transferred, mortgaged, or in any way encumbered for five years. Nor could they take advantage of the provision in the original Homestead Act of 1862 that allowed settlers to buy the land outright before the end of the five-year homestead period.[95] The "Great Father" retained his interest in supervising the transition from tribal membership to citizenship, both in requiring "satisfactory proof" that Native homesteaders had abandoned their tribal relations and in establishing this waiting period before they gained the rights of other homesteaders.[96]

Nor did the Indian Homestead Act solve the problem of resources. As word of the legislation filtered back to Wisconsin, more than a hundred Ho-Chunk men and women in western Wisconsin petitioned the federal government for relief. They introduced themselves as having "dissolved all tribal ties" and desiring to "settle down permanently where we were born and where we now are and to become citizens of this state and of the United States as soon as the necessary legislation can be had defining our rights and privileges as such." They detailed the hardships they faced in making those real: a lack not only of resources to improve land or build schools but of necessities such as food, clothing, and shelter. Short Wing Winneshiek and two other leaders returned to Washington to plead their case for immediate relief in the amount of $25,000, "a small portion of the funds belonging to us under treaty stipulations."[97] Another group, including Roaring Thunder's son and many members of the Decora family, hired Henry Lee on a contingency basis to help them enter homesteads and obtain the money due them from the tribal funds— money without which many could not afford to take or hold such lands.[98]

Getting access to these funds meant wading through the swamps of congressional appropriations, a process that took another six years. Since 1864, Congress had required the Treasury to set aside a proportion of the annuities due the Ho-Chunk for the benefit of the bands in Wisconsin, to be paid to them once they agreed to leave. Those funds had never been paid, but by the late 1870s the amount theoretically past due to the Wisconsin bands added up to more than $300,000. It took several years for allies in Congress to reauthorize these monies in such a way that the Ho-Chunk could take up and improve homesteads in the state.[99] Finally, in 1881, an "Act for the Relief of the Winnebago Indians in Wisconsin, and to aid them to obtain subsistence by agricultural pursuits, and to promote their civilization" mandated the creation of a tribal roll and the distribution of tribal funds to those who had entered homesteads under the 1875 act. The separate allocation of the tribal fund to Ho-Chunks resident in Wisconsin and Nebraska meant, from the perspective of the Office of Indian Affairs, "in legal effect a division of the tribe."[100] A Chicago newspaper went further—probably too far—in declaring that this "practically makes citizens" of the Ho-Chunks now legally residing in Wisconsin.[101]

Perhaps the Wisconsin Ho-Chunks could be said to have gained citizenship somewhere along their journey to landownership and enmeshment in the American world of law. But they did not have it with the clarity of a treaty-defined process, a naturalization before a federal court, or even a certificate drafted by the General Land Office. Perhaps they did not have it at all. But if they did not, and still had the right to take up homesteads, the right to remain in the state, and even the right to vote, then what was citizenship, after all? This ambiguity turned out to be a defining feature of Native citizenship. In 1879, when a congressional committee tabulated the number of citizen Indians by examining treaties and official reports, almost half of the 13,000 Native people it identified as U.S. citizens were "Ottawas and Chippewas" who gained that status by an 1855 treaty. Yet that treaty did not use the word "citizen," nor did it lay out a pathway to that status; it spoke only of the groups' tribal governments being dissolved and their lands allotted. By the late 1870s, apparently, citizenship—whatever it actually granted or implied in terms of rights, privileges, or immunities—seemed to be a logical corollary of those transformations. Yet although the congressional committee enumerating the nation's "Citizen-Indians" included the 160 souls from Minnesota in its reckoning, it did not include the Ho-Chunks in Wisconsin.[102]

In the years after the Ho-Chunk people reestablished their right to remain in Wisconsin, the federal government waged a concerted assault on the bonds connecting tribal nations to their land, parents to their children, and communities to their languages. In 1885, the Major Crimes Act extended federal criminal jurisdiction onto reservations. Allotment laws imposed on Native nations, especially the 1887 Dawes Act, abolished landholding in common and dismantled tribal governments; over the half century after its enactment, Native nations lost about two-thirds of their remaining land. A reinvigorated "civilization" policy coerced and kidnapped Native children into "boarding schools" whose ethos was "to kill the Indian in him, and save the man." While the schools robbed generations of children of their languages, reservation policies punished Native people for maintaining cultural and spiritual traditions and sought to prevent them from traveling freely to visit one another.

During those same years, Reconstruction's expansive vision of national citizenship came under sustained and successful attack. At virtually the same moment in 1873 that Dandy's Band staked their claim in terms of national citizenship, the Supreme Court radically narrowed citizenship's scope and power in the *Slaughterhouse Cases*, limiting "privileges and immunities"—the main distinction between citizens and other residents—to a handful of matters. In the decades that followed, the court went further: in the *Civil Rights Cases* (1883) it overturned the Civil Rights Act of 1875 as an unconstitutional overreach, and in *Plessy v. Ferguson* (1896) its formulation of "separate but equal" granted rigid racial hierarchies the force of federal law. Formal citizenship no longer bespoke a common "family of freedom." Rather, citizenship coexisted in law with racial distinctions determined by state law, local custom, and individual preference. The Supreme Court similarly hedged Native citizenship, ruling in *Elk v. Wilkins* in 1884 that Native people could not seek or gain citizenship of their own volition, only through action by the federal government. This legal apartheid and evacuation of citizenship's promise persisted in constitutional law until the last third of the twentieth century. The irony is painful: Fourteenth Amendment citizenship was designed to create equal status and dignity for African Americans and to exclude most Native Americans; it failed to accomplish its purposes, yet it created the opening through which Ho-Chunk people pressed their successful campaign against exile.

In the years before 1924, the intellectuals of the Society of American Indians, whose Ho-Chunk members included Henry Cloud and Oliver Lamere, continued to wrestle with the problem of Native people's status.[103] As scholar K. Tsianina Lomawaima points out, even the citizenship formally extended under the Dawes Act came with a crucial continuing feature of wardship: the lands allotted under its terms were not fee-simple tracts, such as every other American could own, but held in "trust" on terms that prevented Native owners from offering the land as collateral. For this and other reasons, Native intellectuals sought an escape from federal wardship: "Ward versus citizen looked like the only choice possible."[104] But as historian Philip Deloria suggests, they envisioned citizenship "as a tool to strengthen their claim against the nation and its agents, to preserve individual land in order to remain collectively outside the strictures of American society."[105] Some Ho-Chunk people had been pursuing it this way since the 1840s.

Native citizenship remained a conceptual muddle for the next forty years. During those decades, in historian Lucy Maddox's words, "Indian status was governed by a set of policies and regulations so byzantine and unstable that few claimed to have a good grasp of them." Charles Eastman, one of the early twentieth-century leaders of the Society of American Indians, sounded very much like Attorney General Edward Bates, a half century before, when he wrote, "There has been so much confusing legislation on this matter, that I do not believe there is a learned judge in these United States who can tell an Indian's exact status without a great deal of study, and even then he may be in doubt."[106] Not until the federal government imposed U.S. citizenship on all Native Americans in the 1924 Snyder Act did that question even approach a resolution.[107]

Whatever the Wisconsin Ho-Chunk people's formal status, their transformations did not divorce them from their relations elsewhere. Ties between bands and families in Wisconsin, Nebraska, and other regions remained close. Some people had stayed in Nebraska and taken up allotments or homesteads there or in Minnesota, but even some of those people returned to Wisconsin.[108] John St. Cyr, a naturalized U.S. citizen as of 1870, had already become a landowner in Minnesota, but by 1875 he joined the Ho-Chunk community near Black River Falls as an interpreter and go-between.[109] Mary Crane took up an allotment in Nebraska, but by the late 1870s she too returned to Wisconsin.[110] Connections among far-flung Ho-Chunk communities were so strong and the exchange of gifts and other property so continuous, in fact, that the agent in Nebraska wanted the Indian Office to forbid "the issuing of passes to visiting parties" and to allow agents to arrest and turn back visitors who lacked such passes.[111] But people continued to travel across the Ho-Chunk diaspora, to exchange letters and photographs, and to maintain a sense of connection.

These demands for restrictions and limitations did produce continuing elements of wardship. Officials distrusted the Wisconsin Ho-Chunks' ability to follow through on "civilization." Although the 1881 act provided for a prorated payout to each person on the new roll, the commissioner of Indian Affairs was not convinced the Ho-Chunk people were in earnest about using the money to enter and improve lands. He resolved to divide the money into three installments, not making the second payment until he was satisfied that the recipients had in fact "selected and settled on homestead claims" and "signified their desire and purpose to abandon their tribal relations and adopt the habits and customs of civilized people," as the 1881 act imagined.[112] From the beginning, that is, the Ho-Chunk people's new status came hedged with suspicion, restrictions, and official paternalism.

Yet their achievement was real. For a half century, they had confronted colonial power with their most essential demand: to remain in their homeland, living in relation to one another and the land on their own terms. Considering the forces arrayed against them—settlers who coveted their land and who outnumbered them 100 to 1; layers of government, including a powerful military, that served those settlers' interests—any victory would have been surprising. Now they took up homesteads and formalized settlements in terms that confirmed their right to remain in the territory while at the same time maintaining the essential relations of kin, language, clan, and community that made them a people.

Figure 4.3. Annie Blowsnake Thundercloud, ca. 1882. This photograph represents the survivance of the Ho-Chunk people in the years after they won the right to remain in Wisconsin. It is one of many photographs of Ho-Chunk people at the turn of the century reproduced, identified, and contextualized in Jones et al., *People of the Big Voice*. (Wisconsin Historical Society, WHI-65692)

What historian Amy Lonetree calls her forebears' "heritage of resilience" carried the Ho-Chunk people through the turn of the twentieth century, among the worst years of the encounter between the United States and Indigenous people.[113] And perhaps no artifacts better capture that heritage than the photographs of Ho-Chunk people that Lonetree analyzes. These photographs, taken in a Black River Falls studio, were neither ethnological studies nor romantic fabulations. They were instead commissioned by the Ho-Chunk subjects themselves, who entered Charles Van Schaick's studio just as his other customers did, to represent themselves as they desired.[114]

More than just representing people on their own terms, these photographs now symbolize the survivance of a people. In an extraordinary feat of historical reconstruction, Lonetree and her colleagues—among them photographer Tom Jones and genealogist George A. Greendeer—recovered nearly a thousand glass plates, whose images they shared among Ho-Chunk relatives and friends. Descendants identified most of the subjects of the photographs, offering memories and stories. A photograph of Annie Blowsnake Thundercloud (figure 4.3), taken about 1882, captures her dismay when—after she had prepared for the session in the photographer's studio by sewing an elaborate silk appliqué dress—her mother covered her work with necklaces.

Thundercloud's disappointment was a small, personal tale. But the story's endurance bridges the years between Ho-Chunk people who won the right to remain in their homeland and those who live and work there today. Against the history of colonialism, Annie Blowsnake Thundercloud—her steady gaze, her half-obscured dress, her presence in Black River Falls, and her persistence in the memory of her descendants—embodies Gerald Vizenor's "continuance of stories."[115] It had been the dream of countless agents and bureaucrats to see the Ho-Chunk "dissolve all tribal relations," but those relations remained strong. The status they seized gave them the right to remain, immunity from removal, and protection from some of the worst features of wardship. They established settlements and took up land claims near one another, outside market towns or at the border of American settlement. They maintained relations across their diaspora. They continued to feast, celebrate, and worship together, sustaining ties to kin, clans, and ancestors. And they continued to speak to one another in their mother tongue, the parent speech, the big voice. Citizens of a stolen land, they remained.

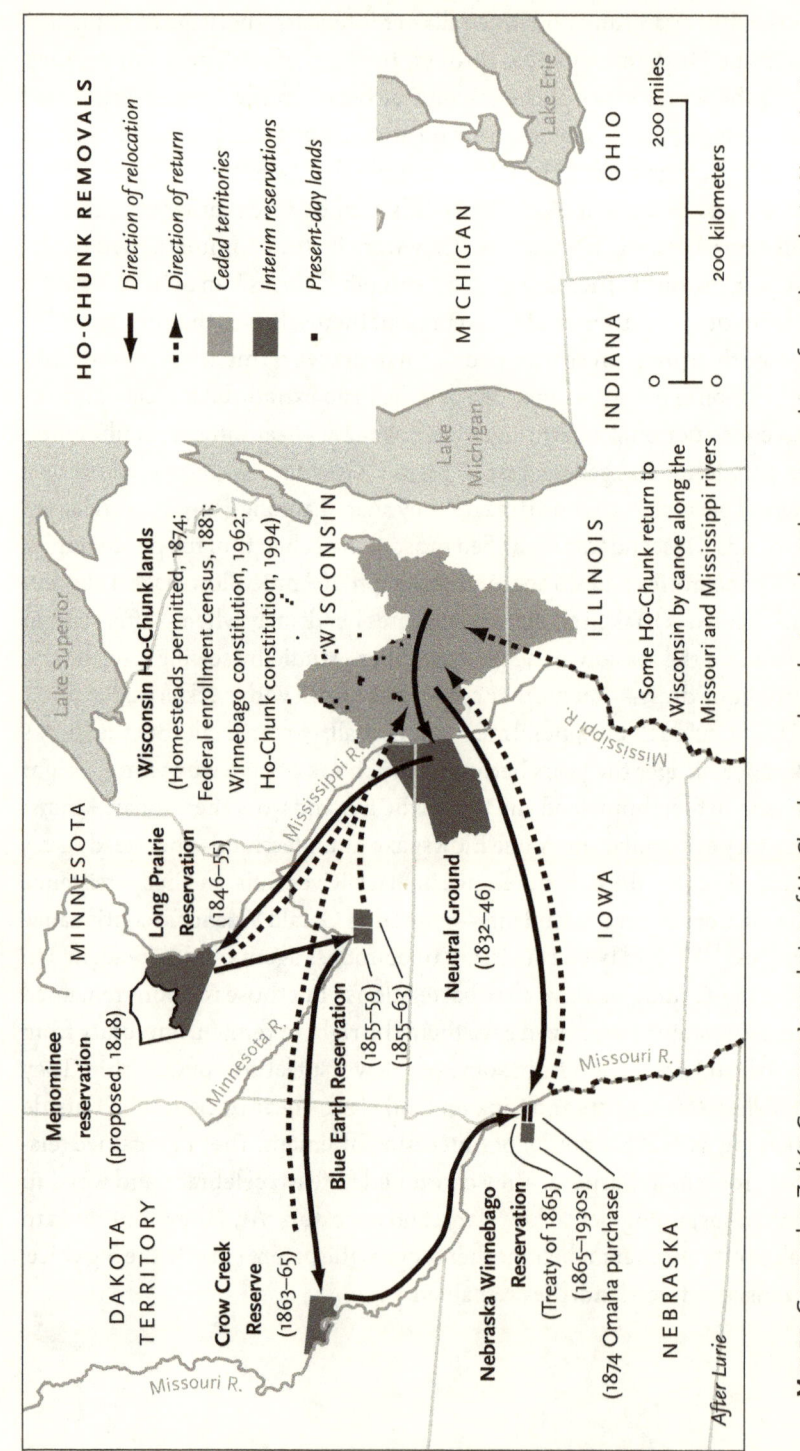

Map 5.1. Geographer Zoltán Grossman's rendering of Ho-Chunk removals and returns, based on a map drawn for anthropologist Nancy Lurie in the 1970s. (Originally published in the Wisconsin Cartographers' Guild, *Wisconsin's Past and Present: A Historical Atlas* [Madison: University of Wisconsin Press, 1998]. Reproduced with permission of Zoltán Grossman.)

EPILOGUE

From the vantage point of 1881, or of today, the story of the Ho-Chunk in Wisconsin can be read as a victory over colonial power. Quietly defying the invaders, repurposing some of their most powerful ideas, the Ho-Chunk reestablished claims to lands that had been stolen from them decades before. This was not the restoration of the old homeland or their sovereignty over it; they continued to live within the colonizers' jurisdiction, often at the margins and interstices of the settler grid. But if one considers the fresh horrors already germinating in U.S. policy makers' minds—the brutal, final round of "Indian Wars"; the forced allotment, detribalization, and massive land loss of the Dawes Act; the assault on sovereignty in virtually every aspect of reservation policy and law; and the cultural genocide of the boarding school system—this achievement of a non-reservation citizenship or something almost indistinguishable from it, with the possibility of land that settlers could not steal, seems extraordinary.

There's no better way to communicate that account of victory than this map of "Ho-Chunk Removals."

Map 5.1 is the basis for the map with which this book began, and through which it first traced the expulsion, diaspora, and return of Ho-Chunk people. That map, as we have seen, represents many (though not all) of their movements and residences during the nineteenth century.

This version includes other elements. It marks the reestablishment, in the twentieth century, of the Ho-Chunk people's territorial and political sovereignty in their ancestral homeland, and it details the lands that now belong to the nation itself. It tells a story of how a people confronted overwhelming

American power, how that struggle divided them into two geographically distinct nations, and how and where they persist into the present day. It is a complex, moving testament to their survivance.

At least, that's how I used to tell the story.

That map was a core element of my first foray into teaching Native American history in the early 2010s, a seminar for first-year students that began as "Native Madison after Removal" and soon became "Ho-Chunk History." This was the students' very first college history class, and the map offered an efficient way, right at the beginning of the semester, to get them thinking about what the story of Ho-Chunk history was and where it had happened. Their assignment was to use anthropologist Nancy Lurie's brief narrative of Ho-Chunk history to plot Ho-Chunk people's movements and migrations onto a simple map of their homelands. Once they had compared and discussed their productions, I would pull out the "Ho-Chunk Removals" map. The conversation that followed would raise questions that historians find essential: Where does a history begin and end? How do historians make sense of a complex and confusing past?

In 2018 the conversation changed. For the first time, I had advertised the course as an advanced reading seminar, and this made it visible to auditors from beyond the campus—among them, a number of Ho-Chunk Nation tribal members. One after another, they wrote to me in the weeks before the course began, and I granted them permission to enroll. On the first day, almost half the people in the room were Ho-Chunk, and three more belonged to other First Nations of Wisconsin. We introduced ourselves and had an initial conversation about who we were and what we could bring to this classroom. I gave them their syllabi, the reading from Lurie, and the assignment to plot the Ho-Chunk people's migrations onto her sketch of their homelands and reservations.

The next week, when we had all settled in, I asked to see what they had produced. And nothing happened.

They had done the reading. They had it in front of them. But the only people who had drawn the maps were two undergraduates.

Confused and a little dispirited, I waited. Finally, as the silence stretched on and my discomfort grew, I handed out the "Ho-Chunk Removals" map. Only then did one woman speak.

"I'd rather talk about a different map." She took a breath. "I want to talk about the map of the places they told us never to go. I want to talk about the stories they told us about why."

The silence that followed felt very loud. Then the woman next to her said, "I want to talk about the places they told us to run and hide if they come for us again."

This book began by asking how the histories of citizenship and of the Civil War era would look different if they took Native histories and stories fully into account. The warnings represented by those imagined maps—places to run, places never to go—offer a disquieting answer, a counterpoint to the narrative of a progressive struggle for equality and the place of citizenship in it. A fuller history of citizenship, a history that takes Ho-Chunk and other Native histories into account, must consider citizenship's genealogy as part of the history of conquest, and the ways citizenship has developed in relation to its opposites, non-citizenship and anti-citizenship. It must examine how those ideas have continued to twine around one another in people's lives and to shape the twentieth- and twenty-first-century world.

The maps my class imagined that day linger in my thoughts, spectral and cautionary. They have reshaped how I understand the history in this book, the history of citizenship, and the history of the United States. My life as a student, a scholar, and—yes—a citizen had taught me to think of citizenship as though the word's most stirring connotations could someday be enacted in daily life, in a social and political order of equality, justice, dignity, and democracy. Thinking of citizenship this way over many years allowed me to understand some important things. I spent years studying how the African American activists of the Civil War era North—people who described themselves as "colored citizens"—imagined and fought for a new kind of place for themselves in what they well understood to be a white republic. They were an integral part of what historian Kate Masur calls "the first civil rights movement," and part of their legacy to their successors in the twentieth century was the black-letter law of equal citizenship.[1]

That story mattered, and matters, for their descendants and for many other people as well. My own ancestors, Jews subject to proscriptions and pogroms in their European homelands, passed through the racialized gates of naturalization to become U.S. citizens at the turn of the twentieth century. They clung to the guarantees of equal citizenship in the United States against the horrors unfolding in twentieth-century Europe and despite the fact that Jim Crow made a mockery of those promises for millions of their African American compatriots. The histories of those mostly separate struggles would fill a small library, and I cannot rehearse them here. But by the time I was born, in 1965, Jim Crow's foes had dismantled much of its legal architecture, and antisemitism had lost much of its cultural legitimacy. Progress was possible, and I learned to see citizenship as one of its banners, perhaps even its defining goal. Over twenty-five years of teaching courses called "Slavery, the Civil War, and Reconstruction" and "Who Is an American?" to undergraduates, that sense of possibility persisted.

But possibility, especially the possibility of the liberal emancipation of citizenship, is not the only history that matters. This book has focused on the creativity and resilience of the Ho-Chunk people during the removal era, as they confronted the forces of colonialism and learned to redeploy some of them—especially landownership and citizenship—for their own purposes. It substantially concludes with the resolution of the half century of crisis brought by the policy of removal, with the victory of part of the Ho-Chunk people over that policy. But my class that day in 2018 insisted on a different framing of that history and a recognition without which any account of Ho-Chunk history—including this book—is incomplete: that the forces of conquest did not cease their work in 1881.

In settler colonial studies, few phrases are quoted more often than Patrick Wolfe's epigrammatic description of settler colonization as "a structure, not an event."[2] By this he meant that settler-colonial processes unfold in complex ways through institutions, interactions, and ideologies and that this unfolding continues long past the initial moment of invasion or dispossession. Without realizing it, I had been offering up the Ho-Chunk experience of colonialism as "the removal era"—as an event. With their alternative maps, the members of the 2018 class were insisting that it had continued to structure their lives.

Most importantly, the maps conjure up histories of citizenship as a vector of violence, especially but not exclusively in the lives of Indigenous people. Whether Americans conceived of them as combatants, as outlaws, or simply as "savages," the Ho-Chunk and other Native Americans were represented as anti-citizens against whom the nation's political and civil community should unite and against whom it must be vigilant. That history did not end in 1881. Native people continue to be disproportionately subject to both state and non-state violence, as reflected in rates of incarceration and experiences of murder and rape. Anti-citizenship also persists in misrepresentations of Native people as fundamentally "savage," premodern, or broken. In newspapers, novels, plays, films, and video games, the "Western" relies on the dualism of "cowboys and Indians." Federal campaigns of indoctrination and child-stealing designed to redress Native "savagery" and "backwardness" began in the nineteenth century, and they manifest today in the extraordinary rate at which state authorities remove Native children from their homes and cultural communities.

The identification of Native people as "savage" anti-citizens has had concrete effects stretching beyond Native American life, providing a template for Americans' subjection of colonial populations and imperial prisoners. At the turn of the twentieth century, President McKinley told the U.S.-appointed governor of the Philippines, future president William Howard Taft, to govern "by analogy to the statutes . . . dealing with the Indian tribes."[3] Later in the twentieth century, U.S. soldiers dubbed other areas of Southeast Asia "Indian Country." The military units that pursued and killed Osama bin Laden codenamed him "Geronimo." And as the U.S. government considered whether it could legally torture "enemy combatants" captured on the battlefield in Afghanistan, Deputy Assistant Attorney General John Yoo sought justification in opinions of the attorney general from the era of the Indian Wars that held that in that arena of conflict, "the laws and customs of civilized warfare may not be applicable."[4] As an indispensable ideological component of the conquest, Native anti-citizenship set the pattern for a broader history of colonialism and empire.

The settler prerogative of vigilante violence, supported or unpunished by government, likewise echoes through the maps of places never to go, places to run and hide. Racist vigilantism has from the beginning been an element of citizenship's claims, legible in this account as early as Henry Dodge's capture of Coming Thunder in his own homeland. But the dyad of squatter and soldier and the figure of the "Indian fighter" were not the only roles that permitted ordinary white men to police non-white people. That anti-citizenship also began in the laws and practices of racial slavery, which treated free and enslaved African Americans as dangers to white lives and communities. Slave patrols, and the laws of racial slavery generally, deputized white men to police the movements and activities of free and enslaved African Americans, a prerogative that persists in the post-emancipation era—our era.

Fourteen years before he screened the racist propaganda film *The Birth of a Nation* in the White House, Woodrow Wilson explained the white supremacist violence of the post-Reconstruction era as integral to the restoration of proper (that is, racialized) civic rights and responsibilities: Black southerners, he explained, "reap[ed] the consquences of ruin, when at last the whites who were real citizens got control again."[5] Vigilante action, often backed up by the institutions of the state—assault, arson, murder, and mob violence—has repeatedly stripped U.S. citizens of their property and their rights, in thousands of lynch mobs, from Atlanta to Brownsville to Duluth, and in campaigns of destruction such as the Tulsa Massacre of 1921. These pogroms and murders have in the main gone unprosecuted.[6] The conviction of three white vigilantes for the 2020 murder of Ahmaud Arbery marks a rare break in this history of impunity, but it also confirms the persistence of racial entitlements that are centuries old: some twenty-first-century citizens continue to imagine that they are Henry Dodge in the lead country and that the land and the law belong to them.[7]

At the territorial border, governments and vigilantes police in the name of the citizenry, and many forms of non-belonging—non-citizenship, but also the racialized policing of citizens—work in relation to one another. The first federal border-control regimes were established in the 1880s and 1890s to police the movement of Chinese immigrants into the United States. In the early twentieth century the focus of this policing shifted to Mexican nationals. The status of these groups differed in the laws of that era: Asian immigrants were barred from naturalization, though their children could gain birthright citizenship (as confirmed by the Supreme Court in *Wong Kim Ark*); Mexican immigrants could and did naturalize as citizens. But both Asian and Mexican immigrants and their descendants endured violent assaults and expulsions at the hands of vigilante and quasi-official mobs.[8] Many also discovered that formal citizenship did not protect them from racialized anti-citizenship. Both groups experienced what historian Mae Ngai calls "alien citizenship," a racial state of perpetual foreignness that can trump even literal U.S. citizenship. Just as the infamous deportations of the 1930s exiled not only Mexican immigrants but also Mexican American U.S. citizens, during World War II the U.S. government incarcerated Japanese nationals and Japanese Americans without regard to their citizenship status.[9]

Governments and citizens alike continue to police the racial borders of citizenship.[10] The federal government exerts enormous and largely unchecked ("plenary") power not only to control the flow of people across international borders but to police and detain people over a vast internal "frontier," stretching 100 miles inland from the nation's borders, which includes about two-thirds of the U.S. population.[11] Within this cordon as beyond it, non-white residents are subject to disproportionate detention, arrest, prosecution, and incarceration. And the policing of who belongs where reverberates through many people's daily lives. "Where are you *really* from?" remains an American refrain, demanded of citizens and non-citizens alike.

One response to this violent history of anti-citizenship and other forms of non-belonging is to insist that people be treated as full or equal citizens. Another response, one that takes a Ho-Chunk history of citizenship more fully into account, might be to say that such violence is part of the history of citizenship itself, rooted in the prerogatives of settlers, the insistence that people abandon their ways of being as a condition for membership, and more generally the distinction between "civilization" and "barbarism."[12] Understood in that light, the Ho-Chunk people's encounter with the United States asks us to do more than question the promises of citizenship. It asks us to question the premise that citizenship is the end and to see it instead as a means—as a tool of both conquest and survivance. Citizenship is not the solution for the structures of settler-colonialism and white supremacy, nor is it the root of those structures. It is a terrain of struggles as messy and multivalent as those the Ho-Chunk confronted in the mid-nineteenth century.

To be a citizen on one's own stolen land is to live the contradictions of that status: its promises of equality; its violent policing of borders; its unwritten rules of "civilization." This was part of what my class was trying to tell me in 2018. And this is the reality the Ho-Chunk people have lived since their victory over the 1873–74 removal. Across the half century that followed, arguably the grimmest period in modern Native American life, they used their comparative autonomy to forge their own path and to sustain their language, values, and community. They do so today in many places, including in their ancestral homeland. From headquarters in Black River Falls, the sovereign and federally recognized Ho-Chunk Nation oversees an archipelago of tribal and trust lands, within the borders of Wisconsin, on which stand health and community centers, elder and veterans' housing, language and heritage programs, courts, hotels, and casinos. That nation's members are citizens of the United States, but never only that. They continue to wrestle with the legacies of centuries of Indian policy and Indian law, and with a widespread presumption that they are fundamentally a race called Indian, not a people and a nation called Ho-Chunk. As they did in the nineteenth century, they continue to negotiate with the United States and to defend their status as a sovereign nation alongside it. They continue to live in relation to one another. They are still Ho-Chunk, and they are still here.

Acknowledgments

From my first meeting with Janice Rice, my understanding of Ho-Chunk history has been shaped by listening to Ho-Chunk people articulate their experiences, interpretations, and values. I offer a heartfelt pinagigi (thank-you) to her and to the other Ho-Chunk members of the Teejop Community History Project—Tara Tindall, Missy Tracy, Kyla Beard, Chloris Lowe III, and Kendra Greendeer—for the time we have spent together. Josie Lee has shared her ideas and insights in ways I wish I could cite more fully. I am particularly grateful to Janice and Josie for their attention to this book in its late stages. Chloris and his Language Division colleague Laura RedEagle suffered my efforts to learn Ho-Chunk pronunciation and syntax, answered many questions, and gave me a lot more to think about besides. Molli Pauliot, an extraordinary student and research assistant, has also been a patient teacher and sounding board. George Greendeer has drawn on his astonishing depth of knowledge to answer my questions about Ho-Chunk history and genealogy. Bill Quackenbush, Ho-Chunk Nation's Tribal Heritage Preservation Officer, graciously allowed me to use the Nation's cartographic work in this book. Chloris Lowe Jr. generously shared his insights into Ho-Chunk history. My UW–Madison colleague Tom Jones visited my seminar each year to share his work with my students. In the pandemic era, Professors Amy Lonetree and Renya Ramirez also generously spent virtual time with my students.

Over a decade ago, when I first sought to learn more about Native American history, Aaron Bird Bear, Miranda Johnson, John Hall, and Larry Nesper rose to the occasion. This project first took form in a series of undergraduate seminars, and the students in those courses profoundly shaped my understanding of the history and its importance. Omar Poler has been a treasured companion during the last five years of this journey, from seminar to the Teejop Community History Project to Our Shared Future.

As I began this work, two scholarly gatherings were crucial. "The World the Civil War Made," convened by Kate Masur and Greg Downs at Penn State's Richards Center, epitomized the generous intensity these extraordinary scholars and friends bring to our field. "Civil War Wests," convened by Adam Arenson and Andrew Graybill at Southern Methodist University's Taos campus and the Autry Museum in Los Angeles, helped me move into conversation with historians of the West and Native America. I also benefited greatly at this and later stages from conversations with Amy Lonetree, Paul Rykken, Libby Tronnes, Andrew Fisher, Patty Loew, Annie Menzel, Malinda Maynor Lowery, Alyssa Mt. Pleasant, Steve Hahn, Joe Genetin-Pilawa, Gingy Scharff, Boyd Cothran, Steve Aron, Megan Nelson, Amy Dru Stanley, Stacey Smith, Fay Yarbrough, Angela Zimmerman, David Chang, Mike Schmudlach, Linda Waggoner, Theresa Schenck, Bob Birmingham, John Broihahn, and Marlin Hawley. I'm so grateful that I was able to speak with Nancy Lurie before her passing. At several points, scholars generously shared their own research, leads, or unpublished scholarship: I wish bountiful karmic return to John Suval, Damon Akins, Justin Gage, Josh Catalano, Kasey Keeler, and Zoltán Grossman. Lawrence Onsager's unpublished M.A. thesis on the 1873–74 removal was an essential starting point.

I also received important feedback from commentators, panelists, and audiences at the Global Nineteenth Century workshop at New York University, the Chabraja Center at Northwestern University, Transnational American Studies at the University of Copenhagen, the Legal History Workshop at the University of Pennsylvania, the University of Wisconsin–Madison's Institute for Research in the Humanities, "Lincoln's Unfinished Work" at Clemson University, "The Many Fourteenth Amendments" at the University of Miami, "Reconstruction" at the Duke University Law School, "Contested Boundaries" at the American University Law School, and meetings of the Society of Civil War Historians, the Danish Historical Association, the Organization of American Historians, the Association for the Study of Ethnohistory, and the Western Historical Association. As I presented work to these audiences, Liz Ellis, Vernon Burton, Eric Foner, Peter Eisenstadt, Kevin Kenny, Andrew Needham, Cathleen Cahill, Maurice Crandall, and Michael Witgen were particularly helpful and encouraging interlocutors. I am grateful to Alaina Roberts and Greg Downs for thoughtful readings as I revised these papers for publication.

The work first began to come together as a book after I was invited to deliver the 2018 Brose Lectures at Penn State's Richards Center. I am grateful to Steve and Janice Brose, to the Richards Center and Bill Blair for the invitation, and to Barby Ann Singer. Other friends read my work, listened to me think it through, or reminded me why what we do is important: I'm so grateful that my world of ideas includes Ari Kelman, Christy Clark-Pujara, Bryant Simon, Kacie Lucchini Butcher, Jim Feldman, Yorel Lashley, Neil Kodesh, Jenni Ratner-Rosenhagen, and Anders Bo Rasmussen. Some of my oldest friends have also read my work, but even without such heroics I'm thankful to have Andrew Lichtenstein, Jeff Kelly-Lowenstein, Evan Notman, David Kris, Vinnie D'Angelo, Hisao Kushi, and their families in my life after all these years. It's an unutterable delight to watch our daughters conspire.

I've had so much help with this research. Cori Simon combed archives across several states; Jesse Gant, Dan Arendt, Molli Pauliot, Mike Kaelin, and Andrew Shaffer pored through archival boxes and scanned countless reels of microfilm. Archival staffs have extended themselves, especially those working for Lee Grady at the Wisconsin Historical Society Archives. I also thank Adam Smith at the Southern Minnesota Historical Center, Elizabeth Finch at the Colby College Museum of Art, Julie Dunn-Morton at the St. Louis Mercantile Library, Rodney A. Ross at the National Archives, and Bill Schuette at the Sauk County Historical Society. My employer, the University of Wisconsin–Madison, has generously supported this work with a Faculty Development Grant, a Kellett Mid-Career Award, a Vilas Distinguished Achievement Professorship, a Senior Fellowship at the Institute for Research in the Humanities, and the Plaenert-Bascom Professorship.

Editors and reviewers at the *Journal of the Civil War Era* and *Western Historical Quarterly* did a great deal to sharpen my thinking: I thank James Brooks, Anne Hyde, Hilary Green, Scott Heerman, and Judy Giesberg for their thoughts at this stage. And it's wonderful to be back at the University of North Carolina Press and to work with Mark Simpson-Vos, María Garcia, and Thomas Bedenbaugh. Two anonymous readers for the press offered incisive and encouraging suggestions that improved the manuscript enormously; if they ever care to identify themselves at the conference bar, I'm picking up the tab.

As I approached the finish line, an A-team of historians read the entire manuscript, sometimes more than once. Ari Kelman helped me articulate the work's deepest implications and urged me not to succumb to the curse of knowledge. Kate Masur brought her characteristic intellectual clarity, rigorous reading, and generous questions. Tim Tyson gave the manuscript his repeated and unstinting literary attention. Walter Johnson suggested its most radical implications. Craig Werner absorbed its content and deduced its structure. Liz Ellis helped me see what was essential, what was missing, and what to burn with fire. I trust they will understand that I have not been able to do everything they suggested. I hope I am somehow able to repay them all.

Pernille Ipsen, the final, indispensable reader of the manuscript, cannot be repaid because debt is not the language of our relation to one another. Every page of this book has been shaped by her clear-eyed, questing, generous view of the world, her belief in the work history can do in it, and her constant question, the one that separates this undertaking from stamp-collecting: What is the meaning of it all? I hope she will never stop asking. My last book was dedicated to her. This one is dedicated to the children we love and have raised in Teejop.

Notes

ABBREVIATIONS

Ann. Rep. U.S. Department of the Interior, Office of Indian Affairs, *Annual Report of the Commissioner of Indian Affairs* (Washington, D.C.: Government Printing Office, 1830–82)

DRNT Microcopy No. T-494, *Documents Relating to the Negotiation of Ratified and Unratified Treaties with Various Tribes of Indians, 1801–69*, Record Group 75, Records of the Bureau of Indian Affairs (Washington, 1960)

LROIA Microcopy No. 234, *Letters Received by the Office of Indian Affairs*, Record Group 75, Records of the Bureau of Indian Affairs, National Archives, Washington, D.C.

TPUS *Territorial Papers of the United States*, 28 vols. (Washington, D.C.: Government Printing Office, 1934–75)

Stat. *U.S. Statutes at Large*

WHC *Wisconsin Historical Collections*, 15 vols. (Madison: State Historical Society, 1854–1915)

INTRODUCTION

1. Petition of "Indians of the Winnebago Tribe, and more particularly described as the descendants of what was known in the year 1837, and subsequent, as Dandy's Band," [May] 1873, *LROIA*, Winnebago Agency, Roll 944.

2. Vizenor, "Aesthetics of Survivance," 1. In recent years, some of these stories have been told by Ho-Chunk scholars who, drawing on deep reservoirs of familial and cultural knowledge, demonstrate what "working from home" can do to illuminate the Ho-Chunk past. See Lonetree, "Heritage of Resilience" (quotation on 45); Ramirez, *Standing Up to Colonial Power*; and Hinzo, "Voicing across Space."

3. For legal scholarship that explicitly treats rights and citizenship as having different meanings and valences in the context of Native sovereignty, see Maltz, "Fourteenth Amendment"; Magliocca, "Cherokee Removal"; Berger, "Birthright Citizenship on Trial"; Epps, "Citizenship Clause"; and Blackhawk, "Federal Indian Law."

4. See Ho-Chunk Nation's *Ho-Chunk Dictionary Online*, http://dictionary.hochunk.org. Native languages appear to have incorporated the new American concept in a variety of ways. Historian Jameson Sweet, for example, shows how nineteenth-century Dakota people developed words with connotations of self-support and self-ownership "to approximate the American concept of citizenship"; Sweet, "Native Suffrage," 101. Undoubtedly the concept has translations of varying degrees of fidelity in numerous other languages. Some Native nations, such as the Citizen Potawatomi Nation, claim the English word today.

5. *Opinion of Attorney General Bates*, 4.

6. Histories of U.S. citizenship frequently treat Native American citizenship not in relation to land-taking or Native sovereignty but as one of many racialized histories of rights claimed and denied; see, for example, R. Smith, *Civic Ideals*. An important exception to this general rule is in accounts of the Dawes Severalty Act (1887), which gave the president of the United States power to divide tribal lands into individual allotments and set allotted landowners on a path to U.S. citizenship; this connection between citizenship and land-taking is so well-known that it features even in works that otherwise treat Native American history only glancingly—see, for example, Lepore, *These Truths*, 337.

Scholars specializing in Indigenous history approach citizenship more skeptically. Historian Frederick Hoxie importantly describes the reimagining of Native people as "potential citizens" rather than as tribal members as a "big lie" that helped (and helps) Americans ignore tribal sovereignty and treaty obligations; Hoxie, "What Was Taney Thinking?," 343. Deborah Rosen thoughtfully analyzes the variety and transformation of state laws regarding Native rights and citizenship from the Revolution to the late nineteenth century and the impact of national citizenship on these diverse regimes; Rosen, *American Indians and State Law*. Some Native groups in the nineteenth century even saw state or national citizenship as such a deep threat to their community integrity that, in the context of invasion and occupation, they concluded they would be better off as wards of the federal government; see Crandall, *These People*. Other important work on the problem of Native citizenship in the Civil War era focused on particular regions or Native nations, including Oberly, *Nation of Statesmen*; Mosteller, "Place, Politics, and Property"; Schneider, "Citizen Lives"; Bowes, *Exiles and Pioneers*; Karamanski, "Citizenship as a Tool"; Kantrowitz, "'Not Quite Constitutionalized'"; Sweet, "Native Suffrage"; and Witgen, *Seeing Red*. Legal scholarship that explicitly treats nineteenth-century rights and citizenship as having different meanings in the context of Native sovereignty includes Maltz, "Fourteenth Amendment"; Magliocca, "Cherokee Removal"; Berger, "Birthright Citizenship on Trial"; Epps, "Citizenship Clause"; and Blackhawk, "Federal Indian Law."

Another body of Indigenous studies scholarship confronts the problem of citizenship in relation to Native sovereignty between the 1880s and the 1920s; key works include Lomawaima, "Mutuality of Citizenship and Sovereignty"; Deloria, "American Master Narratives"; Maddox, *Citizen Indians*; and Bruyneel, *Third Space*.

7. Key works include Wolfe, "Land, Labor, and Difference," "Settler Colonialism," and "Corpus Nullius."

8. On the euphemistic qualities of "removal," see Saunt, *Unworthy Republic*, xi–xix; on "boarding schools," D. Adams, *Education for Extinction*; on genocide, Madley, *American Genocide*; and Ostler, *Surviving Genocide*.

9. Ford, *Settler Sovereignty*, 4–5, 10–11, 17–19; see also Veracini, *Settler-Colonialism*.

10. My account of Ho-Chunk history draws on Lurie, "Winnebago Indians" and "Winnebago"; Onsager, "Removal of the Winnebago Indians"; D. Smith, "Events Leading Up to the Permanent Split"; Tetzloff, "Diminishing Winnebago Estate"; Conzen, "Winnebago Urban System"; Murphy, *Gathering of Rivers* and *Great Lakes Creoles*; Pluth, "Failed Watab Treaty"; Waggoner, *Fire Light, Starring Red Wing!* and "Sibley's Winnebago Prisoners"; Hoelscher, *Picturing Indians*; Jones et al., *People of the Big Voice*; Hinzo, "Voicing across Space"; Arndt, *Ho-Chunk Powwows*; Tronnes, "Corn Moon Migrations"; Coats, "Knights of the Forest"; Ramirez, *Standing Up to Colonial Power*; and Lonetree, "Heritage of Resilience."

The literature on "Indian removal" is vast. An important recent interpretation, focused on Southern removals, is Saunt, *Unworthy Republic*. Dinwoodie, "Evading Indian Removal," offers an analysis of Southern stories in many ways analogous to the Ho-Chunk experience. The crucial work on Northern removals is Bowes, *Land Too Good*. Snyder, "Many Removals," provides an essential historiographical assessment.

11. Saler, *Settlers' Empire*.

12. Boyd Cothran and Ari Kelman, "How the Civil War Became the Indian Wars," *New York Times*, May 25, 2015, https://opinionator.blogs.nytimes.com/2015/05/25/how-the-civil-war-became-the-indian-wars/; see also Cothran, *Remembering the Modoc War*; and Kelman, *Misplaced Massacre* and *For Liberty and Empire*.

13. This work joins the conversation that Elliott West imagined with his framework of a "Greater Reconstruction," exploring the "racial crisis triggered by expansion," the drive to "national consolidation," and "how the two wove together." West, "Reconstructing Race," 12, 21. Works that develop related arguments and explore connections among Civil War, western, and Native American histories include S. Smith, *Freedom's Frontier*; Kelman, *Misplaced Massacre*; Downs and Masur, *World the Civil War Made*; Arenson and Graybill, *Civil War Wests*; Scharff, *Empire and Liberty*; Schneider, "Distinctions That Must Be Preserved"; Hahn, *Nation without Borders*; "The Civil War West: Special Issue," *Journal of the Civil War Era* 6 (December 2016): 481–591; R. White, *Republic for Which It Stands*; Sharfstein, *Thunder in the Mountains*; Nelson, *Three-Cornered War*; and Rasmussen, *Civil War Settlers*.

14. For discussion of the unsettling relation of Native American history to conventional narratives of United States history, see Mt. Pleasant, Wigginton, and Wisecup, "Completing the Turn"; Deloria, "American Master Narratives"; R. White, "New Yorker Nation"; and, more generally, Limerick, *Legacy of Conquest*. For an excellent example of how to explore this disorienting relation, see Lowery, *Lumbee Indians*.

15. Quoted in Le Miere, "'Our Ancestors Tamed a Continent.'"

16. Foner, *Second Founding*; Conn, *History's Shadow*.

17. Fehrenbacher, *Lincoln*, 214.

18. Kantrowitz, "Looking at Lincoln."

19. Lincoln, "Address Delivered at the Dedication of the Cemetery at Gettysburg" and Lincoln to Hahn, March 13, 1864, in Basler, *Collected Works*, 7:21 and 243.

20. Notable exceptions are Nichols, *Lincoln and the Indians*; Berg, *38 Nooses*; and Green, *Lincoln and Native Americans*. For discussion, see Kantrowitz, "Looking at Lincoln."

21. Turner to Sherwood, May 20, 1888, quoted in Billington, "Young Fred Turner," 40–41.

22. Quoted in Jacobs, *Turner's Legacy*, 174.

23. See the essays in Sleeper-Smith et al., *Why You Can't Teach*.

24. Quotations in this and the following paragraph are from Petition of "Indians of the Winnebago Tribe, and more particularly described as the descendants of what was known in the year 1837, and subsequent, as Dandy's Band," [May] 1873, *LROIA*, Winnebago Agency, Roll 944.

25. *Cong. Globe*, 43rd Cong., 1st Sess., 743–44 (1874); "The Winnebagoes," *Milwaukee Daily Sentinel*, February 2, 1874, 1.

CHAPTER 1

1. Tilden, *History of Stephenson County*, 202–3; Jipson, "Story of the Winnebagoes," 213–14, Chicago Historical Society, Chicago, Ill.

2. Tilden, *History of Stephenson County*, 203; Daniel M. Parkinson, "Pioneer Life in Wisconsin," *WHC*, 2:331.

3. For "civilization," see the discussion of the Wisconsin territorial seal, below. For "wandering vagrants," see, e.g., U.S. Congress, Senate, *S. Doc 512, Emigration of Indians*, 3:8.

4. Garvin and Hartmann, *Hoocąk hįįt'ekjawi!*

5. Transcription of the receipt rolls kept by John Kinzie, U.S. agent to the Ho-Chunk, in Jipson, "Story of the Winnebagoes," 265–81; Tanner, *Atlas of Great Lakes Indian History*, 139–46.

6. Material in this and the following paragraph draws on Lurie, "Winnebago"; Radin, *Winnebago Tribe*, 61–70; Murphy, *Gathering of Rivers*, 137–54; and Brown, "Lake Monona," 126.

7. U.S. Congress, Senate, *S. Doc 512, Emigration of Indians*, 4:204.

8. Waggoner, *"Neither White Men nor Indians"*; Murphy, *Gathering of Rivers*, 80.

9. Lurie, "Winnebago," 690; Radin, *Winnebago Tribe*, 1–2; Lurie and Jung, *Nicolet Corrigenda*, 95–112; Birmingham, *Spirits of Earth*; Rosebrough, "Every Family a Nation," 1717.

10. Jipson, "Story of the Winnebagoes," 50–55; Lurie, "Winnebago."

11. Atwater, *Tour to Prairie du Chien*, 121–22.

12. Garvin and Hartmann, *Hoocąk hįįt'ekjawi!*, 424; J. Hall, *Uncommon Defense*, 36.

13. Miller, "Doctrine of Discovery"; Wolfe, "Corpus Nullius"; Konkle, "Indigenous Ownership." For settler criminal jurisdiction over Indigenous people as the essential contest over sovereignty, see Ford, *Settler Sovereignty*.

14. Calloway, *Indian World of George Washington*, 3. See also Ablavsky, "Savage Constitution."

15. The scholarship on the invasion of the Ohio country is vast, but for an introduction that situates it in relation to the history of the Northwest in this era, see Witgen, *Seeing Red*, chs. 1–2.

16. Calloway, *Victory with No Name*; Saler, *Settlers' Empire*, ch. 2.

17. Jipson, "Story of the Winnebagoes," 62. My estimate of the Ho-Chunk population of this village assumes that each of the dwellings described in Jipson's text housed fifteen to twenty people.

18. Jipson, 63–67; Onsager, "Removal of the Winnebago Indians," 28–30.

19. Quoted in Diedrich, *Winnebago Oratory*, 19.

20. Bowes, *Land Too Good*, 11.
21. Kappler, *Laws and Treaties*, 2:130–31, 250–55.
22. Martin, *Sacred Revolt*; Greenberg, "Nose, the Lie, and the Duel."
23. W. Johnson, *Broken Heart*, 41–71.
24. Saunt, *Unworthy Republic*; Garrison, *Legal Ideology of Removal*.
25. Saunt, *Unworthy Republic*, 53–83; Garrison, *Legal Ideology of Removal*, 92–97.
26. Guyatt, *Bind Us Apart*; Seeley, *Right to Remain*, explores the earlier history of plans of removal and separation.
27. Onsager, "Removal of the Winnebago Indians," 32–33; Atwater, *Tour to Prairie du Chien*, 122–23.
28. Moses Strong, "Indian Wars of Wisconsin," *WHC*, 8:250–52.
29. Moses Strong, "Indian Wars of Wisconsin," *WHC* 8:253.
30. Wallace, *Jefferson and the Indians*, 218; J. Hall, *Uncommon Defense*, 73–76.
31. Pelzer, *Henry Dodge*, 8–26.
32. Tesdahl, "Lead, Slavery, and Black Personhood."
33. "Narrative of Morgan L. Martin," *WHC*, 11:397.
34. Jipson, "Story of the Winnebagoes," 93.
35. Strong, "Indian Wars of Wisconsin," 250–59. Strong disputes that the abduction occurred, and Jipson agrees, "Story of the Winnebagoes," 81; but see Tilden, *History of Stephenson County*, 202, for the strong implication that it did.
36. Thomas L. McKenney, "Winnebago War," *WHC*, 5:178–204; Jipson, "Story of the Winnebagoes," 88–92.
37. "Treaty with the Winnebago, Etc., 1828," in Kappler, *Laws and Treaties*, 2:292–94.
38. "Treaty with the Winnebago, 1829," in Kappler, *Laws and Treaties*, 2:300–303; J. Jones, *Winnebago Ethnology*, 147.
39. Treaty journal, August 23–24, 1828, Documents Relating to Ratified Treaty No. 153, Treaty of August 25, 1828, with the Winnebago, and United Potawatomi, Chippewa, and Ottawa Indians, *DRNT*.
40. "Indian Speech at Drummond Island." On this fear, see Ostler, "'To Extirpate the Indians'"; and Harper, "Looking the Other Way."
41. The narrative of the Black Hawk War that follows draws on the research and interpretations in J. Hall, *Uncommon Defense*; Jung, *Black Hawk War*; and Tronnes, "Corn Moon Migrations" and "We Have Buried Our Tomahawks."
42. Tronnes, "Corn Moon Migrations" and "We Have Buried Our Tomahawks."
43. Account of Thomas Clay, "as given by Mr. Oliver Lamere," quoted in "Chief Winneshiek," in Hexom, *Indian History of Winneshiek County*, n.p.
44. John Reynolds to Lewis Cass, September 22, 1832, Documents Relating to the Negotiation of the Treaty of September 15, 1832, with the Winnebago, *DRNT*.
45. Quoted in Bowes, *Land Too Good*, 45.
46. J. Jones, *Winnebago Ethnology*, 147.
47. J. Hall, *Uncommon Defense*, 222.
48. Tronnes, "Corn Moon Migrations," 326–58.
49. J. Jones, *Winnebago Ethnology*, 158.
50. Masur, *Until Justice Be Done*; Seeley, *Right to Remain*, ch. 6.
51. Brush to Cass, December 14, 1835, in U.S. Congress, Senate, *S. Doc. 512, Emigration of Indians*, 3:6–8, Doc. 215.
52. *TPUS*, 27:735–36.

53. Brush to Cass, December 14, 1835, in U.S. Congress, Senate, *S. Doc. 512, Emigration of Indians*, 3:8, Doc. 215.

54. Quoted in Tronnes, "Corn Moon Migrations," 423.

55. "Council near Fort Winnebago, Oct. 12, 1836," *LROIA*, Wisconsin Superintendency, Roll 948, frame 25.

56. Council with Winnebago near Fort Winnebago, October 12, 1836, *LROIA*, Wisconsin Superintendency, Roll 948, frame 28; Herring to Dodge, June 22, 1836, *TPUS*, 27:65; "Proceedings of a council held at Fort Winnebago," September 1, 1837, *LROIA*, Wisconsin Superintendency, Roll 948, frames 180–82.

57. "Proceedings of a council held at Fort Winnebago," September 1, 1837, *LROIA*, Wisconsin Superintendency, Roll 948, frame 184.

58. "Extracts from letter of Major Green," April 3, 1838, *LROIA*, Prairie du Chien Agency, Roll 698, frame 449.

59. "At a council held at Mineral Point September 16, 1838," *LROIA*, Prairie du Chien Agency, Roll 698, frame 514.

60. "The Dandy, the acknowledged orator for the Winnebago Nation," *LROIA*, Prairie du Chien Agency, Roll 698, frame 458.

61. "At a council held at Mineral Point September 16, 1838," *LROIA*, Prairie du Chien Agency, Roll 698, frame 517.

62. "Talk with Winnebagoes at Prairie du Chien, Oct. 5, [18]38," *LROIA*, Wisconsin Superintendency, Roll 948, frames 503–10.

63. Witgen, *Seeing Red*, 256–68; Redix, *Murder of Joe White*, 32–39.

64. "Talk with Winnebagoes at Prairie du Chien, Oct. 5, [18]38," *LROIA*, Wisconsin Superintendency, Roll 948, frame 506.

65. J. Hall, *Uncommon Defense*, 223.

66. Suval, *Dangerous Ground*, ch. 1. See, for example, Bogue, "Iowa Claims Clubs"; and Whaley, *Collapse of Illahee*, 161–68.

67. Rohrbough, *Land Office Business*, 200–220; Suval, *Dangerous Ground*, ch. 1; W. Johnson, *Broken Heart*, 47–48.

68. Quoted in Suval, *Dangerous Ground*, ch. 1.

69. Rohrbough, *Land Office Business*, 141.

70. W. Johnson, *Broken Heart*, 46.

71. Strong, "Indian Wars of Wisconsin," 241.

72. Saler, *Settlers' Empire*, 22–25.

73. Buss, *Winning the West*, 42–70.

74. *Constitution of the State of Illinois*, Art. V, Sec. 1.

75. Tirres, "Ownership without Citizenship," 20–26. By the 1850s, as the growing immigrant populations of the nonslaveholding states added to their demographic edge over the slaveholding states, Southern representatives opposed extending homestead rights to noncitizens. Zolberg, *Nation by Design*, 150–51.

76. See Buss, *Winning the West*, 42–70, esp. 48–49, for the increasing use of "citizens" in settler/squatter petitions in the early nineteenth century. See, for example, Petition by Citizens of Bad Axe, *LROIA*, Winnebago Agency, Roll 932; Petition for Removal of all Winnebago, *LROIA*, Turkey River Agency, Roll 863; and Petition by Residents of Dodge County, *LROIA*, Winnebago Agency, Roll 932.

77. Quoted in Raskin, "Legal Aliens, Local Citizens," 1405.

78. *Stat.*, 24th Cong., 1st Sess., ch. 54 (April 20, 1836), sec. 5.

79. Raskin, "Legal Aliens, Local Citizens," 1407.

80. See, for example, *Cong. Globe*, 39th Cong., 1st Sess., 498–99 (1866). Whatever doubts the foes of birthright citizenship attempted to sow, a full reading of the debates in the *Congressional Globe* for 1866 makes it clear that, for the victorious congressional majority, the birthright citizenship of nearly all children of aliens (excepting only the children of foreign diplomats) represented the continuation of a long-standing and uncontroversial practice. Supporters of the principle even defended its 1866 codification against objections that some of these birthright citizens' parents (notably, Chinese immigrants) might be racially ineligible for citizenship under existing naturalization law. For a full exposition of this point see Kettner, *Development*, ch. 10; and Epps, "Citizenship Clause." For further context, see M. Jones, *Birthright Citizens*.

81. Wisconsin et al., *Revised Statutes*, Title XI, "Of the Internal Police of the State," ch. 28.

82. W. Quigley, "Rumblings of Reform," 743–47.

83. Godwin, *Pleasant Ridge*; Stinson, "Becoming Black, White, and Indian." For an insightful and provocative discussion of whether "settler" is the proper term for nineteenth-century African American migrants, see Miles, "Beyond a Boundary."

84. "Memorandum of a Talk Held at Four Lakes, April 29, 1833," U.S. Congress, Senate, S. Doc. 512, *Emigration of Indians*, 4:203–5.

85. Quoted in Tronnes, "Corn Moon Migrations," 369. See also, for example, *TPUS*, 27:27–31.

86. Report of the Secretary of War, March 1, 1836, U.S. Congress, Senate, S. Doc. 512, *Emigration of Indians* 3:1, Doc. 215.

87. *TPUS*, 27:156–58.

88. *TPUS*, 27:1148

89. *TPUS*, 28:121–24.

90. John T. De La Ronde, "Personal Narrative," *WHC*, 7:363.

91. Quoted in Diedrich, *Winnebago Oratory*, 66.

92. *Ann. Rep.* 1840, 249–51.

93. Saunt, *Unworthy Republic*, xi–xix.

94. Ostler, *Surviving Genocide*, esp. 361–67.

95. Diedrich, *Winnebago Oratory*, 64.

96. Dodge to Crawford, November 14, 1838, *TPUS*, 27:1090–91.

97. Bently to Lowry, May 30, 1840, *LROIA*, Prairie du Chien Agency, Roll 702, frames 290–91.

98. *TPUS*, 28:282–3, 502–3, 814–15.

99. *TPUS*, 28:524–5.

100. *Ann. Rep.* 1850, 6–7.

101. Miller and Reed to Sibley, January 14, 1850, *LROIA*, Winnebago Agency, Roll 932.

102. Briggs to Secretary of War, August 8, 1849, and also Dewey to Ramsay, January 29, 1850, *LROIA*, Winnebago Agency, Roll 932.

103. *Ann. Rep.* 1843, 287, 383.

104. *Ann. Rep.* 1850, 64–71.

105. *Ann. Rep.* 1842, 409; *TPUS*, 28:209–11.

106. *TPUS*, 28:7–8.

107. *TPUS*, 28:296–231.

108. *TPUS*, 28:295–96.

109. Ford, *Settler Sovereignty*, 4–5, 10–11, 17–19.

110. These complex relations of kinship, service as intermediaries, and exploitation are traced in Murphy, *Great Lakes Creoles*; and Waggoner, *"Neither White Men nor Indians."* For a rigorous exploration of the relationship between such histories and the history of settler colonialism, see Witgen, *Seeing Red*, esp. ch. 3.

111. Bowes, *Land Too Good*, 72, 153, 184.

112. *Ann. Rep.* 1854, 57.

113. Cole, "Western Sauk County," 101.

114. Cole, "Western Sauk County," 100–101.

115. "Extracts from letter of Maj. Green . . . 3rd April, 1838," *LROIA*, Prairie du Chien Agency, Roll 698, frame 449.

116. Onsager, "Removal of the Winnebago Indians," 62–3; *TPUS*, 28:912–13; Doty to Crawford, July 13, 1843, *LROIA*, Wisconsin Superintendency, Roll 949, frame 279.

117. Onsager, "Removal of the Winnebago Indians," 64–66.

118. Onsager, 66–67.

119. *TPUS*, 28:814–5

120. *Ann. Rep.* 1846, 40.

121. Onsager, "Removal of the Winnebago Indians," 68.

122. Clark, *Charles Deas*, 14–24. Clark suggests this journey was from Prairie du Chien, but another source suggests Deas also visited Fort Winnebago and traveled down the frozen Rock River, returning "to paint the likenesses of the prominent members of the tribe." Tuckerman, *Book of the Artists*, 428.

123. Kinzie, *Wau-bun*, 65–66.

124. *WHC*, 7:364.

125. Dodge had contemplated this gambit before; see *TPUS*, 27:1074–76.

126. Dart, "Settlement of Green Lake County," *Proceedings of the State Historical Society of Wisconsin*, 263–66.

127. De La Ronde, "Personal Narrative," 7:364–5; Onsager, "Removal of the Winnebago Indians," 70–71.

128. Clark, *Charles Deas*, 14–24.

129. From the U.S. perspective, between 1846 and 1849 this area was the unorganized remainder of the former Iowa Territory.

130. Hatch to Rice, April 24, 1850, U.S. Congress, House, *Rep. No. 501*, 55.

131. Street to Clark, November 28, 1832, June 24, 1833, quoted in Street, "Chapter," 608, 611.

132. Chapman to Brooke, April 3, 1836, *TPUS*, 27:33.

133. Fletcher to Medill, May 18, 1848, *LROIA*, Winnebago Agency, Roll 932.

134. Fletcher to Gorman, September 12, 1854, *LROIA*, Winnebago Agency, Roll 934.

135. *Ann. Rep.* 1854, 57.

136. *Ann. Rep.* 1856, 39–40.

137. *TPUS*, 28:863–64.

138. Petition of the Citizens of the Territory of Wiskonsin, March 4, 1841, Petition of Winnebago Chiefs, September 1841, *LROIA*, Prairie du Chien Agency, Roll 701; Memorial for the Removal of David Loury, June 28, 1843, *LROIA*, Turkey River Agency, Roll 862.

139. *TPUS*, 27:26.

140. *TPUS*, 27:638–39, 852.

141. *TPUS*, 27:760.

142. *TPUS*, 27:27–31; *TPUS*, 28:814–15.

143. *TPUS*, 27:307.

144. Durrie, *History of Madison*, 354–55.

145. "Lake Mendota Indians," interview with Rommelfanger, September 27, 1940, and notes on Rommelfanger, December 31, 1940, Charles E. Brown Papers, box 21, folder 3, Wisconsin Historical Society Archives, Madison, Wisc.

146. "Dane County," Brown Papers, box 21, folder 4; notes on Rommelfanger, December 31, 1940, Brown Papers, box 21, folder 3.

147. *Madison, Dane County, and Surrounding Towns*, 269–70, 395–96; "Lake Wingra and its Borders in the Seventies," Brown Papers, box 22, folder 4.

148. Durrie, *History of Madison*, 179, 191; "Lake Waubesa, Edwards Park," Brown Papers, box 22, folder 3.

149. "Madison Lakes Indians," Brown Papers, box 3, folder "Winnebago"; also "Outlet Group and Village Site," Brown Papers, box 22, folder 2.

150. "Indians on Madison Lakes," *Wisconsin State Journal* (Madison), May 5, 1908, clipping in Brown Papers, box 21, folder 2.

151. Durrie, *History of Madison*, 191.

152. *Madison: The Capital*, 8.

153. Angel Hinzo discusses Glory of the Morning in history and myth in "Voicing across Space," 19–26. The genealogy of the Decora family is discussed in Jipson, "Story of the Winnebagoes"; and Waggoner, *Fire Light* and *Starring Red Wing!*

154. Jipson, "Story of the Winnebagoes," 224–31.

155. *TPUS*, 28:193.

156. *TPUS*, 28:688.

157. *TPUS*, 28:193 and n. 49.

158. See Sleeper-Smith, *Indian Women and French Men*; Murphy, *Great Lakes Creoles*; Witgen, *Seeing Red*; Nesper, *"Our Relations . . . the Mixed Bloods"*; Waggoner, *"Neither White Men nor Indians"*; and Hyde, *Born of Lakes and Plains*.

159. Petition of settlers in the neighborhood of Fort Winnebago, February 9, 1843, and Doty to Crawford, March 27, 1843, *LROIA*, Turkey River Agency, Roll 862.

160. *TPUS*, 28:688

161. *Ann. Rep.* 1844, 55–56.

162. *History of Columbia County*, 702, 705.

163. Blue Wing's patent, September 1, 1852, Accession Nr. WI2100___.127, General Land Office records, Bureau of Land Management, Department of the Interior, https://glorecords.blm.gov/details/patent/default.aspx?accession=WI2100___.127&docClass=STA&sid=lnorvqdb.p1q#patentDetailsTabIndex=1; Wm. H. Canfield, "Map of Sauk County, Wisconsin" (Milwaukee: Louis Lipman Practical Lithographer, 1859), https://lccn.loc.gov/2012593174.

164. "Winnebago Indian Village in Town of Reedsburg," *Reedsburg (Wisc.) Free Press*, December 15, 1921, Brown Papers, box 39, folder "Sauk County 1833–1927."

165. "Winnebago Indian Village in Town of Reedsburg"; F. D. Hurlburt, "Ah-Ho-Cho-Ka (Blue Wing)," Brown Papers, box 39, Sauk Folder 1; Krug, *History of Reedsburg*, 271; Cole, "Western Sauk County," 100.

166. Treaty with the Winnebago, 1837, in Kappler, *Laws and Treaties*, 2:498.

CHAPTER 2

1. Treaty with the Winnebago, 1859, in Kappler, *Laws and Treaties*, 2:790.
2. Wolcott to Thompson, August 16, 1861, Wolcott to Dole, August 16, 1861, and Thompson to Wolcott, August 21, 1861, *LROIA*, Winnebago Agency, Roll 935.
3. See introduction, n. 7.
4. Epps, "Citizenship Clause."
5. Fehrenbacher, *Dred Scott Case*, 340–54, 445–47. "Degraded class" comes from an unpublished opinion Taney had written twenty-five years earlier, when he was attorney general of the United States; Fehrenbacher, *Dred Scott Case*, 340.
6. Hinks, *To Awaken*. Exploration of the constitutional claims and status of free African Americans are at the core of Schoeppner, *Moral Contagion*, and M. Jones, *Birthright Citizens*. See also Seeley, *Right to Remain*, ch. 6; Masur, *Until Justice Be Done*, ch. 2; Pryor, *Colored Travelers*; and Kantrowitz, *More Than Freedom*.
7. Anbinder, *Nativism and Slavery*. On the complexities of immigration and citizenship in law and practice, see Parker, *Making Foreigners*.
8. Wolfe, "Land, Labor, and Difference."
9. Ablavsky, "'With the Indian Tribes,'" 1057.
10. Quoted in Wallace, *Jefferson and the Indians*, 78.
11. Articles of Confederation, March 1, 1781, Art. IX.
12. Guyatt, *Bind Us Apart*; Snyder, *Great Crossing*.
13. Wallace, *Jefferson and the Indians*, 223.
14. Novak, "Transformation of Citizenship"; Welke, *Borders of Belonging*.
15. *Opinion of Attorney General Bates on Citizenship*.
16. Masur, "State Sovereignty and Migration," 589.
17. Masur, *Until Justice Be Done*, 14–15.
18. See Kettner, *Development*, 256–63.
19. W. Quigley, "Rumblings of Reform," 743; Masur, *Until Justice Be Done*, 230–45.
20. Hoxie, "What Was Taney Thinking?," 342; Young, "Indian Removal and Land Allotment," 35.
21. Journal of the Proceedings, Documents Relating to the Negotiation of the Treaty of October 13, 1846, with the Winnebago Indians, *DRNT*, 22, 41.
22. Journal of the Proceedings, 34–35, 37, 64.
23. Fletcher to Harvey, June 1, 1848, Morgan to Medill, June 3, 1848, Fletcher to Harvey, June 4, 1848, Rice to Medill, June 15, 1848, Fletcher to Harvey, June 24, 1848; Morgan to Medill, July 6, 1848, Harvey to Commissioner, July 15, July 17, 1848, Levi to the President, n.d. [July 1848], *LROIA*, Winnebago Agency, Roll 932; Heilbron, "Making a Motion Picture," 157; *Collections of the Minnesota Historical Society*, 8:382–85; McDermott, "Old Fort Snelling," 215–16.
24. Heilbron, "Making a Motion Picture"; Folwell, *History of Minnesota*, 1:311–12; *Collections of the Minnesota Historical Society*, 8:382–85; *Ann. Rep.* 1851, 8, 61–62; Fletcher to [?], September 12, 1854, *LROIA*, Winnebago Agency, Roll 934.
25. Harvey to Commissioner, July 15, July 17, 1848, *LROIA*, Winnebago Agency, Roll 932.
26. Whaley, *Collapse of Illahee*, 161–82.
27. Lindsay, *Murder State*, 271.
28. Madley, *American Genocide*.
29. M. Adams, *Who Belongs?*, 96–104.

30. Witgen, *Infinity of Nations* and *Seeing Red*; Murphy, *Gathering of Rivers* and *Great Lakes Creoles*; Sleeper-Smith, *Indian Women and French Men*; Karamanski, "Citizenship as a Tool."

31. Low, *Imprints*, 23–36; see also Clifton, *Pokagons*.

32. Silverman, *Red Brethren*; Oberly, *Nation of Statesmen*.

33. Silverman, *Red Brethren*, 174–75; *WHC*, 4:296–97 (1859).

34. Quoted in Oberly, *Nation of Statesmen*, 71.

35. "An Act for the Relief of the Stockbridge Tribe of Indians," March 3, 1843, 5 *Stat.* 645.

36. "Sketch of the Brothertown Indians," *WHC*, 4:296–97 (1859).

37. Silverman, *Red Brethren*, 192–95.

38. Karamanski, "Citizenship as a Tool," 125–31. See also Bowes, *Land Too Good*, 201–4; and Rosen, *American Indians and State Law*, 128–52.

39. Oberly, *Nation of Statesmen*, 75–85; Silverman, *Red Brethren*, 184; Gates, "Indian Allotments," 164.

40. Quoted in Silverman, *Red Brethren*, 184–85.

41. Karamanski, "Citizenship as a Tool," 122–23; Bowes, *Land Too Good*, 201–2.

42. Rosen, *American Indians and State Law*, 132–41; *Constitution of the State of Wisconsin*, Art. III, Sec. 1.

43. *Debates and Proceedings of the Minnesota [Democratic] Constitutional Convention*, 430–31.

44. Rosen, *American Indians and State Law*, 137–41.

45. Oberly, *Nation of Statesmen*, 62–78.

46. Sweet, "Native Suffrage," 103.

47. Sweet, 99. See also Hauptman, "American Indians and the Right to Vote."

48. *Debates and Proceedings of the [Republican] Constitutional Convention*, 347; Rosen, *American Indians and State Law*, 138.

49. *Cong. Globe*, 35th Cong., 1st Sess., 1325 (1858).

50. H. Hall, *H. P. Hall's Observations*, 51.

51. I have explored this dynamic in postbellum "civilization" policy in Kantrowitz, "'Citizen's Clothing.'" On this anxiety generally in antebellum American culture, see Halttunen, *Confidence Men*, 56–91.

52. Quoted in Prucha, *Great Father*, 324.

53. *Ann. Rep.* 1843, 285; *Ann. Rep.* 1842, 409–12.

54. Murphy, *Gathering of Rivers*, ch. 5.

55. Decision of the chiefs relative to their annuity for 1836, July 16, 1835, *LROIA*, Winnebago Agency, Roll 931.

56. Rayman, "David Lowry," 110.

57. *Ann. Rep.* 1838, 519–20.

58. Petition, May 12, 1845, *LROIA*, Turkey River Agency, Roll 863.

59. *Ann. Rep.* 1844, 122; Lang and Taylor, *Report of a Visit*, 6–10.

60. Schoolcraft, *Historical and Statistical Information*, 1:498.

61. *TPUS*, 28:60–61. Henry Gratiot, agent to the Rock River Ho-Chunk earlier in the decade, attributed a good deal of hostility and suspicion between settlers and Ho-Chunks to "the want of good interpreters." Jipson, "Story of the Winnebagoes," 118–20, Chicago Historical Society, Chicago, Ill.

62. *Ann. Rep.* 1849, 93. Even in the 1850s, a longtime agent was dismayed to find Ho-Chunk students and their government-employed teacher conversing not in English but in French. Fletcher to Gorman, January 21, 1856, *LROIA*, Winnebago Agency, Roll 934.

63. Rice to Brown, March 2, 1850, *LROIA*, Winnebago Agency, Roll 932.

64. *Ann. Rep.* 1843, 383.

65. Jipson, "Story of the Winnebagoes," 218.

66. *Ann. Rep.* 1850, 6–7, O. Brown to Ramsey, April 15, 1850, U.S. Congress, House, *Rep. No. 501*.

67. Commissioner's report, August 12, 1853, Documents Relating to the Negotiation of an Unratified Treaty of August 6, 1853, with the Winnebago Indians, *DRNT*. See also Pluth, "Failed Watab Treaty."

68. *Ann. Rep.* 1853, 57–58, 67–74. See also Pluth, "Failed Watab Treaty."

69. Pluth, "Failed Watab Treaty."

70. "George W. Manypenny (1853–57)," in Kvasnicka and Viola, *Commissioners of Indian Affairs*, 57–67.

71. Catalano, "Uneven Ground."

72. Interview between the Commissioner of Indian Affairs and the Winnebago Delegation, Documents Relating to the Negotiation of the Treaty of February 27, 1855, with the Winnebago Indians, *DRNT*.

73. Treaty with the Winnebago, 1855, in Kappler, *Laws and Treaties*, 2:690–93.

74. *Ann. Rep.* 1843, 284–488.

75. *TPUS*, 28:121–24.

76. Doty to Spencer, November 13, 1841, quoted in Journal of the Proceedings, Documents Relating to the Negotiation of the Treaty of October 13, 1846, with the Winnebago Indians, *DRNT*, 50

77. *TPUS*, 28:124.

78. Petition by Winnebago Chiefs, 1849, *LROIA*, Winnebago Agency, Roll 932 ("principal chief"); Petition, January 18, 1856, *LROIA*, Winnebago Agency, Roll 934 ("president").

79. Fletcher to Cochran, November 24, 1848, *LROIA*, Winnebago Agency, Roll 932.

80. "Report on the condition of the Winnebago Agency for the month of January 1856," *LROIA*, Winnebago Agency, Roll 934.

81. Petition, January 18, 1856, *LROIA*, Winnebago Agency, Roll 934.

82. Cullen to Abercrombie, November 27, 1858, December 16, 1858; Cullen to Denver, December 23, 1858, *LROIA*, Winnebago Agency, Roll 934.

83. Fletcher to Gorman, September 13, 1855, McMahan to Thomson, January 15, 1858, *LROIA*, Winnebago Agency, Roll 934.

84. In late 1857, a settler named Jackson Rowley, accusing a Ho-Chunk man of stealing $100 in goods, held the man's wife for ransom. She told the agent that Rowley raped her while in captivity. Neither Fletcher nor the regional superintendent took any action on this claim; they only informed Rowley that by taking matters into his own hands he had forfeited any claim for compensation by the U.S. government. Fletcher to Cullen, December 1, 1857, Statement, December 21, 1857; Cullen to Mix, December 21, 1857, *LROIA*, Winnebago Agency, Roll 934.

85. *Ann. Rep.* 1847, 144–46; *Ann. Rep.* 1848, 459–62; *Ann. Rep.* 1856, 5.

86. "An Act to extend the laws of the State over the Indian Tribes within the boundaries of the State, and to confine them to their own lands," *General Laws of the State of Minnesota*, 103.

87. *Ann. Rep.* 1858, 35–36.
88. "Relation of Indians to Citizenship," 7 *Op. Att'y Gen.* 746, 1856; Nesper, *"Our Relations . . . the Mixed Bloods,"* esp. 96–99.
89. "Relation of Indians to Citizenship," 746.
90. Fehrenbacher, *Dred Scott Case*.
91. Cushing, *Speech Delivered in Faneuil Hall*, 45, 43.
92. Hoxie, "What Was Taney Thinking?," 330.
93. Art. VII, Treaty with the Chippewa, 1854, in Kappler, *Laws and Treaties*, 2:648–52.
94. "Relation of Indians to Citizenship," 755; italics mine.
95. Generations of scholars have traced the complexities of Democratic Party politics in this era. For a recent perspective, see Landis, *Northern Men with Southern Loyalties*.
96. This paragraph is indebted to the insights of Hoxie, "What Was Taney Thinking?"
97. *Ann. Rep.* 1858, 38.
98. Hughes, *Blue Earth County*, 96–97.
99. *Ann. Rep.* 1857, 46–48.
100. Bowes, *Exiles and Pioneers*.
101. Suval, *Dangerous Ground*, esp. chs. 7–8.
102. Miner and Unrau, *End of Indian Kansas*, xiv.
103. Quoted in Report of the Committee on Territorial Affairs, 1879, appendix A, in U.S. Congress, House, *Misc. Doc. No. 18*, 38.
104. Bowes, *Exiles and Pioneers*.
105. Treaty with the Wyandot, 1855, in Kappler, *Laws and Treaties*, 2:677. But note that in the same year, under the same commissioner, the Odawa and Ojibwe of Michigan traded tribal organization for individual allotment without citizenship. Treaty with the Ottawa and Chippewa, 1855, in Kappler, *Laws and Treaties*, 2:725. Subsequent treaties offered other approaches: the Treaty with the Sioux (actually two Dakota bands), 1858, instead contemplated the individual incorporation of any members of the bands who wished to dissolve their tribal ties and take up homesteads; once they did so, they became U.S. citizens. On the arguments over these and related policies in the postwar decades, see Genetin-Pilawa, *Crooked Paths to Allotment*.
106. Bowes, *Exiles and Pioneers*, 217.
107. Holzer, *Lincoln-Douglas Debates*, 109.
108. Tilden, *History of Stephenson County*, 201–2.
109. Mix to Cullen, December 6, 1858, *LROIA*, Winnebago Agency, Roll 934.
110. Coats, "Knights of the Forest," 87.
111. McMahan to Cullen, January 15, 1858, *LROIA*, Winnebago Agency, Roll 934.
112. Mix to Cullen, December 6, 1858, *LROIA*, Winnebago Agency, Roll 934.
113. "Parting Interview of the Winnebagoes, April 18, 1859," Documents Relating to the Negotiation of the Treaty of April 15, 1859, with the Winnebago Indians, *DRNT*.
114. Waggoner, "Sibley's Winnebago Prisoners," 28.
115. *Ann. Rep.* 1860, 79.
116. Agent to Dole, July 18, 1861, *LROIA*, Winnebago Agency, Roll 935.
117. "Winnoshik" to Commissioner of Indian Affairs, November 29, 1859, *LROIA*, Winnebago Agency, Roll 934.
118. Cullen to Greenwood, May 27, 1589, *LROIA*, Winnebago Agency, Roll 934.
119. Cullen to Greenwood, May 27, 1589.
120. Treaty with the Winnebago, 1859, in Kappler, *Treaties and Laws*, 2:790–92.

121. *Ann. Rep.* 1858, 35–36.

122. "Winnoshik" to Commissioner of Indian Affairs, November 29, 1859.

123. "Winnoshik" to Commissioner of Indian Affairs, November 29, 1859.

CHAPTER 3

1. Details on Roaring Thunder's activities in this and the following paragraph: "A Conference between Governor Salomon and the Winnebago Chiefs," *Semi-Weekly Wisconsin* (Milwaukee), August 21, 1863, 2; "The Indian Council," *Wisconsin Pinery* (Stevens Point), July 29, 1863, 1. On the U.S.-Dakota War and its aftermath: Berg, *38 Nooses*; Wingerd, *North Country*, 301–45; Chomsky, "Military Injustice."

2. Beck, *Columns of Vengeance*.

3. Berg, *38 Nooses*; Chomsky, "Military Injustice."

4. Berg, *38 Nooses*; Waggoner, "Sibley's Winnebago Prisoners," 29–35; Bachman, *Northern Slave, Black Dakota*, 15.

5. Bachman, *Northern Slave, Black Dakota*, 236–39, citing unpublished record of trials in the U.S. House records, 248n50; Waggoner, "Sibley's Winnebago Prisoners," 36, 44.

6. Quote in Waggoner, "Sibley's Winnebago Prisoners," 38; Coats, "Knights of the Forest," 87, 55–58.

7. Coats, "Knights of the Forest," 62.

8. Act of February 21, 1863, "An Act for the Removal of the Winnebago Indians, and for the Sale of their Reservation in Minnesota for their Benefit," 12 *Stat.* ch. 53, 658–60 (1863); Lass, "Removal of the Sioux and Winnebago," 354.

9. "About the Winnebagoes," *Mankato (Minn.) Record*, May 2, 1863, 2.

10. Art. IV, Treaty with the Winnebago, 1859, in Kappler, *Treaties and Laws*, 2:791.

11. "About the Winnebagoes," *Mankato (Minn.) Record*, May 2, 1863, 2.

12. Lass, "Removal of the Sioux and Winnebago," 361–62; notes on J. B. Hubbell in *St. Paul Dispatch*, September 7, 1901, in Thomas Hughes Papers, box 3, folder 8, Southern Minnesota Historical Center, Mankato, Minn.

13. Hughes, *Indian Chiefs*, 121–22.

14. "Personal," *St. Paul Daily Press*, May 22, 1863, 4.

15. Sibley to Selfridge, May 23, 1863, *LROIA*, Winnebago Agency, Roll 936.

16. Sibley to Selfridge, May 23, 1863.

17. "Going, Going, Gone," *St. Paul Daily Press*, May 28, 1863, 4; Lass, "Removal of the Sioux and Winnebago." In 1935, Joseph LaMere testified that 600 died in the two years following the expulsion, *Congressional Record*, 74th Cong., 12496 (August 5, 1935).

18. Blackhawk quoted in Hughes, *Indian Chiefs*, 122.

19. "St. Peter Correspondence" and "Oak Grove Township," *Mankato (Minn.) Weekly Union*, July 17, 1863, 2–3; *Ann. Rep.* 1863, 312.

20. Frank Kennedy interview, Hughes Papers, box 3, folder 8.

21. George Covel interview, Hughes Papers, box 3, folder 8.

22. Hughes, *Indian Chiefs*, 129–30.

23. "Valuable Lands for Sale," *Wisconsin State Journal*, May 13, 1863, 4.

24. *Mankato Record*, May 23, 1863, 2.

25. *Mankato Record*, May 30, 1864, 2.

26. While Minnesota settlers who had welcomed the Treaty of 1859 waited eagerly for the Blue Earth lands to become available, the long wait between the signing of the

treaty and the first steps in enacting its plan of allotment sowed doubts among the Ho-Chunk about the government's intentions. Baker to Dole, July 18, 1861, *LROIA*, Winnebago Agency, Roll 935. Without certificates to guarantee their ownership of eighty-acre plots, even the people most eager to take up allotments—the mixed-descent people deemed most "civilized" by the United States—hesitated to undertake the work of agricultural improvement of their lands "until they receive their certificates." Ann. Rep. 1862, 93.

27. *Constitution of the State of Minnesota*, Art. VII, Sec. 1.

28. "About the Winnebago," *Mankato Weekly Record*, May 9, 1863, 3.

29. Petition of James Caldwell and others, August 8, 1864, *LROIA*, Winnebago Agency, Roll 937.

30. Porter to Dole, June 8, 1863, *LROIA*, Winnebago Agency, Roll 936.

31. Beveridge to Dole, June 22, 1863, *LROIA*, Winnebago Agency, Roll 936.

32. Beveridge outlined these claims in a letter to Secretary of the Interior Harlan, August 17, 1865, *LROIA*, Winnebago Agency, Roll 938.

33. Quarles, *Negro in the Civil War*, 183ff.

34. Board of Commissioners, *Minnesota in the Civil and Indian Wars*, 560.

35. Bishop to Ramsey, June 19, 1863 (copy), Beveridge to Dole, July 30, 1863, *LROIA*, Winnebago Agency, Roll 936; Foyles to Dole, June 25, 1864, Mix to Usher, July 3, 186[3—misfiled], *LROIA*, Winnebago Agency, Roll 937; Board of Commissioners, *Minnesota in the Civil and Indian Wars*, 560.

36. Ann. Rep. 1864, 394; Ann. Rep. 1866, 298–99; Ann. Rep. 1869, 446–48.

37. "Madison Lakes Indians," typescript, Brown Papers, box 3, folder "Winnebago," Wisconsin Historical Society Archives, Madison; also "Lake Mendota Indians," March 1931, Brown Papers, box 21, folder 3; *Madison, Dane County, and Surrounding Towns*, 300.

38. "Lake Mendota Indians," March 1931, interview with Rommelfanger, September 27, 1940, and notes on Rommelfanger, December 31, 1940, Brown Papers, box 21, folder 3.

39. Ann. Rep. 1862, 333–34.

40. Salomon to Usher, July 21, 1863, *LROIA*, Winnebago Agency, Roll 936.

41. Ann. Rep. 1863, 34.

42. Kingston to Salomon, July 19, 1863, Citizens of Juneau County to General T. C. H. Smith, n.d. [1863], Davis to Dole, August 4. 1863, *LROIA*, Winnebago Agency, Roll 936.

43. Salomon to Usher, July 24, 1863, *LROIA*, Winnebago Agency, Roll 936; details in "The Indian Council," *Wisconsin Pinery*, July 29, 1863, 1.

44. Salomon to Pope, July 2, 1863, in Ann. Rep. 1863, 359–60.

45. Ann. Rep. 1866, 299.

46. Quotation in Ann. Rep. 1869, 446–668; Ann. Rep. 1870, 323–24.

47. "The Indian Council," 1.

48. "A Conference between Governor Salomon and the Winnebago Chiefs," *Semi-Weekly Wisconsin*, August 21, 1863, 2.

49. "A Conference between Governor Salomon and the Winnebago Chiefs," 2.

50. "The Indian Council," 1.

51. Ann. Rep. 1863, 358–61; Cogswell to Dole, September 27, 1863, *LROIA*, Winnebago Agency, Roll 936.

52. Ann. Rep. 1865, 53. See the first official report of this agent in Ann. Rep. 1866, 298–99.

53. Higginson, *Army Life in a Black Regiment*, 60.

54. Foner, *Reconstruction*.

55. "An Act to protect all Persons in the United States in their Civil Rights, and furnish the Means of their Vindication," 14 *Stat.* 27–30 (April 9, 1866).

56. There was, as historian Kate Masur shows, somewhat less to "citizens" here than met the eye: the emphasis on the rights of citizens in the bill's first section actually represented a retreat from Trumbull's more expansive draft version. He had wanted to bar racial discrimination against all inhabitants, ensuring that, whether they were citizens or not, all residents of the United States would have the same federally enforceable legal and property rights. Trumbull's more expansive version fell before his colleagues' fears that it would prevent states from limiting immigrants' ability to purchase land and would overrule laws that discriminated against Chinese immigrants, who were racially ineligible for naturalization and whom California's white politicians and workers targeted with increasing hostility. Masur, *Until Justice Be Done*, 314–15, 322–23. Most of the Civil Rights Act, and the Fourteenth Amendment, concerned the rights of "persons"; citizens had special "privileges and immunities," to be sure, but beginning in the early 1870s the Supreme Court whittled away at this category until it contained very little.

57. *Cong. Globe*, 39th Cong., 1st Sess., 498–99 (1866).

58. *Cong. Globe*, 497–98, 574.

59. McPherson, *Battle Cry*, 450–53.

60. On the redeployment, see Downs, *After Appomattox*.

61. Bruyneel, *Third Space*, 33–44; Prucha, *Great Father*, 427–34; Kvasnicka and Viola, *Commissioners of Indian Affairs*, 102–3. Important works on the status of enslaved and formerly enslaved people in these nations include Miles, *Ties That Bind*; Naylor, *African Cherokees*; Yarbrough, *Race and the Cherokee Nation* and "'Dis Land Which Jines'"; Schreier, "Indian or Freedman?"; Micco, "'Blood and Money'"; Krauthamer, *Black Slaves, Indian Masters*; and Roberts, *I've Been Here*. For further ways Native nations responded to the impact of U.S. pressures on their own regimes of citizenship, see M. Adams, *Who Belongs?*; Sturm, *Blood Politics*; and Reed, *Serving the Nation*.

62. U.S. Congress, House, *Misc. Doc. No. 18*, 47, asserts that there were 13,653 by 1868; I have subtracted from that number those ostensibly made citizens after early 1866. See chapter 4 for a critical discussion of these numbers.

63. *Cong. Globe*, 39th Cong., 1st Sess., 527–28 (1866).

64. *Cong. Globe*, 498–99.

65. *Cong. Globe*, 506, 522.

66. Bowes, *Land Too Good*, 224–25.

67. *Cong. Globe*, 39th Cong., 1st Sess., 506 (1866).

68. *Cong. Globe*, 506.

69. *Cong. Globe*, 1683, 1700–1703.

70. *Cong. Globe*, 525.

71. Kvasnicka and Viola, *Commissioners of Indian Affairs*, 105, citing *Ann. Rep.* 1866, 1–2.

72. Madley, *American Genocide*, 331.

73. Lindsay, *Murder State*, 286–90. But see Schneider, "Citizen Lives," xii–xiii.

74. *Cong. Globe*, 39th Cong., 1st Sess., 573 (1866).

75. *Cong. Globe*, 39th Cong., 1st Sess., 574 (1866).

76. *Cong. Globe*, 39th Cong., 1st Sess., 573 (1866).

77. *Cong. Globe*, 39th Cong., 1st Sess., 527 (1866).

78. *Debates and Proceedings of the Minnesota [Democratic] Constitutional Convention*, 430–31; *Constitution of the State of Minnesota*, Art. VII, Sec. 1; *Cong. Globe*, 39th Cong., 1st Sess., 526 (1866).

79. Treaty with the Winnebago, 1865, in Kappler, *Laws and Treaties*, 2:874.

80. *Cong. Globe*, 39th Cong., 1st Sess., 526 (1866).

81. *Cong. Globe*, 527.

82. U.S. Department of the Interior, Census Office, *Eighth Census . . . Instructions to U.S. Marshals*.

83. *Cong. Globe*, 39th Cong., 1st Sess., 572 (1866).

84. *Cong. Globe*, 39th Cong., 1st Sess., 2894 (1866).

85. *Cong. Globe*, 39th Cong., 1st Sess., 573 (1866).

86. 14 *Stat.* 27–30 (April 9, 1866).

87. *Cong. Globe*, 39th Cong., 1st Sess., 2893–94 (1866).

88. *Cong. Globe*, 39th Cong., 1st Sess., 2869 (1866).

89. *Cong. Globe*, 39th Cong., 1st Sess., 2894–95 (1866).

90. *Cong. Globe*, 39th Cong., 1st Sess., 2890 (1866).

91. *Cong. Globe*, 39th Cong., 1st Sess., 2895 (1866). On sovereignty in this context, see Ford, *Settler Sovereignty*.

92. U.S. Congress, *Condition of the Indian Tribes*, 3–8; on the Doolittle Commission and its report, see Kelsey, "Doolittle Report"; and Oman, "Beginning of the End."

93. *Cong. Globe*, 39th Cong., 1st Sess., 2896–97 (1866).

94. *Cong. Globe*, 39th Cong., 1st Sess., 2892–93 (1866).

95. The enforcement acts did more than this, however; claiming extensive election fraud in Democrats' Northern urban strongholds, Republicans sought to bolster their chances by deploying a large number of federal officers to oversee elections in those places. D. Quigley, *Second Founding*.

96. On the postwar colonial oversight of reservation life, see Prucha, *Great Father*; and Cahill, *Federal Mothers and Fathers*.

97. The essential explication of free-labor ideology is Foner, *Free Soil*. Crucial works exploring the wartime and postbellum elaboration of this ideology with reference to freed-people and other (non-Indian) groups include Rose, *Rehearsal for Reconstruction*; Stanley, *From Bondage to Contract*; and Masur, *Example for All the Land*, 51–86. Quotation: White to Atkinson, February 21, 1862, in Rose, *Rehearsal for Reconstruction*, 41.

98. *Ann. Rep.* 1857, 46–48.

99. *Cong. Globe*, 39th Cong., 1st Sess., 498 (1866).

100. "President Ulysses S. Grant's First Inaugural Address (March 4, 1869)," National Park Service website, accessed June 29, 2022, https://www.nps.gov/articles/000/president-ulysses-s-grant-s-first-inaugural-address-march-4-1869.htm.

101. Hyman, "Survival at Crow Creek"; *Ann. Rep.* 1863, 323; Sully to Asst. Adj. Gen., May 28, 1864, Furnas to Thompson, August 8, 1864, *LROIA*, Winnebago Agency, Roll 937; Burbank to Taylor, August 7, 1865, *LROIA*, Winnebago Agency, Roll 938.

102. Thompson to Mix, April 20, 1864, Balcombe to Dole, June 21, 1864, Balcombe to Thompson, September 23, 1864, *LROIA*, Winnebago Agency, Roll 937; Balcombe to Dole, March 22, 1865, *LROIA*, Winnebago Agency, Roll 938.

103. October 1, 1864, *LROIA*, Winnebago Agency, Roll 937, frames 1463–1508.

104. Treaty with the Winnebago, 1865, in Kappler, *Laws and Treaties*, 2:874.

105. Petition of members of Winnebago Nation to Abraham Lincoln, June 10, 1864, *LROIA*, Winnebago Agency, Roll 937.

106. Beck, *Columns of Vengeance*.

107. *Roster of Nebraska Volunteers*, 227–29. See also Jipson, "Story of the Winnebagoes," 232–34, Chicago Historical Society, Chicago, Ill.

108. Board of Commissioners, *Minnesota in the Civil and Indian Wars*, 560.

109. Petition, January 25, 1867, *LROIA*, Winnebago Agency, Roll 940.

110. Petition, August 5, 1867, *LROIA*, Winnebago Agency, Roll 940.

111. Petition, January 30, 1867, *LROIA*, Winnebago Agency, Roll 940.

112. Petition, December 24, 1868, *LROIA*, Winnebago Agency, Roll 942.

113. *Laws and Regulations Adopted by the Winnebago Tribe*.

114. Prucha, *Great Father*, 488–92, quotation on 491; Genetin-Pilawa, *Crooked Paths to Allotment*.

115. Prucha, *Great Father*, 501–33.

116. *Ann. Rep.* 1870, 241.

117. *Ann. Rep.* 1870, 228–29.

118. *Ann. Rep.* 1872, 218.

119. *Ann. Rep.* 1871, 436.

120. Sellers, "Diary of Joseph A. Paxson," pt. 1, 177.

121. Mathewson to Taylor, November 19, 1866, *LROIA*, Winnebago Agency, Roll 940.

122. Denman to Taylor, April 22, 1867, *LROIA*, Winnebago Agency, Roll 940.

123. Sellers, "Diary of Joseph A. Paxson," pt. 1, 189.

124. *Ann. Rep.* 1870, 228.

125. *Ann. Rep.* 1870, 227.

126. Sellers, "Diary of Joseph A. Paxson," pt. 2.

127. *Ann. Rep.* 1874, 408ff.

128. Kantrowitz, "'Citizen's Clothing.'"

129. Sellers, "Diary of Joseph A. Paxson," pt. 2, 244–45.

130. *Ann. Rep.* 1870, 229.

131. In this sense, the Ho-Chunk took part in creating what Kevin Bruyneel calls a "third space of sovereignty," a political location "neither simply inside nor outside the American political system." Bruyneel, *Third Space*, xvii.

132. *Report of the Joint Delegation*, 36.

133. *Report of the Joint Delegation*, 29.

134. Evenson and Trayte, "Dress and Interaction," 110.

135. *Second Annual Report of the Joint Delegation*, 45–47; see also, for example, *Ann. Rep.* 1875, 715.

136. *Ann. Rep.* 1872, 415, 602.

137. *Ann. Rep.* 1878, 786.

138. On Lakota women as the late nineteenth-century bearers of "traditional" culture, particularly clothing, see Bol, "Lakota Beaded Costumes," 365.

139. *Ann. Rep.* 1873, 185.

140. Chakrabarty, *Provincializing Europe*.

141. Miscellaneous claims for allotments, July 10, 1866, *LROIA*, Winnebago Agency, Roll 939.

142. Beveridge to Vanvalkenberg, October 13, 1865, *LROIA*, Winnebago Agency, Roll 938. About half the households were headed by women. The total did not appear to include those serving in the Minnesota regiments, such as John St. Cyr. See Harlan to Acting, September 16, 1865, *LROIA*, Winnebago Agency, Roll 938; and Harlan to Beveridge, August 8, 1866, *LROIA*, Winnebago Agency, Roll 939.

143. Beveridge to Harlan, August 17, 1865, *LROIA*, Winnebago Agency, Roll 938.

144. Windom to Browning, April 6, 1867, *LROIA*, Winnebago Agency, Roll 940.

145. *Cong. Globe*, 41st Cong., 2nd sess., 4053–54 (1870).

146. Beveridge to Cooley, March 24, 1866, *LROIA*, Winnebago Agency, Roll 939; Beveridge to Bogy, March 2, 1867, Beveridge to Browning, March 4, 1867, *LROIA*, Winnebago Agency, Roll 940; Commissioner, General Land Office, to Parker, February 3, 1870, *LROIA*, Winnebago Agency, Roll 942. For other successful claims to land, see Beveridge to Commissioner, March 27, 1867, Commissioner to Sir, June 8, 1867, *LROIA*, Winnebago Agency, Roll 940.

147. U.S. Congress, House, *Act for the Benefit of Certain Half-Breed*. See also U.S. Congress, Senate, *Joint Resolution for the Relief*.

148. "An Act making Appropriations for the current and contingent expenses of the Indian Department . . . ," sec. 9–10, 16 *Stat.* 335 (July 15, 1870).

149. List of Winnebago Indian Families That Became Citizens of the United States, Records of the Bureau of Indian Affairs, 1793–1999, National Archives, accessed at https://catalog.archives.gov/id/7582792. See, for comparison, the discussion of mixed-descent Anishinaabe people's "asserting a dual citizenship, as Indian and American" in Witgen, *Seeing Red*, 287.

150. "A Novel Event—Fifty-One Indians Naturalized in Minnesota," *Portland (Maine) Daily Press*, October 20, 1870, 1. For an example, see Naturalization Certificate for Mary Paro, *LROIA*, Winnebago Agency, Roll 944, frame 120; and Twitchell to Parker, March 17, 1871, *LROIA*, Winnebago Agency, Roll 943.

151. See certificates in *LROIA*, Winnebago Agency, Roll 943, frames 137–159.

152. "A Schedule containing the names of certain Winnebago Indians," February 1871, *LROIA*, Winnebago Agency, Roll 943.

153. Sanborn to Walker, March 13, 1872, *LROIA*, Winnebago Agency, Roll 943.

154. Certificate of Naturalization for Joseph La Gree, January 3, 1872, *LROIA*, Winnebago Agency, Roll 943.

155. Twitchell to Parker, March 17, 1871, *LROIA*, Winnebago Agency, Roll 943; Thomas to Clum, May 12, 1871, *LROIA*, Winnebago Agency, Roll 943.

156. Copp, *Public Land Laws*, 283–85.

157. Copp, 284.

158. Asher, *Beyond the Reservation*, 76–77.

159. Thomas to Clum, May 12, 1871, *LROIA*, Winnebago Agency, Roll 943.

160. *Ann. Rep.* 1871, 450.

161. U.S. Congress, Senate, Committee on the Judiciary, *S. Rpt. No. 268*, 2, 11.

CHAPTER 4

1. Thomas to commanding officer, January 16, 1874, *LROIA*, Winnebago Agency, Roll 945.

2. U.S. Congress, House, *Misc. Doc. No. 167*, 405–6; Hunt to Smith, December 29, 1873, *LROIA*, Winnebago Agency, Roll 945.

3. "Petition of Wm. Amery and other citizens," January 31, 1866, Petitions, Remonstrances, and Resolutions to the Wisconsin Legislature, 1836–2010, Wisconsin Historical Society Archives, Madison, Wisc.

4. U.S. Congress, House, *Ex. Doc. No. 216*; "Removal of the Indians," *Mauston (Wisc.) Star*, August 4, 1870, 1.

5. *Cong. Globe*, 42nd Cong., 2nd Sess., 2194 (1872).

6. *Ann. Rep.* 1870, 323.

7. Griffith to Parker, December 16, 1869, *LROIA*, Winnebago Agency, Roll 942.

8. *Ann. Rep.* 1874, 31–32.

9. "An Interesting Case," *Dubuque Daily Times*, June 21, 1872, 2; "Indian Mary," *Winona (Minn.) Daily Republican*, April 16, 1873, 3; "Removal of the Winnebagoes," *Winona Daily Republican*, April 25, 1873, 3; "Indian Department Once Existed at Albion College," *Albion Recorder*, January 17, 2002, http://www.albionmich.com/history/histor_notebook/R020117.shtml.

10. "The Winnebago at the Capital," *Milwaukee Sentinel*, February 27, 1873, 2. See Viola, *Diplomats in Buckskin*.

11. "About the Indians," *Prairie du Chien Courier*, March 4, 1873, 2.

12. "Removal of the Winnebagoes," *Prairie du Chien Courier*, April 8, 1873, 2.

13. "The Winnebago at the Capital," 1.

14. Beach to Barber, October 17, 1872, *LROIA*, Winnebago Agency, Roll 943.

15. Spaulding to Grant, September 1, 1873, *LROIA*, Winnebago Agency, Roll 944; Rykken, "Spaulding's Funeral."

16. U.S. Congress, House, *Misc. Doc. No. 167*, 401.

17. H. W. Lee to H. R. Blum, May 1, 1873, *LROIA*, Winnebago Agency, Roll 944.

18. Petition of "Indians of the Winnebago Tribe, and more particularly described as the descendants of what was known in the year 1837, and subsequent, as Dandy's Band," [May] 1873, *LROIA*, Winnebago Agency, Roll 944.

19. Petition of "Indians of the Winnebago Tribe, and more particularly described as the descendants of what was known in the year 1837, and subsequent, as Dandy's Band."

20. "Winnebago Council," *Sparta (Wisc.) Herald*, June 3, 1863.

21. White to Smith, August 4, 1873, *LROIA*, Winnebago Agency, Roll 944.

22. Delano to Commissioner of Indian Affairs, July 10, 1873, *LROIA*, Winnebago Agency, Roll 944.

23. Bradley to White, November 12, 1873, *LROIA*, Winnebago Agency, Roll 944.

24. White to Smith, August 4, 1873, *LROIA*, Winnebago Agency, Roll 944.

25. "The Winnebago Indians," *Badger State Banner* (Black River Falls), July 5, 1873, 2.

26. "Indian Council," *Wisconsin State Register* (Portage), June 21, 1873, 2.

27. Telegram, C. A. Hunt to E. P. Smith, July 8, 1873, *LROIA*, Winnebago Agency, Roll 944.

28. *Wisconsin State Register*, July 5, 1873, 2. See, similarly, *La Crosse (Wisc.) Daily Republican and Leader*, April 14, 1873, 1.

29. "The Winnebagoes," *Wisconsin State Register*, July 19, 1873, 2.

30. *Wisconsin State Register*, July 5, 1873, 2.

31. *Cong. Globe*, 42nd Cong., 2nd Sess., 2194 (1872); Kantrowitz, *More Than Freedom*, 351.

32. *Cong. Globe*, 42nd Cong., 2nd Sess., 2194–95 (1872).

33. *Cong. Globe*, 41st Cong., 2nd Sess., 5587 (1870).
34. *Cong. Globe*, 42nd Cong., 3rd Sess., 432 (1873).
35. *Cong. Globe*, 29th Cong., 2nd Sess., 190 (1847).
36. "Winnebago Indians," *Prairie du Chien Courier*, September 16, 1873, 2.
37. *Cong. Globe*, 42nd Cong., 2nd Sess., 2200 (1872).
38. *Cong. Globe*, 42nd Cong., 3rd Sess., 372–73 (1873).
39. *Cong. Globe*, 42nd Cong., 3rd Sess., 373 (1873).
40. *Cong. Globe*, 42nd Cong., 3rd Sess., 484 (1873).
41. *Cong. Globe*, 42nd Cong., 3rd Sess., 372 (1873).
42. *Cong. Globe*, 42nd Cong., 3rd Sess., 3827 (1873).
43. *Cong. Globe*, 42nd Cong., 3rd Sess., 372–73 (1873).
44. *Cong. Globe*, 42nd Cong., 3rd Sess., 375, 377 (1873); U.S. Congress, Senate, *Journal of the Senate of the United States* 68, no. 113 (January 7, 1873); Walker, "Moral and Social Reforms," 314.
45. "About the Indians," *Prairie du Chien Courier*, March 4, 1873, 2.
46. "The Winnebagoes and Their Future," *Sparta Herald*, March 18, 1873, 1.
47. Smith to Lee, June 13, 1873, quoted in "The Indian Removal Questions," *Wisconsin State Register*, July 12, 1873, 2.
48. U.S. Congress, House, *Misc. Doc. No. 167*, 403.
49. Delano to Smith, July 10, 1873, quoted in "Removal of the Winnebagoes," *Juneau County (Wisc.) Argus*, August 21, 1873, 2.
50. "The Winnebago Pow-Wow," *Sparta Herald*, July 22, 1873, 4.
51. "Returned from the Indian Country," *Trempeleau County (Wisc.) Republican*, August 22, 1873, 2.
52. Hunt to Smith, August 22, 1873, *LROIA*, Winnebago Agency, Roll 944.
53. "Winnebago Council," *Sparta Herald*, June 3, 1863.
54. See notes 1 and 2, above.
55. "Revmoal [*sic*] of the Winnebagoes," *Wisconsin State Register*, December 27, 1873, 2.
56. U.S. Congress, House, *Misc. Doc. No. 167*, 408; "Yankee Bill's" later patent for the same Monroe County land described in this document can be found in the records of the U.S. General Land Office at https://glorecords.blm.gov/details/patent/default.aspx?accession=WI1100___.137&docClass=STA&sid=sttv5qmd.d4f#patentDetailsTabIndex=1.
57. Thomas to Asst. Adj. Gen., Department of Dakota, January 2, 1874, Microcopy No. 666, *Letters Received by the Office of the Adjutant General*, Roll 133.
58. "Revmoal [*sic*] of the Winnebagoes," 2.
59. "The Indian Difficulty," *Reedsburg Free Press*, January 2, 1874, 2 (quotations); Writ of Habeas Corpus, December 27, 1873, Hunt to Smith, December 29, 1873, *LROIA*, Winnebago Agency, Roll 945; "The Winnebagoes," *Reedsburg Free Press*, December 26, 1873, 2; "Gathering Them In," *Sparta Herald*, December 30, 1873, 4.
60. Cash to Thomas, copy, December 27, 1873, Microcopy No. 666, *Letters Received by the Office of the Adjutant General*, Roll 133.
61. "The Indian Difficulty," 2.
62. Thomas to Asst. Adj. Gen., Dept. of Dakota (copy), December 28, 1873, Microcopy No. 666, *Letters Received by the Office of the Adjutant General*, Roll 133.
63. Sheridan to Sherman, copy, January 3, 1874, *LROIA*, Winnebago Agency, Roll 945.
64. Delano to Belknap, January 5, 187[4], *LROIA*, Winnebago Agency, Roll 945.
65. *Congressional Record*, 43rd Cong., 1st. Sess., 743–44 (1874).

66. "The Winnebagoes," *Milwaukee Daily Sentinel*, February 2, 1874, 1.
67. Hunt to Smith, May 4, 1874, *LROIA*, Winnebago Agency, Roll 945.
68. Bradley to Smith, May 11, 1874, *LROIA*, Winnebago Agency, Roll 945.
69. Bradley to White, October 1, 1874, *LROIA*, Winnebago Agency, Roll 945.
70. Bon to Smith, July 13, 1874, *LROIA*, Winnebago Agency, Roll 945.
71. Bradley to Smith, November 5, 1874, *LROIA*, Winnebago Agency, Roll 945.
72. "An Indian Talk," *Sparta Herald*, May 19, 1874, 1.
73. "Winnebagoes Returned," *Juneau County Argus*, July 16, 1874, 3.
74. *Prairie du Chien Courier*, May 12, 1874, 3.
75. *Winona Daily Republican*, August 3, 1874, 3.
76. Petition, June 26, 1874, *LROIA*, Winnebago Agency, Roll 945.
77. Telegram, Hunt to Smith, April 4, 1874, *LROIA*, Winnebago Agency, Roll 945.
78. Telegram, Hunt to Smith, May 4, 1874, *LROIA*, Winnebago Agency, Roll 945.
79. Hunt to Smith, May 8, 1874, *LROIA*, Winnebago Agency, Roll 945.
80. *Ann. Rep.* 1874, 337.
81. "The Indians," *Reedsburg Free Press*, April 9, 1874, 3.
82. Telegram, Hunt to Smith, April 1, 1874, *LROIA*, Winnebago Agency, Roll 945.
83. "The Indians," *Trempeleau County Republican*, January 9, 1874, 3 (quotation); Onsager, "Removal of the Winnebago Indians," 273.
84. "Indian Dodge," *Sparta Herald*, April 7, 1874, 1.
85. "Wisconsin," *Milwaukee Daily Sentinel*, November 9, 1874, 2.
86. "Lo at School," *Reedsburg Free Press*, January 9, 1874, 3.
87. "Political," *Milwaukee Daily Sentinel*, November 5, 1875, 1.
88. Bradford to Grant, January 7, 1875, *LROIA*, Winnebago Agency, Roll 946.
89. Petition of Walking Cloud and others, March 10, 1875, Affidavit of John M. St. Cyr, March 26, 1875, *LROIA*, Winnebago Agency, Roll 946.
90. "Legislative Summary," *Wisconsin State Journal*, January 26, 1875, 1; "Wisconsin Legislature," *Milwaukee Daily Sentinel*, February 13, 1875, 1.
91. "The Winnebago Indians in Wisconsin," *Wisconsin State Register*, February 27, 1875, 1.
92. 18 *Stat.* 420 (March 3, 1875); for discussion of the "Indian Homestead Act," see Fisher, *Shadow Tribe*, 91–92.
93. The Center for Legislative Archives (National Archives, Washington, D.C.) holds a bound volume of the minutes of the Committee on Indian Affairs, but that volume contains no discussions of these provisions in February, nor any minutes from February 14, 1875, through the end of the session. The center does not possess the corresponding docket volume. Author correspondence with Rodney A. Ross, Center for Legislative Archives, June 14, 2012.
94. "Sensible Indians," *Daily Inter Ocean* (Chicago), May 31, 1875; "Stevens Point," *Milwaukee Daily News*, February 1, 1876, 1.
95. 18 *Stat.* 420, sec. 15–16 (March 3, 1875).
96. K. Tsianina Lomawaima points to similar limitations on Native people's property rights under later regimes of allotment and even citizenship; Lomawaima, "Mutuality of Citizenship and Sovereignty."
97. Petition of Walking Cloud and others, March 10, 1875, *LROIA*, Winnebago Agency, Roll 946.
98. Lee to Delano, May 13, 1875, *LROIA*, Winnebago Agency, Roll 946; U.S. Congress, Senate, *Doc. 144*, 1:6, 2:2–5.

99. Merrell to Dear Sir, May 17, 1875, *LROIA*, Winnebago Agency, Roll 946; Cameron to Delano, July 1, 1875, *LROIA*, Winnebago Agency, Roll 946; U.S. Congress, Senate, Committee on Indian Affairs, *S. Rpt. No. 747* and *S. Rpt. No. 253*.

100. Leeds to Secretary of the Interior, Aril 13, 1878, in U.S. Congress, Senate, Committee on Indian Affairs, *S. Rpt. No. 253*.

101. "Winnebago Indians," *Daily Inter Ocean*, January 8, 1881, 1–2; 21 *Stat.* 315, January 18, 1881; U.S. Congress, Senate, *Doc. 144*, 36; *Copp's Land Owner*, March 15, 1884, 405–6.

102. Appendix A, "Report of the Committee on Territorial Affairs," 1879, in U.S. Congress, House, *Misc. Doc. No. 18*, 47; Treaty with the Ottawa and Chippewa, 1855, in Kappler, *Laws and Treaties*, 2:725–31.

103. Ramirez, *Standing Up to Colonial Power*; Lamere, "Indian Culture of the Future."

104. Lomawaima, "Mutuality of Citizenship and Sovereignty," 333–34.

105. Deloria, "American Master Narratives," 10.

106. Quoted in Maddox, *Citizen Indians*, 107.

107. But see Lomawaima, "Mutuality of Citizenship and Sovereignty," for important cautions.

108. List of Nebraska allotments to Wisconsin Winnebago, January 28, 1876, *LROIA*, Winnebago Agency, Roll 946.

109. Petition of Winneshiek and Black Hawk, February 9, 1876, *LROIA*, Winnebago Agency, Roll 946.

110. "Local Brevities," *Winona Daily Republican*, June 24, 1879, 3; *Stat.*, ch. 177, 68th Cong., 1st Sess. (May 24, 1924).

111. *Ann. Rep.* 1883, 107.

112. *Ann. Rep.* 1883, xxvii–xxviii.

113. Lonetree, "Heritage of Resilience."

114. Jones et al., *People of the Big Voice*. See also Hoelscher, *Picturing Indians*.

115. Jones et al., *People of the Big Voice*, 44; Vizenor, "Aesthetics of Survivance," 1.

EPILOGUE

1. Kantrowitz, *More Than Freedom*; Masur, *Until Justice Be Done*.

2. Wolfe, "Settler Colonialism."

3. Quoted in Williams, "United States Indian Policy," 829; Immerwahr, *How to Hide an Empire*, ch. 1.

4. Cothran, "Enduring Legacy," 571.

5. Wilson, "Reconstruction," 11.

6. Cecelski and Tyson, *Democracy Betrayed*; Ellsworth, *Death in a Promised Land*; Tyson, *Blood of Emmett Till*.

7. W. Johnson, "Guns in the Family."

8. Lew-Williams, *Chinese Must Go*; B. Johnson, *Revolution in Texas*.

9. Ngai, *Impossible Subjects*.

10. Bosniak, "Varieties of Citizenship."

11. "Know Your Rights: 100 Mile Border Zone," American Civil Liberties Union website, accessed June 28, 2022, https://www.aclu.org/know-your-rights/border-zone/.

12. Wallerstein, "Citizens All?"

Bibliography

ARCHIVAL MATERIALS

Chicago Historical Society, Chicago, Ill.
    Norton Jipson, "The Story of the Winnebagoes," unpublished manuscript
Southern Minnesota Historical Center, Mankato, Minn.
    Thomas Hughes Papers
Wisconsin Historical Society Archives, Madison, Wisc.
    American Indian Classified File, ca. 1850s–ca. 1950s
    Charles E. Brown Papers, 1889–1945
    Petitions, Remonstrances, and Resolutions to the Wisconsin Legislature, 1836–2010

GOVERNMENT PUBLICATIONS

Congressional Globe
Congressional Record
Constitution of the State of Illinois. November 16, 1818. Washington City [D.C.]: D. E. Krafft, 1818.
Constitution of the State of Minnesota. Adopted in convention, on Friday, August 28, 1857. St. Paul, Minn.: S. E. Goodrich, 1857.
Constitution of the State of Wisconsin, Adopted in Convention, at Madison, on the First Day of February, in the Year of Our Lord 1848. Madison, Wisc.: Beriah Brown, 1848.
Debates and Proceedings of the Minnesota [Democratic] Constitutional Convention including the Organic Act of the Territory. St. Paul, Minn.: Earle S. Goodrich, 1857.
Debates and Proceedings of the [Republican] Constitutional Convention for the Territory of Minnesota: To Form a State Constitution Preparatory to Its Admission into the Union as a State. St. Paul, Minn.: George W. Moore, 1858.
General Laws of the State of Minnesota; Passed and Approved during the First Session of the State Legislature. St. Paul, Minn.: Earle S. Goodrich, 1858.

Kappler, Charles J., comp. *Indian Affairs: Laws and Treaties.* 5 vols. Washington, D.C.: Government Printing Office, 1903–41.

Laws and Regulations Adopted by the Winnebago Tribe of Indians, in Council Held at the Winnebago Agency, Nebraska, July 21st, A.D. 1868. Omaha: Daily Herald, 1868.

Opinion of Attorney General Bates on Citizenship. Washington: Government Printing Office, 1862.

Territorial Papers of the United States. 28 vols. Washington, D.C.: Government Printing Office, 1934–75.

U.S. Congress. *Condition of the Indian Tribes: Report of the Joint Special Committee, Appointed under Joint Resolution of March 3, 1865. With an Appendix.* Washington, D.C.: Government Printing Office, 1867.

U.S. Congress. House. *An Act for the Benefit of Certain Half-Breed and Mixed Bloods of the Winnebago Tribe of Indians.* H.R. 416, 39th Cong., 1st Sess., 1866.

———. *Ex. Doc. No. 216. Stray Bands of Indians.* 41st Cong., 2nd Sess., 1870.

———. *Misc. Doc. No. 18. Allotment of Lands in Severalty among Indian Tribes.* 47th Cong., 2nd Sess., 1883.

———. *Misc. Doc. No. 167. Indian Affairs.* 44th Cong., 1st. Sess., 1876.

———. *Rep. No. 501. Removal of the Winnebagoes.* 31st Cong., 1st Sess., 1850.

U.S. Congress. Senate. Committee on Indian Affairs. *S. Rpt. No. 253. Report to Accompany Bill S. 323.* 46th Cong., 2nd Sess., 1880.

———. Committee on Indian Affairs. *S. Rpt. No. 747. Report to Accompany Bill S. 1124.* 45th Cong., 3rd Sess., 1879.

———. Committee on the Judiciary. *S. Rpt. No. 268.* 41st Cong., 3rd Sess., 1870.

———. *Doc. 144. Henry W. Lee.* 56th Cong., 1st Sess., 1900.

———. *Joint Resolution for the Relief of Certain Winnebago Indians Residing in Minnesota.* S.J.Res.96. 40th Cong., 2nd Sess., 1868.

———. *Journal of the Senate of the United States.*

———. *S. Doc. 512. Correspondence on the Subject of the Emigration of Indians.* 5 vols. Washington: Duff Green, 1834–35. 23rd Cong., 1st Sess., 1834–35.

U.S. Department of Justice. *Opinions of the Attorney-General.*

U.S. Department of the Interior. Census Office. *Eighth Census, United States—1860. Instructions to U.S. Marshals. Instructions to Assistants.* Washington, D.C.: Geo. W. Bowman, 1860.

———. General Land Office. Patent and survey records. https://glorecords.blm.gov/default.aspx.

———. Office of Indian Affairs. *Annual Report of the Commissioner of Indian Affairs.* Washington, D.C.: Government Printing Office, 1830–82.

U.S. Statutes at Large.

Wisconsin, C. S. Jordan, M. Frank, and C. Minton Baker. *The Revised Statutes of the State of Wisconsin: Passed at the Second Session of the Legislature, Commencing January 10, 1849.* Southport, Wisc.: C. L. Sholes, 1849.

GOVERNMENT RECORDS IN MICROFORM

Microcopy No. T-494. *Documents Relating to the Negotiation of Ratified and Unratified Treaties with Various Tribes of Indians, 1801–69.* Record Group 75, Records of the Bureau of Indian Affairs. National Archives, Washington, D.C., 1960.

Microcopy No. 234. *Letters Received by the Office of Indian Affairs, 1824–1880.*
    Record Group 75, Records of the Bureau of Indian Affairs.
    National Archives, Washington, D.C.
    Letters Received, Northern Superintendency
    Letters Received, Prairie du Chien Agency
    Letters Received, Turkey River Agency
    Letters Received, Winnebago Agency
    Letters Received, Wisconsin Superintendency
Microcopy No. 666. *Letters Received by the Office of the Adjutant General, 1870–1880.* 1873:
    Roll 133. Records of the Adjutant General.
    National Archives, Washington, D.C., 1966.

PERIODICALS

Albion (Mich.) Recorder
Annals of Iowa
Badger State Banner
    (Black River Falls, Wisc.)
Copp's Land Owner (Washington, D.C.)
Daily Inter Ocean (Chicago)
Dubuque Daily Times
Juneau County (Wisc.) Argus
LaCrosse (Wisc.) Daily Republican
    and Leader
Mankato (Minn.) Record
Mankato (Minn.) Weekly Union
Mauston (Wisc.) Star
Milwaukee Daily News

Milwaukee Sentinel
Portland (Maine) Daily Press
Prairie du Chien Courier
Reedsburg (Wisc.) Free Press
Semi-Weekly Wisconsin (Milwaukee)
Sparta (Wisc.) Herald
St. Paul Daily Press
Trempeleau County (Wisc.) Republican
Winona (Minn.) Daily Republican
Wisconsin Archaeologist
Wisconsin Pinery (Stevens Point)
Wisconsin State Journal (Madison)
Wisconsin State Register (Portage)

BOOKS, THESES, AND DISSERTATIONS

Adams, David. *Education for Extinction: American Indians and the Boarding School Experience, 1875–1928.* Lawrence: University Press of Kansas, 1995.

Adams, Mikaëla M. *Who Belongs? Race, Resources, and Tribal Citizenship in the Native South.* New York: Oxford University Press, 2016.

Anbinder, Tyler. *Nativism and Slavery: The Northern Know Nothings and the Politics of the 1850s.* New York: Oxford University Press, 1992.

Arenson, Adam, and Andrew R. Graybill, eds. *Civil War Wests: Testing the Limits of the United States.* Berkeley: University of California Press, 2015.

Arndt, Grant. *Ho-Chunk Powwows and the Politics of Tradition.* Lincoln: University of Nebraska Press, 2016.

Asher, Brad. *Beyond the Reservation: Indians, Settlers, and the Law in Washington Territory, 1853–1889.* Norman: University of Oklahoma Press, 1999.

Atwater, Caleb. *Remarks Made on a Tour to Prairie du Chien.* Columbus, Ohio: Isaac N. Whiting, 1831.

Bachman, Walt. *Northern Slave, Black Dakota: The Life and Times of Joseph Godfrey.* Bloomington, Minn.: Pond Dakota Press, 2013.

Basler, Roy P., ed. *The Collected Works of Abraham Lincoln*. 7 vols. New Brunswick: Rutgers University Press, 1953.

Beck, Paul N. *Columns of Vengeance: Soldiers, Sioux, and the Punitive Expeditions, 1863–1864*. Norman: University of Oklahoma Press, 2013.

Berg, Scott W. *38 Nooses: Lincoln, Little Crow, and the Beginning of the Frontier's End*. New York: Vintage, 2012.

Birmingham, Robert A. *Spirits of Earth: The Effigy Mound Landscape of Madison and the Four Lakes*. Madison: University of Wisconsin Press, 2002.

Board of Commissioners. *Minnesota in the Civil and Indian Wars, 1861–1865*. 2nd ed. St. Paul, Minn.: Pioneer Press, 1891.

Bowes, John P. *Exiles and Pioneers: Eastern Indians in the Trans-Mississippi West*. New York: Cambridge University Press, 2007.

———. *Land Too Good for Indians: Northern Indian Removal*. Norman: University of Oklahoma Press, 2016.

Bruyneel, Kevin. *The Third Space of Sovereignty: The Postcolonial Politics of U.S.–Indigenous Relations*. Minneapolis: University of Minnesota Press, 2007.

Buss, James Joseph. *Winning the West with Words: Language and Conquest in the Lower Great Lakes*. Norman: University of Oklahoma Press, 2011.

Cahill, Cathleen. *Federal Mothers and Fathers: A Social History of the United States Indian Service, 1869–1933*. Chapel Hill: University of North Carolina Press, 2011.

Calloway, Colin G. *The Indian World of George Washington: The First President, the First Americans, and the Birth of the Nation*. New York: Oxford University Press, 2018.

———. *The Victory with No Name: The Native American Defeat of the First American Army*. New York: Oxford University Press, 2015.

Cecelski, David S., and Timothy B. Tyson. *Democracy Betrayed: The Wilmington Race Riot of 1898 and Its Legacy*. Chapel Hill: University of North Carolina Press, 1998.

Chakrabarty, Dipesh. *Provincializing Europe: Postcolonial Thought and Historical Difference*. Princeton, N.J.: Princeton University Press, 2000.

Clark, Carol. *Charles Deas and 1840s America*. Norman: University of Oklahoma Press, 2009.

Clifton, James A. *The Pokagons, 1683–1983: Catholic Potawatomi Indians of the St. Joseph River Valley*. Lanham, Md.: University Press of America, 1984.

Coats, Catherine M. "'Extermination or Removal': The Knights of the Forest and Ethnic Cleansing in Early Minnesota." M.A. thesis, St. Cloud State University, 2017.

Cole, Harry Ellsworth. *A Standard History of Sauk County, Wisconsin*. Chicago: Lewis Publishing Company, 1918.

Collections of the Minnesota Historical Society. 17 vols. St. Paul: Minnesota Historical Society Press, 1872–1920.

Conn, Steven. *History's Shadow: Native Americans and Historical Consciousness in the Nineteenth Century*. Chicago: University of Chicago Press, 2004.

Copp, Henry N. *Public Land Laws Passed by Congress from March 4, 1869, to March 3, 1875, with Important Decisions of the Secretary of the Interior, and Commissioner of the General Land Office*. Washington, D.C.: Henry N. Copp, 1875.

Cothran, Boyd. *Remembering the Modoc War: Redemptive Violence and the Making of American Innocence*. Chapel Hill: University of North Carolina Press, 2014.

Crandall, Maurice S. *These People Have Always Been a Republic: Indigenous Electorates in the U.S.–Mexico Borderlands, 1598–1912*. Chapel Hill: University of North Carolina Press, 2019.

Cushing, Caleb. *Speech Delivered in Faneuil Hall, Boston, October 27, 1857. Also, Speech Delivered in City Hall, Newburyport, October 31, 1857*. Boston: Boston Post, 1857.

Diedrich, Mark. *Ho-Chunk Chiefs: Winnebago Leadership in an Era of Crisis*. Rochester, Minn.: Coyote Books, 2001.

———. *Winnebago Oratory: Great Moments in the Recorded Speech of the Hochungra, 1742–1887*. Rochester, Minn.: Coyote Books, 1991.

Downs, Gregory P. *After Appomattox: Military Occupation and the Ends of War*. Cambridge, Mass.: Harvard University Press, 2015.

Downs, Gregory P., and Kate Masur, eds. *The World the Civil War Made*. Chapel Hill: University of North Carolina Press, 2015.

Durrie, Daniel S. *A History of Madison, the Capital of Wisconsin; Including the Four Lake Country to July 1874*. Madison, Wisc.: Atwood and Culver, 1874.

Ellsworth, Scott. *Death in a Promised Land: The Tulsa Race Riot of 1921*. Baton Rouge: Louisiana State University Press, 1982.

Fehrenbacher, Donald. *The Dred Scott Case: Its Significance in American Law and Politics*. New York: Oxford University Press, 2001.

———, ed. *Abraham Lincoln: Speeches and Writings, 1832–1858*. New York: Library of America, 1989.

Fisher, Andrew H. *Shadow Tribe: The Making of Columbia River Indian Identity*. Seattle: University of Washington Press, 2010.

Folwell, William Watts. *A History of Minnesota*. 4 vols. St. Paul: Minnesota Historical Society, 1921.

Foner, Eric. *Free Soil, Free Labor, Free Men: The Ideology of the Republican Party before the Civil War*. New York: Oxford University Press, 1970.

———. *Reconstruction, 1863–1877: America's Unfinished Revolution*. New York: Harper and Row, 1988.

———. *The Second Founding: How the Civil War and Reconstruction Remade the Constitution*. New York: W. W. Norton, 2019.

Ford, Lisa. *Settler Sovereignty: Jurisdiction and Indigenous People in America and Australia, 1788–1836*. Cambridge, Mass.: Harvard University Press, 2010.

Garrison, Tim Alan. *The Legal Ideology of Removal: The Southern Judiciary and the Sovereignty of Native American Nations*. Athens: University of Georgia Press, 2002.

Garvin, Cecil, and Iren Hartmann. *Hoocąk hijt'ekjawi! A Ho-Chunk Language Text- and Workbook for Beginners*. N.p., n.d.

Genetin-Pilawa, Joseph C. *Crooked Paths to Allotment: The Fight over Federal Indian Policy after the Civil War*. Chapel Hill: University of North Carolina Press, 2012.

Godwin, Shawn. *Pleasant Ridge: A Rural African-American Community in Grant County, Wisconsin*. Madison: State Historical Society of Wisconsin/Old World Wisconsin, 2000.

Green, Michael S. *Lincoln and Native Americans*. Carbondale: Southern Illinois University Press, 2021.

Guyatt, Nicholas. *Bind Us Apart: How Enlightened Americans Invented Racial Segregation*. New York: Basic Books, 2016.

Hahn, Steven. *A Nation under Our Feet: Black Political Struggles in the Rural South from Slavery to the Great Migration*. Cambridge, Mass.: Harvard University Press, 2003.

———. *A Nation without Borders: The United States and Its World in an Age of Civil Wars, 1830–1910*. New York: Penguin Books, 2016.

Hall, Harland Page. *H. P. Hall's Observations, Being More or Less a History of Political Contests in Minnesota from 1849 to 1904*. St. Paul, Minn.: n.p., 1904.

Hall, John W. *Uncommon Defense: Indian Allies in the Black Hawk War*. Cambridge, Mass.: Harvard University Press, 2009.

Halttunen, Karen. *Confidence Men and Painted Women: A Study of Middle-Class Culture in America, 1830–1870*. New Haven, Conn.: Yale University Press, 1982.

Hexom, Charles Philip, comp. *Indian History of Winneshiek County*. Decorah, Iowa: A. K. Bailey and Son, 1913.

Higginson, Thomas Wentworth. *Army Life in a Black Regiment*. 1869. Reprint, New York: W. W. Norton, 1984.

Hinks, Peter P. *To Awaken My Afflicted Brethren: David Walker and the Problem of Antebellum Slave Resistance*. University Park: Pennsylvania State University Press, 1997.

Hinzo, Angel Mae. "Voicing across Space: Subverting Colonial Structures in Ho-Chunk/Winnebago Tribal History." Ph.D. diss., University of California, Davis, 2016.

The History of Columbia County, Wisconsin. Chicago: Western Historical Company, 1880.

Hoelscher, Steven D. *Picturing Indians: Photographic Encounters and Tourist Fantasies in H. H. Bennett's Wisconsin Dells*. Madison: University of Wisconsin Press, 2008.

Holzer, Harold, ed. *The Lincoln-Douglas Debates*. New York: Fordham University Press, 2004.

Hughes, Thomas. *History of Blue Earth County and Biographies of Its Leading Citizens*. Chicago: Middle West Publishing Co., 1901.

———. *Indian Chiefs of Southern Minnesota*. Mankato, Minn.: Free Press Company, 1927.

Hyde, Anne F. *Born of Lakes and Plains: Mixed-Descent Peoples and the Making of the American West*. New York: W. W. Norton, 2022.

———. *Empires, Nations, and Families: A History of the North American West, 1800–1860*. Lincoln: University of Nebraska Press, 2011.

Immerwahr, Daniel. *How to Hide an Empire: A History of the Greater United States*. New York: Picador, 2019.

Jacobs, Wilbur R., ed. *Frederick Jackson Turner's Legacy: Unpublished Writings in American History*. San Marino, Calif.: Huntington Library, 1965.

Johnson, Benjamin Heber. *Revolution in Texas: How a Forgotten Rebellion and Its Bloody Suppression Turned Mexicans into Americans*. New Haven, Conn.: Yale University Press, 2005.

Johnson, Walter. *The Broken Heart of America: St. Louis and the Violent History of the United States*. New York: Basic Books, 2020.

Jones, J. A. *Winnebago Ethnology*. New York: Garland, 1974.

Jones, Martha S. *Birthright Citizens: A History of Race and Rights in Antebellum America*. New York: Cambridge University Press, 2018.

Jones, Tom, Michael Schmudlach, Matthew Daniel Mason, Amy Lonetree, and George A. Greendeer. *People of the Big Voice: Photographs of Ho-Chunk Families by Charles Van Schaick, 1879–1942*. Madison: Wisconsin Historical Society Press, 2011.

Jung, Patrick J. *The Black Hawk War of 1832*. Norman: University of Oklahoma Press, 2008.

Kantrowitz, Stephen. *More Than Freedom: Fighting for Black Citizenship in a White Republic, 1829–1889*. New York: Penguin Press, 2012.

Kelman, Ari. *For Liberty and Empire: How the Civil War Bled into the Indian Wars*. New York: Basic Books, forthcoming.

———. *A Misplaced Massacre: Struggling over the Memory of Sand Creek*. Cambridge, Mass.: Harvard University Press, 2013.

Kettner, James. *The Development of American Citizenship, 1608–1870*. Chapel Hill: University of North Carolina Press, 1978.

Kiernan, Ben. *Blood and Soil: A World History of Genocide and Extermination from Sparta to Darfur*. New Haven, Conn.: Yale University Press, 2009.

Kinzie, Mrs. John H. [Juliette]. *Wau-bun: The "Early Day" in the Northwest*. Chicago: Rand, McNally, 1901.

Krauthamer, Barbara. *Black Slaves, Indian Masters: Slavery, Emancipation, and Citizenship in the Native American South*. Chapel Hill: University of North Carolina Press, 2013.

Krug, Merton Edwin. *History of Reedsburg and the Upper Baraboo Valley*. Madison, Wisc.: Democratic Printing Co., 1929.

Kvasnicka, Robert M., and Herman J. Viola, eds. *The Commissioners of Indian Affairs, 1824–1977*. Lincoln: University of Nebraska Press, 1977.

Landis, Michael Todd. *Northern Men with Southern Loyalties: The Democratic Party and the Sectional Crisis*. Ithaca: Cornell University Press, 2014.

Lang, John D., and Samuel Taylor. *Report of a Visit to Some of the Tribes of Indians, Located West of the Mississippi River*. New York: Mahlon Day, 1843.

Lepore, Jill. *These Truths: A History of the United States*. New York: W. W. Norton, 2018.

Lew-Williams, Beth. *The Chinese Must Go: Violence, Exclusion, and the Making of the Alien in America*. Cambridge, Mass.: Harvard University Press, 2018.

Limerick, Patricia. *The Legacy of Conquest: The Unbroken Past of the American West*. New York: W. W. Norton, 1987.

Lindsay, Brendan C. *Murder State: California's Native American Genocide, 1846–1873*. Lincoln: University of Nebraska Press, 2012.

Low, John N. *Imprints: The Pokagon Band of Potawatomi Indians and the City of Chicago*. East Lansing: Michigan State University Press, 2016.

Lowery, Malinda Maynor. *The Lumbee Indians: An American Struggle*. Chapel Hill: University of North Carolina Press, 2018.

Lurie, Nancy O. "The Winnebago Indians: A Study in Cultural Change." Ph.D. diss., Northwestern University, 1952.

Lurie, Nancy O., and Patrick Jung. *The Nicolet Corrigenda: New France Revisited*. Long Grove, Ill.: Waveland Press, 2009.

Maddox, Lucy. *Citizen Indians: Native American Intellectuals, Race, and Reform*. Ithaca, N.Y.: Cornell University Press, 2005.

Madison, Dane County, and Surrounding Towns; Being a History and Guide. Madison, Wisc.: Wm. J. Park, 1877.

Madison: The Capital of Wisconsin, Its Progress, Capabilities and Destiny. Madison, Wisc.: Rublee and Gary, 1855.

Madley, Benjamin. *An American Genocide: The United States and the California Indian Catastrophe*. New Haven, Conn.: Yale University Press, 2016.

Martin, Joel. *Sacred Revolt: The Muskogees' Struggle for a New World*. Boston: Beacon Press, 1991.

Masur, Kate. *An Example for All the Land: Emancipation and the Struggle over Equality in Washington*. Chapel Hill: University of North Carolina Press, 2010.

———. *Until Justice Be Done: America's First Civil Rights Movement, from the Revolution to Reconstruction*. New York: W. W. Norton, 2021.

McPherson, James M. *Battle Cry of Freedom: The Civil War Era*. New. York: Oxford University Press, 1988.

Miles, Tiya. *Ties That Bind: The Story of an Afro-Cherokee Family in Slavery and Freedom.* Berkeley: University of California Press, 2006.

Miner, H. Craig, and William E. Unrau. *The End of Indian Kansas: A Study of Cultural Revolution, 1854–1871.* Lawrence: University Press of Kansas, 1978.

Mosteller, Kelli Jean. "Place, Politics, and Property: Negotiating Allotment for the Citizen Potawatomi, 1861–1891." Ph.D. diss., University of Texas, 2013.

Murphy, Lucy Eldersveld. *A Gathering of Rivers: Indians, Métis, and Mining in the Western Great Lakes, 1737–1832.* Lincoln: University of Nebraska Press, 2000.

———. *Great Lakes Creoles: The French–Indian Community on the Northern Borderlands, Prairie du Chien, 1750–1860.* New York: Cambridge University Press, 2014.

Naylor, Celia E. *African Cherokees in Indian Territory: From Chattel to Citizens.* Chapel Hill: University of North Carolina Press, 2008.

Nelson, Megan Kate. *The Three-Cornered War: The Union, the Confederacy, and Native Peoples in the Fight for the West.* New York: Simon and Schuster, 2020.

Nesper, Larry. *"Our Relations . . . the Mixed Bloods": Indigenous Transformation and Dispossession in the Western Great Lakes.* Albany: State University of New York Press, 2021.

Ngai, Mae. *Impossible Subjects: Illegal Immigrants and the Making of Modern America.* Princeton, N.J.: Princeton University Press, 2004.

Nichols, David. *Lincoln and the Indians: Civil War Policy and Politics.* 1978. Reprint, St. Paul: Minnesota Historical Society Press, 2012.

Oberly, James W. *A Nation of Statesmen: The Political Culture of the Stockbridge-Munsee Mohicans, 1815–1972.* Norman: University of Oklahoma Press, 2005.

O'Brien, Jean M. *Firsting and Lasting: Writing Indians Out of Existence in New England.* Minneapolis: University of Minnesota Press, 2010.

Onsager, Lawrence W. "The Removal of the Winnebago Indians from Wisconsin in 1873–1874." M.A. thesis, Loma Linda University, 1985.

Ostler, Jeffrey. *Surviving Genocide: Native Nations and the United States from the American Revolution to Bleeding Kansas.* New Haven, Conn.: Yale University Press, 2019.

Parker, Kunal M. *Making Foreigners: Immigration and Citizenship Law in America, 1600–2000.* New York: Cambridge University Press, 2015.

Pelzer, Louis. *Henry Dodge.* Iowa City: State Historical Society of Iowa, 1911.

Proceedings of the State Historical Society of Wisconsin at Its Fifty-Seventh Annual Meeting, Held October 21, 1909. Madison: State Historical Society of Wisconsin, 1910.

Prucha, Francis Paul. *The Great Father: The United States Government and American Indians.* Lincoln: University of Nebraska Press, 1984.

Pryor, Elizabeth Stordeur. *Colored Travelers: Mobility and the Fight for Citizenship before the Civil War.* Chapel Hill: University of North Carolina Press, 2016.

Quarles, Benjamin. *The Negro in the Civil War.* New York: Da Capo, 1989. First published in 1953.

Quigley, David. *Second Founding: New York City, Reconstruction, and the Making of American Democracy.* New York: Hill and Wang, 2003.

Radin, Paul. *The Winnebago Tribe.* Lincoln: Bison Books/University of Nebraska Press, 1990. First published in 1923.

Ramirez, Renya K. *Standing Up to Colonial Power: The Lives of Henry Roe and Elizabeth Bender Cloud.* Lincoln: University of Nebraska Press, 2018.

Rasmussen, Anders Bo. *Civil War Settlers: Scandinavians, Citizenship, and American Empire, 1848–1870.* New York: Cambridge University Press, 2022.

Redix, Erik M. *The Murder of Joe White: Ojibwe Leadership and Colonialism in Wisconsin*. East Lansing: Michigan State University Press, 2014.
Reed, Julie L. *Serving the Nation: Cherokee Sovereignty and Social Welfare, 1800–1907*. Norman: University of Oklahoma Press, 2016.
Report of the Joint Delegation Appointed by the Committees on the Indian Concern of the Yearly Meetings of Baltimore, Philadelphia, and New York . . . to Visit the Indians under the Care of Friends in the Northern Superintendency, State of Nebraska, 7th & 8th Mos., 1869. Baltimore: J. Jones, 1869.
Roberts, Alaina. *I've Been Here All the While: Black Freedom on Native Land*. Philadelphia: University of Pennsylvania Press, 2021.
Rohrbaugh, Malcolm J. *The Land Office Business: The Settlement and Administration of American Public Lands, 1789–1837*. New York: Oxford, 1968.
Rose, Willie Lee. *Rehearsal for Reconstruction: The Port Royal Experiment*. 1964. Reprint, Athens: University of Georgia Press, 1999.
Rosebrough, Amy. "Every Family a Nation: A Deconstruction and Reconstruction of the Effigy Mound 'Culture' of the Western Great Lakes of North America." Ph.D. diss., University of Wisconsin–Madison, 2009.
Rosen, Deborah. *American Indians and State Law: Sovereignty, Race, and Citizenship, 1790–1880*. Lincoln: University of Nebraska Press, 2007.
Roster of Nebraska Volunteers from 1861 to 1869. Hastings, Neb.: Wigton and Evans, 1888.
Rushforth, Brett. *Bonds of Alliance: Indigenous and Atlantic Slaveries in New France*. Chapel Hill: University of North Carolina Press, 2012.
Saler, Bethel. *The Settlers' Empire: Colonialism and State Formation in America's Old Northwest*. Philadelphia: University of Pennsylvania Press, 2015.
Saunt, Claudio. *Unworthy Republic: The Dispossession of Native Americans and the Road to Indian Territory*. New York: W. W. Norton, 2020.
Scharff, Virginia, ed. *Empire and Liberty: The Civil War and the West*. Berkeley: University of California Press, 2015.
Schneider, Khal Ross. "Citizen Lives: California Indian Country, 1855–1940." Ph.D. diss., University of California, Berkeley, 2006.
Schoeppner, Michael A. *Moral Contagion: Black Atlantic Sailors, Citizenship, and Diplomacy in Antebellum America*. New York: Cambridge University Press, 2019.
Schoolcraft, Henry B. *Historical and Statistical Information respecting the History, Condition, and Prospects of the Indian Tribes of the United States*. 6 vols. Philadelphia: Lippincott, Grambo and Co., 1851–57.
Second Annual Report of the Joint Delegation Appointed by the Committees on the Indian Concern of the Yearly Meetings of Ohio and Genesee: And Approved by the General Conference of Delegates from the Indian Committees of the Yearly Meetings of Baltimore, Philadelphia, New York, Indiana, Ohio and Genesee, Respectively, Which Met at Philadelphia, 5th mo., 6th, 1870. Rochester, N.Y.: Democratic Book and Job Print House, 1870.
Seeley, Samantha. *Race, Removal, and the Right to Remain: Migration and the Making of the United States*. Chapel Hill: University of North Carolina Press, 2021.
Sharfstein, Daniel J. *Thunder in the Mountains: Chief Joseph, Oliver Otis Howard, and the Nez Perce War*. New York: W. W. Norton, 2017.
Silverman, David. *Red Brethren: The Brothertown and Stockbridge Indians and the Problem of Race in Early America*. Ithaca: Cornell University Press, 2010.

Sleeper-Smith, Susan. *Indian Women and French Men: Rethinking Cultural Encounter in the Western Great Lakes.* Amherst: University of Massachusetts Press, 2001.

Sleeper-Smith, Susan, Juliana Barr, Jean M. O'Brien, Nancy Shoemaker, and Scott Manning Stevens, eds. *Why You Can't Teach United States History without American Indians.* Chapel Hill: University of North Carolina Press, 2015.

Smith, David Lee. "The Events Leading Up to the Permanent Split within the Winnebago Tribe, 1800–1815." M.A. thesis, University of California, Los Angeles, 1986.

Smith, Rogers. *Civic Ideals: Conflicting Visions of Citizenship in U.S. History.* New Haven, Conn.: Yale University Press, 1997.

Smith, Stacey L. *Freedom's Frontier: California and the Struggle over Unfree Labor, Emancipation, and Reconstruction.* Chapel Hill: University of North Carolina Press, 2013.

Snyder, Christina. *Great Crossing: Indians, Settlers, and Slaves in the Age of Jackson.* New York: Oxford University Press, 2017.

Stanley, Amy Dru. *From Bondage to Contract: Wage Labor, Marriage, and the Market in the Age of Slave Emancipation.* New York: Cambridge University Press, 2010.

Sturm, Circe. *Blood Politics: Race, Culture, and Identity in the Cherokee Nation of Oklahoma.* Berkeley: University of California Press, 2002.

Suval, John. *Dangerous Ground: Squatters, Statesmen, and the Antebellum Rupture of American Democracy.* New York: Oxford University Press, 2022.

Tanner, Helen Hornbeck. *Atlas of Great Lakes Indian History.* Chicago: Newberry Library, 1987.

Tetzloff, Jason. "The Diminishing Winnebago Estate in Wisconsin: From White Contact to Removal." M.A. thesis, University of Wisconsin–Eau Claire, 1991.

Tilden, M. H. *The History of Stephenson County, Illinois.* Chicago: Western Historical Company, 1880.

Tronnes, Libby Rose. "Corn Moon Migrations: Ho-Chunk Belonging, Removal, and Return in the Early Nineteenth-Century Western Great Lakes." Ph.D. diss., University of Wisconsin–Madison, 2017.

Tuckerman, Henry Theodore. *Book of the Artists: American Artist Life, Comprising Biographical and Critical Sketches of American Artists.* New York: G. P. Putnam and Son, 1867.

Tyson, Timothy B. *The Blood of Emmett Till.* New York: Simon and Schuster, 2017.

Veracini, Lorenzo. *Settler-Colonialism: A Theoretical Overview.* New York: Palgrave Macmillan, 2010.

Viola, Herman J. *Diplomats in Buckskin: A History of Indian Delegations in Washington City.* Washington, D.C.: Smithsonian Institution Press, 1981.

Waggoner, Linda M. *Fire Light: The Life of Angel De Cora, Winnebago Artist.* Norman: University of Oklahoma Press, 2008.

———. *Starring Red Wing! The Incredible Career of Lilian St. Cyr, the First Native American Film Star.* Lincoln: Bison Books/University of Nebraska Press, 2019.

———, ed. *"Neither White Men nor Indians": Affidavits from the Winnebago Mixed-Blood Claims Commissions, Prairie du Chien, Wisconsin, 1838–1839.* Roseville, Minn.: Park Genealogical Books, 2002.

Wallace, Anthony F. C. *Jefferson and the Indians: The Tragic Fate of the First Americans.* Cambridge, Mass.: Harvard University Press, 2001.

Welke, Barbara Young. *Law and the Borders of Belonging in the Long Nineteenth Century United States.* New York: Cambridge University Press, 2010.

Whaley, Gray H. *Oregon and the Collapse of Illahee: U.S. Empire and the Transformation of an Indigenous World, 1792–1859*. Chapel Hill: University of North Carolina Press, 2010.

White, Richard. *The Republic for Which It Stands: The United States during Reconstruction and the Gilded Age, 1865–1896*. New York: Oxford University Press, 2017.

White, Sophie. *Wild Frenchmen and Frenchified Indians: Material Culture and Race in Colonial Louisiana*. Philadelphia: University of Pennsylvania Press, 2012.

Wingerd, Mary Lethert. *North Country: The Making of Minnesota*. Minneapolis: University of Minnesota Press, 2010.

Wisconsin Cartographers' Guild. *Wisconsin's Past and Present: A Historical Atlas*. Madison: University of Wisconsin Press, 1998.

Wisconsin Historical Collections. 15 vols. Madison: State Historical Society of Wisconsin, 1854–1915.

Witgen, Michael John. *An Infinity of Nations: How the Native New World Shaped Early North America*. Philadelphia: University of Pennsylvania Press, 2012.

———. *Seeing Red: Indigenous Land, American Expansion, and the Political Economy of Plunder in North America*. Chapel Hill: University of North Carolina Press, 2022.

Yarbrough, Fay. *Race and the Cherokee Nation: Sovereignty in the Nineteenth Century*. Philadelphia: University of Pennsylvania Press, 2008.

Zolberg, Aristide. *A Nation by Design: Immigration Policy in the Fashioning of America*. New York: Russell Sage Foundation with the Harvard University Press, 2006.

JOURNAL ARTICLES AND ESSAYS IN EDITED VOLUMES

Ablavsky, Gregory. "The Savage Constitution." *Duke Law Journal* 63 (February 2013): 999–1089.

———. "'With the Indian Tribes': Race, Citizenship, and Original Constitutional Meanings." *Stanford Law Review* 70 (April 2018): 1025–76.

Berger, Bethany R. "Birthright Citizenship on Trial: *Elk v. Wilkins* and *United States v. Wong Kim Ark*." *Cardozo Law Review* 37 (2016): 1185–1258.

Billington, Ray A. "Young Fred Turner." *Wisconsin Magazine of History* 46 (Autumn 1962): 38–48.

Blackhawk, Maggie. "Federal Indian Law as Paradigm within Public Law." *Harvard Law Review* 132 (May 2019): 1791–877.

Bogue, Allen G. "The Iowa Claims Clubs: Symbol and Substance." *Mississippi Valley Historical Review* 45 (September 1958): 231–53.

Bol, Marsha Clift. "Lakota Beaded Costumes of the Early Reservation Era." In *Arts of Africa, Oceania, and the Americas: Selected Readings*, edited by Janet Catherine Berlo and Lee Anne Wilson, 363–70. Englewood Cliffs, N.J.: Prentice Hall, 1993.

Bosniak, Linda. "Varieties of Citizenship." *Fordham Law Review* 75 (2007): 2449–53.

Brown, Charles E. "Lake Monona." *Wisconsin Archaeologist* 1, no. 4 (new series) (December 1922): 119–67.

Catalano, Joshua. "Digitally Analyzing the Uneven Ground: Language Borrowing among Indian Treaties." *Current Research in Digital History* 1 (2018), https://crdh.rrchnm.org/essays/v01-02-digitally-analyzing-the-uneven-ground/.

Chomsky, Carol. "The United States–Dakota War Trials: A Study in Military Injustice." *Stanford Law Review* 43 (1990): 13–98.

Cole, H. E. "Summary of the Archaeology of Western Sauk County." *Wisconsin Archaeologist* 1, no. 3 (new series) (August 1922): 81–111.

Conzen, Kathleen Neils. "The Winnebago Urban System: Indian Policy and Townsite Promotion on the Upper Mississippi." In *Cities and Markets: Studies in the Organization of Human Space*, edited by Rondo Cameron and Leo F. Schnore, 269–310. Lanham, Md.: University Press of America, 1997.

Cothran, Boyd. "Enduring Legacy: U.S.–Indigenous Violence and the Making of American Innocence in the Gilded Age." *Journal of the Gilded Age and Progressive Era* 14 (2015): 562–73.

Deloria, Philip J. "American Master Narratives and the Problem of Indian Citizenship in the Gilded Age and Progressive Era." *Journal of the Gilded Age and Progressive Era* 14 (2015): 3–12.

Dinwoodie, Jane. "Evading Indian Removal in the American South." *Journal of American History* 108 (June 2021): 17–41.

Epps, Garrett. "The Citizenship Clause: A 'Legislative History.'" *American University Law Review* 60, no. 2 (2010): 331–88.

Evenson, Sandra Lee, and David J. Trayte. "Dress and Interaction in Contending Cultures: Eastern Dakota and Euroamericans in Nineteenth-Century Minnesota." In *Religion, Dress and the Body*, edited by Linda B. Arthur, 95–116. New York: Berg/Oxford, 1999.

Gates, Paul W. "Indian Allotments Preceding the Dawes Act." In *The Frontier Challenge: Responses to the Trans-Mississippi West*, edited by John G. Clark, 141–70. Lawrence: University Press of Kansas, 1971.

Greenberg, Kenneth S. "The Nose, the Lie, and the Duel in the Antebellum South." *American Historical Review* 95 (February 1990): 57–74.

Greendeer, Kendra. "The Land Remembers Native Histories." *Edge Effects*, November 21, 2019. https://edgeeffects.net/native-histories/.

Harper, Rob. "Looking the Other Way: The Gnadenhutten Massacre and the Contextual Interpretation of Violence." *William and Mary Quarterly* 64 (July 2007): 621–44.

Hauptman, Laurence M. "American Indians and the Right to Vote: *United States v. Elm* (1877), Its Origins, and Its Impact." *Journal of the Gilded Age and Progressive Era* 20 (April 2021): 234–51.

Heilbron, Bertha L. "Making a Motion Picture in 1848: Henry Lewis on the Upper Mississippi." *Minnesota History* 17 (June 1936): 131–58.

Hoxie, Frederick. "What Was Taney Thinking? American Indian Citizenship in the Era of *Dred Scott*." *Chicago-Kent Law Review* 82 (2007): 329–59.

Hyman, Colette A. "Survival at Crow Creek, 1863–1877." *Minnesota History* 61, no. 4 (Winter 2008–9): 148–61.

"Indian Speech at Drummond Island," June 30, 1828. In *Historical Collections: Collections and Researches Made by the Michigan Pioneer and Historical Society*, vol. 23, 144–48. Lansing: Michigan Historical Society, 1895.

Johnson, Walter. "Guns in the Family." *Boston Review*, March 23, 2018. https://bostonreview.net/articles/walter-johnson-guns-family/.

———. "On Agency." *Journal of Social History* 37 (Autumn 2003): 113–24.

Kantrowitz, Stephen. "'Citizen's Clothing': Reconstruction, Ho-Chunk Persistence, and the Politics of Dress." In *Civil War Wests: Testing the Limits of the United States*, edited by Adam Arenson and Andrew R. Graybill, 242–64. Berkeley: University of California Press, 2015.

———. "Looking at Lincoln from the Effigy Mound." In *Lincoln's Unfinished Work: The New Birth of Freedom from Generation to Generation*, edited by Orville Vernon Burton and Peter Eisenstadt, 184–201. Baton Rouge: Louisiana State University Press, 2022.

———. "'Not Quite Constitutionalized': The Meanings of 'Civilization' and the Limits of Native American Citizenship." In *The World the Civil War Made*, edited by Gregory P. Downs and Kate Masur, 75–105. Chapel Hill: University of North Carolina Press, 2015.

Karamanski, Theodore J. "State Citizenship as a Tool of Indian Persistence: A Case Study of the Anishinaabeg of Michigan." *Michigan Historical Review* 37 (Spring 2011): 119–38.

Kauanui, J. Kēhaulani. "'A Structure, Not an Event': Settler Colonialism and Enduring Indigeneity." *Lateral* 5, no. 1 (Spring 2016). https://csalateral.org/issue/5-1/forum-alt-humanities-settler-colonialism-enduring-indigeneity-kauanui/.

Kelsey, Harry. "The Doolittle Report of 1867: Its Preparation and Shortcomings." *Arizona and the West* 17, no. 2 (Summer 1975): 107–20.

Konkle, Maureen. "Indigenous Ownership and the Emergence of U.S. Liberal Imperialism." *American Indian Quarterly* 32 (Summer 2008): 297–323.

Lamere, Oliver. "The Indian Culture of the Future." *Quarterly Journal of the Society of American Indians* 1, no. 4 (October–December 1913): 361–63.

Lass, William E. "The Removal of the Sioux and Winnebago Indians." *Minnesota History* 38 (December 1963): 353–64.

Le Miere, Jason. "Donald Trump Says 'Our Ancestors Tamed a Continent' and 'We Are Not Going to Apologize for America.'" *Newsweek*, May 25, 2018. https://www.newsweek.com/donald-trump-tame-continent-america-945121.

Lomawaima, K. Tsianina. "The Mutuality of Citizenship and Sovereignty: The Society of American Indians and the Battle to Inherit America." *American Indian Quarterly* 37 (Summer 2013): 333–51.

Lonetree, Amy. "A Heritage of Resilience: Ho-Chunk Family Photographs in the Visual Archive." *Public Historian* 41 (February 2019): 34–50.

Lurie, Nancy O. "Winnebago." In *Handbook of North American Indians*, vol. 15, *Northeast*, edited by Bruce G. Trigger, 690–707. Washington: Smithsonian Institution Press, 1978.

Magliocca, Gerald N. "The Cherokee Removal and the Fourteenth Amendment." *Duke Law Journal* 53 (December 2003): 875–965.

Maltz, Earl M. "The Fourteenth Amendment and Native American Citizenship." *Constitutional Commentary* 17 (2000): 555–73.

Masur, Kate. "State Sovereignty and Migration before Reconstruction." *Journal of the Civil War Era* 9 (December 2019): 588–611.

McDermott, John Francis. "A Journalist at Old Fort Snelling: Some Letters of 'Solitaire' Robb." *Minnesota History* 31, no. 4 (1950): 209–21.

Micco, Melinda. "'Blood and Money': The Case of Seminole Freedmen and Seminole Indians in Oklahoma." In *Crossing Waters, Crossing Worlds: The African Diaspora in Indian Country*, edited by Tiya Miles and Sharon Holland, 121–44. Durham: Duke University Press, 2006.

Miles, Tiya. "Beyond a Boundary: Black Lives and the Settler-Native Divide." *William and Mary Quarterly* 76, no. 3 (July 2019): 417–26.

Miller, Robert J. "The Doctrine of Discovery, Manifest Destiny, and American Indians." In *Why You Can't Teach United States History without American Indians*, edited by Susan Sleeper-Smith, Juliana Barr, Jean M. O'Brien, Nancy Shoemaker, and Scott Manning Stevens, 87–100. Chapel Hill: University of North Carolina Press, 2015.

Mt. Pleasant, Alyssa, Caroline Wigginton, and Kelly Wisecup. "Forum: Materials and Methods in Native American and Indigenous Studies: Completing the Turn." *William and Mary Quarterly* 75, no. 2 (April 2018): 207–36.

Novak, William J. "The Legal Transformation of Citizenship in Nineteenth-Century America." In *The Democratic Experiment: New Directions in American Political History*, edited by Meg Jacobs, William J. Novak, and Julian E. Zelizer, 85–119. Princeton, N.J.: Princeton University Press, 2009.

Oman, Kerry R. "The Beginning of the End: The Indian Peace Commission of 1867–1868." *Great Plains Quarterly* 22 (Winter 2002): 35–51.

Ostler, Jeffrey. "'To Extirpate the Indians': An Indigenous Consciousness of Genocide in the Ohio Valley and Lower Great Lakes, 1750s–1810." *William and Mary Quarterly* 72 (October 2015): 587–622.

Pluth, Edward J. "The Failed Watab Treaty of 1853." *Minnesota History* 57 (Spring 2000): 2–22.

Quigley, William P. "Rumblings of Reform: Northern Poor Relief Legislation in Antebellum America, 1820–1860." *Capital University Law Review* 26 (1997): 739–74.

Raskin, Jamin B. "Legal Aliens, Local Citizens: The Historical, Constitutional and Theoretical Meanings of Alien Suffrage." *University of Pennsylvania Law Review* 141, no. 4 (1993): 1391–470.

Rayman, Ronald. "David Lowry and the Winnebago Indian School, 1833–1848." *Journal of Presbyterian History* 56 (Summer 1978): 108–19.

Rykken, Paul. "Spaulding's Funeral." *Wisconsin Magazine of History* 105 (Fall 2021): 24–35.

Schneider, Khal. "Distinctions That Must Be Preserved: On the Civil War, American Indians, and the West." *Civil War History* 62 (March 2016): 36–54.

Schreier, Jesse T. "Indian or Freedman? Enrollment, Race, and Identity in the Choctaw Nation, 1896–1907." *Western Historical Quarterly* 42 (Winter 2011): 458–79.

Sellers, James L., ed. "Diary of Joseph A. Paxson, Physician to the Winnebago (Part I)." *Nebraska History* 27 (1946): 143–204.

———. "Diary of Joseph A. Paxson, Physician to the Winnebago (Part II)." *Nebraska History* 27 (1946): 244–75.

Snyder, Christina. "Many Removals: Re-evaluating the Arc of Indigenous Dispossession." *Journal of the Early Republic* 41, no. 4 (Winter 2021): 623–50.

Stinson, Jennifer Kirsten. "Becoming Black, White, and Indian in Wisconsin Farm Country, 1850s–1910s." *Middle West Review* 2, no. 2 (Spring 2016): 53–84.

Street, Ida M. "A Chapter of Indian History." *Annals of Iowa* 3, no. 8 (1999): 601–23.

Sweet, Jameson. "Native Suffrage: Race, Citizenship, and Dakota Indians in the Upper Midwest." *Journal of the Early Republic* 39, no. 1 (Spring 2019): 99–109.

Tesdahl, Eugene R. H. "Lead, Slavery, and Black Personhood in Wisconsin." *Wisconsin Magazine of History* 102 (Summer 2019): 17–27.

Tirres, Allison Brownell. "Ownership without Citizenship: The Creation of Noncitizen Property Rights." *Michigan Journal of Race and Law* 19 (2013): 1–52.

Tronnes, Libby. "We Have Buried Our Tomahawks Very Deep in the Ground and in the Sky: Rock River Ho-Chunk Peacekeeping in the 1832 'Black Hawk War.'" *Western Historical Quarterly* 53, no. 3 (Fall 2022): 1–22.

Vizenor, Gerald. "Aesthetics of Survivance: Literary Theory and Practice." In *Survivance: Narratives of Native Presence*, edited by Gerald Vizenor, 1–23. Lincoln: University of Nebraska Press, 2008.

Waggoner, Linda M. "Sibley's Winnebago Prisoners: Deconstructing Race and Recovering Kinship in the Dakota War of 1862." *Great Plains Quarterly* 33 (Winter 2013): 25–48.

Walker, George Harold. "Moral and Social Reforms in Congress." *The Chautauquan* 14 (December 1891): 314–17.

Wallerstein, Immanuel. "Citizens All? Citizens Some! The Making of the Citizen." *Comparative Studies in Society and History* 45 (October 2003): 650–79.

West, Elliott. "Reconstructing Race." *Western Historical Quarterly* 34 (Spring 2003): 6–26.

White, Richard. "New Yorker Nation." *Reviews in American History* 47 (June 2019): 159–67.

Williams, Walter L. "United States Indian Policy and the Debate over Philippine Annexation: Implications for the Origins of American Imperialism." *Journal of American History* 66 (March 1980): 810–31.

Wilson, Woodrow. "The Reconstruction of the Southern States." *The Atlantic*, January 1901.

Wolfe, Patrick. "Corpus Nullius: The Exception of Indians and Other Aliens in US Constitutional Discourse." *Postcolonial Studies* 10, no. 2 (2007): 127–51.

———. "Land, Labor, and Difference: Elementary Structures of Race." *American Historical Review* 106 (June 2001): 866–905.

———. "Settler Colonialism and the Elimination of the Native." *Journal of Genocide Research* 8 (December 2006): 387–409.

Yarbrough, Fay. "'Dis Land Which Jines Dat of Ole Master's': The Meaning of Citizenship for the Choctaw Freedpeople." In *Civil War Wests: Testing the Limits of the United States*, edited by Adam Arenson and Andrew R. Graybill, 224–41. Berkeley: University of California Press, 2015.

Young, Mary. "Indian Removal and Land Allotment: The Civilized Tribes and Jacksonian Justice." *American Historical Review* 64 (October 1958): 31–45.

Index

Ablavsky, Gregory, 63
abolition movement, 83–84, 107
Ackerman, Abraham, 44–45
Adams, John Quincy, 26
African Americans: citizenship of, 3, 39–40, 60, 62–64, 80–84, 96, 102, 108–9, 119, 134, 141–43, 155–56, 163, 165; Civil War military service of, 102, 106–7; as "degraded class," 62, 108, 182n5; equality promised in Reconstruction, 1, 7, 12, 119, 141; limits on rights of free African Americans, 31, 39, 61–62, 65–66, 165; Abraham Lincoln on, 9
Alabama, 22, 66
allotments: and alienation of common land, 59, 87; and alienation of land to settlers, 72, 87; and Blue Earth reservation, 57, 58–59, 87, 89, 100, 101–3, 122, 127, 128, 130, 131, 135, 187n26; citizenship linked with, 58–59, 72, 82–83, 86–87, 102, 112–13, 128, 155, 174n6, 185n105; and civilization, 80, 89, 103, 119, 122, 124, 187n26; in Mississippi, 69; and Office of Indian Affairs, 77, 101–2, 103; policies of, 111; and Treaty of 1859, 87, 89
American Fur Company, 45, 50, 54
American Revolution, 63
antisemitism, 164

Arbery, Ahmaud, 166
Articles of Confederation (1781), 30, 62, 64
Atcherson family, 100
Atkinson, Henry, 52

Baraboo River, 45, 49, 52, 56, 133, 147
barbarism, civilization distinguished from, 14, 37, 52, 167
Bates, Edward, 64, 156
Beach, Horace, 136, 138
belonging: forms of non-belonging, 166–67; in Ho-Chunk language, 2; lexicon of, 10; national belonging, 62, 108
Benton, Thomas Hart, 22, 35
Beveridge, Francis, 102, 127, 187n32
Big Hawk (Ho-Chunk leader), 133, 134, 146, 147, 148
Big Mouth (Ho-Chunk leader), 75
bin Laden, Osama, 165
Birth of a Nation, The (film), 165
Blackhawk, John, 99–100
Black Hawk (Sauk leader), 28, 151
Black Hawk War of 1832, 8–9, 28–30, 45
Black River, 103
Black River Falls, 138, 151, 153, 157, 159, 167
Blue Earth reservation: and allotments, 57, 58–59, 87, 89, 100, 101–3, 122, 127, 128,

Blue Earth reservation (*continued*)
130, 131, 135, 187n26; Ho-Chunk people banished from, 93, 94, 98, 103, 120, 128; Ho-Chunk people moved to, 57, 77–79, 97; Ho-Chunk people's movement beyond borders of, 79–80; sale of western half of, 89; settlers squatting on, 100–101, 128; settlers' threats to, 79–80, 84, 87, 98, 184n84; and Treaty of 1855, 77–78, 79, 94, 120; and Treaty of 1859, 186–87n26; and U.S.-Dakota War of 1862, 96–97; and Coming Thunder Winneshiek, 57, 78, 91–92, 94

Blue Wing (Aahucoga), 54, 56, 135, 147–48, 151

Bowes, John, 21, 44, 85

Brant, Joseph, 10

British Band, 28–30, 38

Brothertown people, 40, 70–71, 72, 73

Bruyneel, Kevin, 190n131

Burr, Aaron, 25

California, 69, 113, 115, 188n56

California Volunteers, 69

Cass, Lewis, 22, 27

Catalano, Joshua, 77

Cherokees, 22, 42, 66, 71, 110–11, 113

Chickasaws, 22

Chinese immigrants, 61, 166, 179n80, 188n56

Chinooks, 69

Choctaws, 22, 66, 69

Christianity: Americans as Christian people, 111, 144; and former slaves, 119; Native American adoption of, 52, 54, 70, 72; and Nebraska Ho-Chunk reservation supervision, 123–24

Citizen Potawatomi Nation, 174n4

citizenship: of African Americans, 3, 39–40, 60, 62–64, 80–84, 96, 102, 108–9, 119, 134, 141, 143, 155–56, 163, 165; alien citizenship, 166; allotments linked with, 58–59, 72, 82–83, 86–87, 102, 112–13, 128, 155, 174n6, 185n105; anti-citizenship, 61–63, 65, 72, 102, 163, 164–66; assimilation and incorporation implied by, 1, 59, 63; birthright citizenship, 39, 61, 62, 166, 179n80; of Brothertown people, 71; and civilization, 91, 102, 114, 116, 125, 134, 138, 140, 149–50; and civil rights bill, 107–10; Civil War linked with, 3, 102; coercive nature of, 59; and colonial encounter, 3; definitions and meanings of, 2–3, 4, 37–38, 59, 60, 64–65, 72, 73, 80, 90–91, 96, 107–16, 117, 155, 163, 167; and dispossession and exile, 59–60, 84; exclusion of Native people in unorganized territories claimed by U.S., 117; histories of, 3, 10, 163, 164, 174n6; Ho-Chunk people's experiments with, 5, 11, 44, 52, 54, 60, 72; and Ho-Chunk petition of 1873, 1–3, 5, 7, 10–12, 49, 138–39, 145–46, 155; implications for Native Americans, 2, 4, 7, 12, 59–60, 61, 64, 71–73, 108–15, 118, 120, 131, 143–44, 156, 174n6; incorporation of noncitizens, 38, 39, 65, 80, 178n75; internal contradictions of, 3; landownership's relationship to, 1, 2, 4, 5, 52, 54, 56, 59, 60, 64–65, 69, 72, 77, 84, 87, 134, 138, 140, 146–51, 153–55, 161, 164, 194n96; liberal emancipation of, 164; and military service, 102; national citizenship, 2, 4, 7, 96, 107–9, 111–14, 115, 116–17, 128, 130, 131, 136, 155; Office of Indian Affairs on, 74–75, 109; racial prohibitions on, 62, 82, 141; renouncing tribal rule and, 115–16; Senate report of 1870 on, 131, 138; and settlement, 64–65; state citizenship, 62, 64, 72, 81, 82; and taxation, 64, 72, 113, 115–17, 118, 128; as tool of conquest, 2, 59–60; translation in Ho-Chunk language, 2, 174n4; treaty rights' relationship to, 2, 108, 138–39, 142, 174n7; and tribal sovereignty, 59, 63, 174n7; and unequal status, 64; and U.S. territorial expansion, 4, 110; and voting rights of Native Americans, 40, 101; whiteness conflated with, 73, 80

civilization: and allotments, 80, 89, 103, 119, 122, 124, 187n26; barbarism distinguished from, 14, 37, 52, 167; and citizenship, 91, 102, 114, 116, 125, 134, 138, 140, 149–50; Thomas Commuck on, 71; and former slaves, 119; and gendered division of labor, 37, 75, 126; Ho-Chunk people's embrace of, 1, 3, 11, 124–27, 128, 130, 138, 190n131; George Washington Manypenny on, 77–78; Office of Indian Affairs on, 74, 119, 125, 126; policies of, 57–58, 73, 111, 112, 119, 123; and private property, 37, 80; settler colonialism's definition of, 14, 37, 43, 52, 70, 71, 72–74, 75, 85, 134, 167; John St. Cyr on, 122; and voting rights, 101; Coming Thunder Winneshiek on, 60, 89–90, 91

Civil Rights Act of 1866, 107–16, 117, 118, 119–20, 128, 188n56

Civil Rights Act of 1875, 155

Civil Rights Cases (1883), 155

civil rights movement, 3, 163

Civil War era: definition of citizenship following, 3, 65, 107–16, 117, 163; and Indian removal, 60; Abraham Lincoln on, 12; and military service, 102–3, 106, 121; and Native survivance, 5; violence of, 7

Clackamas, 69

Clark, Carol, 180n122

Clark, William, 30

Cloud, Henry, 156

Coggswell, Amos, 74

collectively owned lands, transformed to private property, 2, 4, 35, 37, 57–59, 72, 73, 77

"colonization" movement, 62

Colorado Territory, 117

Commuck, Thomas, 71

Conness, John, 113, 114, 115

Covel, George, 100

Cowan, James, 136

Crane, Mary (Hotokawinga), 136, 145, 157

Creeks, 22, 110

Crow Creek Reserve, 94, 98–100, 103, 105, 115, 120, 128, 134, 149

Cullen, William, 80, 84–85, 90–91, 119, 120, 123

Cushing, Caleb, 81–83, 84

Dakotas: and allotments, 80, 185n105; and Christianity, 72; and citizenship concept, 174n4; and Ho-Chunk people, 17, 43, 97; and Minnesota, 96, 114; movement beyond reservation borders, 79–80; U.S.-Dakota War of 1862, 7, 8, 93, 94, 96–97, 104, 106, 111; U.S. mapping of territory, 30

Dakota Territory, 7, 94

Dandy's Band, 2, 3, 11, 12, 49, 138–39, 155

Dawes Severalty Act (1887), 59, 155, 156, 161, 174n6

Deas, Charles, 46, 49, 180n122

Declaration of Independence, 63

Decora, Peter, 52, 54, 56

Decorah, Wakan, 32

DeKauri, Blind, 33

De Korrie, Little, 67

De La Ronde, John, 54

Deloria, Philip, 156

Democratic Party: complexity of politics, 185n95; and conquest of land, 21–22, 84; and election fraud, 189n95; and immigrants, 63; and mixed-descent people, 73, 74; and presidential election of 1856, 83; and rights for white people, 21, 83–84

Descarrie, Sabrevoir, 52

dispossession and exile: and citizenship, 59–60, 84; and landownership, 87; of settler-colonial elimination, 3, 5, 11; violence of, 7, 14, 21, 25, 27

Doctrine of Discovery, 19

Dodge, Henry: and capture and imprisonment of Coming Thunder Winneshiek, 13–14, 18, 87, 165; and Peter Decora, 52, 54; and Democratic Party, 21–22; and Indian removal, 21–22, 30, 40–42, 45–46, 50, 52; and Roaring Thunder, 42, 46, 49, 180n125; as squatter-warlord, 25, 34; on traders, 50; and treaty rights, 33–34; and War of 1812, 25

Doolittle, James, 118–19, 131

Doty, James, 50, 71

Douglas, Stephen, 85, 86

Douglass, Frederick, 102–3

Dred Scott v. Sandford (1857), 12, 60, 61–62, 81–83, 108, 149, 182n5

Eastman, Charles, 156

Edmunds, George, 144

Index 215

education: and agency schools, 75–76, 89, 122, 125; boarding school system, 3, 155, 161; English-language education, 76, 89; Ho-Chunk acceptance of, 151; Ho-Chunk resistance to, 75–76; and Morrill Act, 110; of people recently freed from slavery, 119

Elk v. Wilkins (1884), 156

Enforcement Acts, 119, 144, 189n95

Enlightenment, 34–35

federal government: border-control regimes of, 166; land policies of, 34–35; Native groups as wards of, 90, 94, 98, 114, 117, 118, 120, 127, 131, 143–44, 156–57, 159, 174n7; naturalization law of, 38, 61, 81; policies on Native life, 59; and settler conquest of Native lands, 4

federal militia law of 1792, 38

Fehrenbacher, Donald, 182n5

Fifteenth Amendment, 119

Fifty-Fourth Massachusetts, 102–3

First Nations of Wisconsin, 162

Fletcher, Jonathan, 79–80, 119, 184n84

Fletcher, Joseph, 49

Foner, Eric, 189n95

Fort Snelling, 14, 26, 67, 99

Fort Winnebago, 45

Fourteenth Amendment, 39, 65, 116–18, 130–31, 138, 143–44, 148, 156, 188n56

Fox River, 30, 45

free-labor ideology, 119, 189n95

free people of African birth or ancestry, 61, 66

"free soil" claims, 5, 60, 61, 82, 86, 96, 110

gendered division of labor, 37, 75, 126

General Land Office, 35, 54, 130, 155

genocide, 3, 42, 65, 69, 113, 161

Georgia, 22, 66, 109

Glory of the Morning, 52

gold rush, 69, 113

Grant, Ulysses S., 120, 123, 138

Gratiot, Henry, 32, 183n61

Great Nemaha Agency, 67

Greendeer, George A., 159

Guthrie, James, 120

Hall, John, 23

Harlan, James, 110–11, 127, 143, 187n32

Hazelton community, 72

Higginson, Thomas Wentworth, 107

Ho-Chunk homeland: and British alliances, 19; changes in, 15, 134; continued residence in, 5, 15; defense of, 28; experiences of Abraham Lincoln in, 8–9; expulsion from, 1, 2, 8, 14–15, 21, 30, 40–41; and French alliances, 19; geography of, 15, 18; lead diggings in, 13–14, 18, 23, 25, 26, 34, 45; long removal era, 5–7, 11–12; and Red Banks, 18; and settlers' claims in Wisconsin, 7, 9, 14, 35, 37, 40, 70–71, 135; settlers' invasion of, 4, 5, 10, 11, 14, 15, 20, 23, 25–27, 30–32, 40, 70–71, 86–87; and Treaty of 1829, 26, 28, 86; and Treaty of 1832, 8, 30, 40, 50, 87; and Treaty of 1837, 32–33, 40, 42, 45, 52, 56, 66–67; U.S. acknowledgment of territorial claims of, 5; U.S. conquest of, 23; U.S. designation as Indiana Territory, 20; U.S. distribution of annuities for, 26, 29, 32, 33, 44, 58, 75, 78, 79, 97, 98, 121, 127, 128, 130, 139, 151, 153, 154; U.S. mapping of, 23, 34–35; U.S. military occupation of, 8, 30; and U.S. military removal, 5, 11, 41, 67, 78; U.S. threat to, 19, 20; and U.S. treaties of 1816 and 1821, 21; violence of dispossession, 7, 14, 21, 25, 27

Ho-Chunk Nation, 162, 167

Ho-Chunk people: on agency schools, 75, 183n55; allegiance pledged to U.S. government, 1, 128; on Americans as Mąįxete (Big Knives), 19, 21, 28; American characterization as "wandering vagrants" and "vagabonds," 14, 30–32, 42–43, 44, 56, 77, 94, 115, 127, 135, 140, 142, 147, 150–51; Anglo-American clothing styles adopted by, 125–27; bands of, 2, 15, 17, 51, 67, 75–76, 78, 79, 85, 89, 90, 93–94, 106; Bear clan, 32, 78; and Black Hawk War, 28–29; British alliances of, 18, 19, 20, 21, 25, 27–28; burial mounds of, 18, 51; burial practices of, 18, 44–45, 100; civilization embraced by, 1, 3, 11,

124–27, 128, 130, 138, 190n131; Civil War military service of, 103, 121, 127; colonial pressures on cultural and political lives of, 5, 84–85; continuing identity of, 138; and corn cultivation, 15, 17, 20, 43, 89; in Crow Creek Reserve, 94, 98, 99–100, 103, 105, 115, 120, 128; Charles Deas's portraits of, 46, 180n122; diaspora of, 94, 125–26, 130–31, 157, 159, 161; and English-language education, 76; exclusion from citizenship, 98; French alliances of, 18, 19; geographical self-determination of, 94; histories of, 10–12, 164, 166–67; and hunting game, 15, 17–18, 27, 40, 43, 51, 56, 89, 103, 104, 135; and kinship relations, 150, 157, 159; land-use patterns of, 51, 76–77; lead diggings of, 13–14, 18, 23; leadership structure of, 78, 85, 90; and maple sugar, 51, 89, 104; marriage alliances of, 17, 18; and Medicine Lodge ceremonies, 124–25; naturalization of, 128, 130–31, 135, 136, 146, 153, 157; outlaw status of, 1–2, 11, 94, 115; patrilineal clans of, 2, 15, 18, 78; peace negotiations with John Quincy Adams, 26; performance of citizens' dress, 126; relations with other Native nations, 17, 18; removal to Nebraska reservation, 11, 94, 114–15, 121–26, 130–31, 133–34, 136, 138, 139–40, 149, 157, 161; reputation of, 18; resilience of, 5, 159, 164; and rice gathering, 40, 51, 52; seasonal itineraries of, 14, 15, 17, 37, 40, 43, 45, 51, 56, 57, 76, 89, 103, 106, 115, 135; and self-determination, 91, 94, 115; and self-support, 128, 130; and smallpox epidemic, 30; social structure of, 15, 17; sovereignty of, 21, 23, 25, 98, 106; and state jurisdiction, 66; territorial and political sovereignty, 161–62; Thunder clan of, 15; and traders, 18, 19, 44, 50, 51, 52, 138; and Treaty of 1837, 1, 11; understanding of citizenship policies, 2–3, 65; and U.S.-Dakota War of 1862, 97; U.S. officials' census of, 58; values of, 26; villages of, 15, 17, 20, 40, 51–52, 54, 56, 87, 176n17; voting rights of, 12, 151; wardship status of, 90, 94, 98, 120, 127, 131, 140, 143–44, 157, 159; and written legal code adopted by tribal council, 122–24

Ho-Chunk resistance: defiance of federal plans for cultural transformation, 1, 91; to education, 75–76; to Long Prairie Reservation, 76–77; map of, 7; in removal era, 2, 5, 11, 12, 32–34, 40, 42–44, 50, 67, 106, 115, 127, 131, 133, 134–35, 142–43, 145, 149, 161, 164; Roaring Thunder as face of, 2, 45, 46, 49; and Coming Thunder Winneshiek, 60

Ho-Chunk survivance: maps representing, 161–63, 164; photographs representing, 159; in removal era, 5, 11, 164; Roaring Thunder on, 105–6; and settler colonialism, 3; stories of, 2, 159, 162–63, 173n2

Ho-Chunk women: clothing of, 126–27; corn cultivation of, 17; home production of, 75, 126; lead digging of, 18; marriages with the French, 19, 52, 54; marriages with traders, 50, 52; U.S. military's abduction of, 26

Homestead Act of 1862, 35, 110, 130, 146, 153
Howard, Jacob, 117–18
Howe, Timothy, 135, 136, 140, 141–45
Hoxie, Frederick, 84, 174n7
Hunt, Charles, 139, 140, 145–47, 150–51
Hurlburt, F. D., 56
Huujopka (Four Legs), 27–28

Illinois Supreme Court, 39
immigrants: as "alien," 61, 82; Catholic immigrants, 62–63; and citizenship, 3, 38–39, 62–63, 166, 179n80; and "Know Nothing" movement, 63; naturalization of, 38, 61, 63, 109, 163, 179n80; population in nonslaveholding states, 178n75; in settler society, 39; voting rights for free white immigrant men, 38–39
Indiana, 44
Indiana Territory, 20, 67
Indian Country: effect of Civil War on, 92; federal authority over, 111, 113, 117; and Kansas-Nebraska Act, 85; U.S. agents sent to, 64; U.S. conquest of, 8, 19–21, 110, 111

Indian Homestead Act of 1875, 153–54, 194n93
Indian Peace Commission, 123, 128
Indian Question, 118
Indian removal: and concession of "consent," 145–49; death, displacement, and lasting trauma of, 11, 15, 30–32, 41–42, 133–34, 146, 148; dispossession and exile of, 3, 5, 11; of Ho-Chunk people from Wisconsin, 2, 5, 11, 12, 32–34, 40, 42, 43–44, 46, 50, 54, 67, 106, 134–36, 138–43, 145–46, 161; of Ho-Chunk people to Nebraska reservation, 11, 94, 114–15, 121–26, 130–31, 133–34, 136, 138, 139–40, 149, 157, 161; Ho-Chunk resistance during removal era, 2, 5, 11, 12, 32–34, 40, 42–44, 50, 67, 106, 115, 127, 131, 133, 134–35, 142–43, 149, 161, 164; lack of white citizens' opposition to, 22; long removal era, 5–7, 11–12; philanthropic sentiment on, 22; politics of, 22, 141–45; in South, 42, 66; strategies of, 43–44; and U.S. military, 1–2, 5, 11, 40, 41–42, 43, 45, 67, 78, 99–100, 133–34, 143, 144–50; and U.S. territorial expansion, 21, 60–61
Indian Removal Act (1830), 22, 42, 60, 65–66, 84
Indian Territory, 42–43, 59, 85–86, 110–11, 113
Indian Wars, 161, 165
Iowa (state), 5, 43, 66, 115, 135, 180n129
Iowas, 67, 120
Iowa Territory, 67, 180n129

Jackson, Andrew, 21–22, 84
Jefferson, Thomas, 25, 34–35, 63, 64
Jipson, Norton, 176n17, 177n35
Johnson, Andrew, 107, 116, 118
Jones, Tom, 159

Kalapuyas, 69
Kansas, 7, 60, 85–86, 112–13
Kansas-Nebraska Act (1854), 85
Kennedy, Frank, 100
Kinzie, John, 42, 46

Kinzie, Juliette, 46
Knights of the Forest, 98
"Know Nothing" movement, 63
Ku Klux Klan, 107, 144

Lake Koshkonong, 28
Lake Michigan, 70
Lamere, Oliver, 156
Land Ordinance of 1784, 19
landownership: citizenship's relationship to, 1, 2, 4, 5, 52, 54, 56, 59, 60, 64–65, 69, 72, 77, 84, 87, 134, 138, 140, 146–51, 153–55, 161, 164, 194n96; Ho-Chunk people's experiments with, 5, 15, 44, 52, 54, 56, 72; noncitizens' eligibility for, 38; transformation of collectively owned lands to private property, 2, 4, 35, 37, 57–59, 72, 73, 77
land-taking, 3, 174n6
Lane, James, 112–13, 115
Lasallier, Baptiste, 87, 89, 130
Lee, Henry, 133, 138–39, 145, 146, 151, 153, 154
Lincoln, Abraham: and Black Hawk War, 28–29, 38; and Stephen Douglas, 86; as president, 92; settler stories told by, 8–9, 10, 12; and U.S.-Dakota War of 1862, 96, 97; and Coming Thunder Winneshiek, 121
Little Elk (Ho-Chunk leader), 19, 23, 27, 76, 79
Little Hill (Ho-Chunk leader), 66, 100
Little Priest (Ho-Chunk leader), 79, 90, 97, 100, 120, 121
Little Soldier (Ho-Chunk leader), 33
Little Turtle, 10
Lomawaima, K. Tsianina, 156, 194n96
Lonetree, Amy, 159
Long Prairie reservation, 67, 76–77, 78, 79, 89, 99, 136
Louisiana Territory, 25
Lowry, David, 41, 75
Lurie, Nancy, 162

Maddox, Lucy, 156
Madison, Wisconsin, 17, 35, 46, 51–52
Madley, Benjamin, 69
Major Crimes Act of 1885, 155

Manifest Destiny, 5, 8
Mankato, Minn., 87, 91, 96, 97–98
Manypenny, George Washington, 77–78, 80, 86, 112, 119, 120, 123
Masur, Kate, 107, 163, 188n56
Maznopinka, 97
McKinley, William, 165
Menominee people, 17, 20, 23, 28, 40, 70, 104
Meskwakis, 17, 23, 28, 67, 135
Mexican Cession, 60
Miami Confederacy, 20, 44
Michigan Territory, 27, 34, 66, 70–72
Minnesota: criminal law and Native people, 109; and Dakota people, 96, 114; Ho-Chunk allotments in, 127, 128; Ho-Chunk citizenship in, 7, 127–28, 134, 139, 153, 155, 157; Ho-Chunk people banned from, 93; Ho-Chunk people's expulsion from, 98–100, 101, 114, 115; Ho-Chunk resistance to removal in, 43, 115, 127; Ho-Chunk treaty lands in, 8; petition for statehood, 74; settlers' conquest of Native lands in, 5; state constitution of, 72–73, 101; voting rights for mixed-descent people, 73; Coming Thunder Winneshiek in, 57. *See also* Blue Earth reservation
Minnesota Territory, 67, 72
Mississippi, 22, 66, 69
Mississippi River, 22, 30, 33, 41–42
Missouri Compromise, 82
Mix, Charles, 90, 91
mixed-descent people: and allotments, 89, 94, 101–2; and Blue Earth reservation, 100–101, 135, 187n26; and citizenship, 52, 73, 81; and Civil War military service, 121, 122; education of, 76; as intermediaries, 52, 101, 122; and landownership, 52, 94; and relations between settlers and Ho-Chunk people, 14–15, 101; and treaty rights, 29; and voting rights, 73, 101
Monekasdayhekah, 97
Moore, Marcus, 101
Morrill Act, 110
Myott, Catherine, 52

Native Americans: attitudes of settlers toward, 50; as British subjects, 63; cultural assimilation of, 1, 63; cultural incompatibility of, 63; cultural self-determination of, 19; detribalization of, 59; "Doctrine of Discovery" imposed on, 19; as domestic aliens, 81; erasure of Native histories from U.S. history, 8–10; exclusion from citizenship of Native people in unorganized territories claimed by U.S., 117; histories of, 7–8, 10, 163; Ho-Chunk persistence challenging stories of disappearance, 5; implications of citizenship for, 2, 4, 7, 12, 59–60, 61, 64, 71–73, 108–15, 118, 131, 143–44, 156, 174n6; pauper and vagrant status of, 30–32, 150–51; political incorporation of, 1; representations of, 164–65; settler panic about possible pan-Indian rising, 46; squatters in conflict with, 34; in stories of U.S. territorial expansion, 7–8; and traders, 18, 19, 44, 50, 70, 73; Frederick Jackson Turner on, 9–10; U.S. military massacres at Bear River and Sand Creek, 111; as wards, 90, 94, 98, 114, 117, 118, 120, 127, 131, 143–44, 156–57, 159, 174n7
Native nations: and citizenship status, 56, 59–60, 81; Civil War involvement of, 110; confederations and alliances of, 20–21; federal recognition of, 72, 73; Jacob Howard on, 117–18; U.S. diplomacy with, 109; U.S. Indian policies on, 110, 117, 119; U.S. jurisdiction over, 7, 19, 110, 112, 113, 114, 116, 117, 118–19, 131; U.S. mapping of territories of, 23, 25–26; U.S. purchasing land through treaties with, 21; in War of 1812, 20, 25
Native political sovereignties: American authorities' attempts to break up, 2; assertion of U.S. jurisdiction over, 110, 112, 113, 114, 116, 117, 118–19, 131, 143; and citizenship, 59, 63, 109, 174n7; Indian Removal Act's assault on, 22; as "quasi foreign nations," 117–18; as self-determining bodies, 4; in the South, 22, 69; and state laws, 65

Index 219

Native sovereignty over land: and anti-citizenship, 63; effect of Civil War on, 111; and self-determination, 4, 91; and settler colonialism, 4, 22; and speculators, 112; and U.S. jurisdiction, 118; U.S. Supreme Court on, 61. *See also* settler conquest of Native lands

Native survivance, 5, 8, 12

nativism, 63

Nebraska: removal of Ho-Chunk people to reservation in, 11, 94, 114–15, 121–26, 130–31, 133–34, 136, 138, 139–40, 149, 157, 161; settlers' conquest of Native lands in, 5

Negro Seaman laws, 62

Nelson, Rensselaer, 128

Nesper, Larry, 81

Neutral Ground: expulsion of Ho-Chunk people to, 41–43, 45, 49, 50, 54, 66–67, 75–76, 80, 89, 122; on western banks of Mississippi River, 30, 33, 41, 42

New York, 65–66

New York Indian Militia, 70

Ngai, Mae, 166

nonracial equality, 62, 84, 109, 111, 136, 141–42, 144, 149

non-white people, paternal oversight and tutelage of, 119, 120, 123

Northern Paiutes, 113

Northwest Ordinance of 1787, 19, 25, 34, 35

Northwest Territory, 20, 38, 64, 70, 71–72

Oberly, James, 73

Odawas, 71–72, 136, 185n105

Office of Indian Affairs: and allocation of tribal funds, 154, 157; allotment policies of, 77, 101–2, 103; on citizenship, 74–75, 109; on civilization, 74, 119, 125, 126; on cultural transformation, 77; on education, 75–76; Ho-Chunk petition of 1873, 1–3, 5, 7, 10–12, 49, 138–39, 145–46, 155; on Indian removal, 106; on Indian Territory, 43

Ojibwes, 23, 26, 40, 72, 80, 185n105

Omahas, 67, 120

Omaha Scouts, 121, 136

Oneidas, 40, 70

Oregon Territory, 69, 113–14

Ostler, Jeffrey, 42

Otoe (Chiwere), 67

outlaws, Ho-Chunk people's status as, 1, 11, 94, 115

Pacific Railroad Act, 110

Paquette, Pierre, 52

Paxson, Joseph, 124, 125

Pecatonica River, 15, 86

Pierce, Franklin, 79

Plessy v. Ferguson (1896), 155

Pokagon, Leopold, 70

Pokégnek Bodéwadmik (the Pokagon Band of Potawatomi Indians), 70

Pomeroy, Samuel, 112

Pontiac, 10

Pope, John, 106

Potawatomis: and allotment, 112–13; Citizen Potawatomi Nation, 174n4; and Ho-Chunk people, 17, 20, 67; and Indian removal, 42, 44, 135; and Treaty of Chicago, 70; U.S. mapping of territory, 23; in Wisconsin, 40, 106, 135

Powhatan, 10

Prairie du Chien: conference of Ho-Chunk band leaders in, 136; Ho-Chunk retaliations near, 26; as regional trading center, 18, 23, 50; and treaty negotiations, 30; Treaty of Prairie du Chien (1825), 23, 25–26; in War of 1812, 20

Pre-emption Act (1830), 34, 35, 38

Pre-emption Act (1841), 38, 81–82

private property: as American ideal, 2; and civilization, 37, 80; transformation of collectively owned lands to, 2, 4, 35, 37, 57–59, 72, 73, 77

Prophetstown, 20

Quinney, John W., 72

Ramsey, Alexander, 114–15, 131

Raskin, Jamin, 29

Reconstruction: equality of African Americans promised in, 1, 7, 12, 119, 141; Ho-Chunk people on, 11, 134; implications of citizenship in laws of, 2, 4, 12,

142, 145, 148–49, 155; opposition to, 107, 141; and U.S. jurisdiction over defeated states, 7, 110; Elliott West on, 175n16
Red Bird (Ho-Chunk leader), 26
Red Cloud, 10
Red Cloud's War, 111
Republican Party: on citizenship, 141–44, 148; and election fraud, 189n95; on emancipation, 119; and national civil rights bill, 107–9, 116, 119; and opposition to slavery, 82, 83, 86; on standard of civilization, 74
Revels, Hiram, 141
Roaring Thunder (Wakąjaxetega): arrest of, 46, 49; band of, 49–50; clothing of, 46; "Dandy" as American moniker for, 2, 46; Charles Deas's portraits of, 46, 49; death of, 131; and Henry Dodge, 42, 46, 49, 180n125; as face of Ho-Chunk resistance, 2, 45, 46, 49; and Menominee people, 104; on peaceful relations, 105–6; resistance to removal, 42, 49, 94; and Edward Salomon, 93–94, 104–6; settler accounts of, 46, 49; son of, 154; and treaty negotiations, 32–33, 45, 93; and Yellow Thunder, 54
Rock River, 15, 26, 28, 30, 32, 41
Rosen, Deborah, 174n7
Rowley, Jackson, 184n84
Roy, Vincent, 81–83

Salomon, Edward, 93–94, 104–6, 145
Sauks, 17, 20, 23, 28, 30, 42, 67, 135
Saunt, Claudio, 41
Scott, Dred, 81–82, 83
Second Minnesota Cavalry, 103
Second Minnesota Infantry, 103
settler colonialism: citizenship as practice of, 4; in Civil War era, 5; as elimination, 3, 5, 11, 59, 65; and Ho-Chunk survivance, 3; Andrew Jackson's vision of, 21–22; Abraham Lincoln's involvement in, 8–9; local histories of, 111–16; in post-emancipation U.S., 110; relations of trade and labor requiring presence of Native people, 3–4, 14–15, 50, 52, 54, 70, 105–6, 134, 138, 147; squatters and soldiers as founding dyad of, 14, 20, 23, 25; structures of, 167; Frederick Jackson Turner's involvement in, 9–10; and U.S. program of "civilization," 14, 37, 43, 52, 70, 71, 72–74, 75, 85, 134, 167; in the West, 142; Patrick Wolfe on, 164
settler conquest of Native lands: effect on Ho-Chunk people, 14; history of, 3–4, 5, 8–9, 20, 65, 92, 114–15, 163; ideology of, 63, 86; right of, 61, 110; and squatters' land claims, 34–35, 37, 38
settler population: competing claims of, 115; concept of citizenship used by, 2, 4; demand for western territories, 5, 83; growth of, 2, 51, 135, 157; Ho-Chunk people abused by, 11, 13, 21, 135; Ho-Chunk people defended by, 11–12, 146, 147–49, 151; Ho-Chunk people's retaliation on, 25–26; as invaders, 2, 4, 5, 10, 13–14, 20, 25–27, 30–32, 40, 134, 135; panic about possible pan-Indian rising, 46; squatters sheltering in U.S. forts, 26; squatters violating Ho-Chunk treaty lines, 13–14, 21, 23, 25–26, 27, 34, 86–87
settler society: attitudes toward Ho-Chunk people, 46, 50, 51, 56, 134, 146, 147–50, 157; cleavages within, 50, 134; Ho-Chunk homeland overcome by, 30, 37; Ho-Chunk people in spaces at margins of, 14–15, 44, 49–50, 103, 105, 159; and Ho-Chunk people's experiments with landownership, 5, 15, 44, 52, 54, 56; Ho-Chunk people's social conflict with, 44–46; land-use patterns of, 51; and Native groups' experimentation with citizenship, 59–60; Native people materially enmeshed in, 116; population growth in, 39; and settler grid, 35, 43, 50, 79, 103
settler vigilantism: and citizenship claims, 165; and expulsion of Ho-Chunk people, 104, 134, 151; in Ho-Chunk homeland, 23; Ho-Chunk people's citizenship as protection against, 56; on paupers and vagrants, 31–32; threats of, 5, 13, 14, 45, 79, 87, 93, 97–98, 184n84
Sheridan, Philip, 148

Sherman, William Tecumseh, 148
Sibley, Henry, 99, 100
Silverman, David, 72
Sitting Bull, 10
Slaughterhouse Cases, 155
slavery: abolition of, 106; challenges in courts, 81; and Cherokee people, 111; and Civil War era, 5, 92; and cotton cultivation, 69–70; and emancipation, 96, 110, 119; imperatives for maintaining, 62; and lands of Indian Territory, 85; and Northwest Ordinance, 25; and popular sovereignty, 85; proslavery defenses of, 22; and Republican Party, 82, 83, 86; in West, 60, 83
Smith, Edward, 140, 145
Snake Skin (Ho-Chunk leader), 27, 33
Snyder Act of 1924, 156
Society of American Indians, 156
South (U.S. region): Black Codes in, 107, 119–20, 163–64; citizenship for African Americans in, 134, 141–42; cotton cultivation in, 5, 22, 69–70; Indian removal in, 42, 66; Native political sovereignties in, 22, 69; opposition to homestead rights for noncitizens, 178n75
South Dakota, 5
sovereignty. *See* Native political sovereignties; Native sovereignty over land
Spaulding, Jacob, 138, 151
state laws: discrimination against non-white residents, 64, 66, 67; legal statuses of residents, 65–66; and Native rights and citizenship, 65, 66, 69, 81, 108, 109, 114, 115, 174n7; of settlement, 39, 64–65
St. Clair, Arthur, 20
St. Cyr, John M., 89–90, 91, 103, 121–24, 130, 151, 157, 191n142
St. Cyr, Michel, 52
Stockbridge-Munsee Mohicans, 40, 70–71, 72, 73
Strong, Moses, 177n35
Suval, John, 34
Sweet, Jameson, 73, 174n4

Taft, William Howard, 165
Taney, Roger, 61–62, 82, 83, 84, 108, 182n5

taxation, and citizenship, 64, 72, 113, 115–17, 118, 128
Tecumseh, 10, 20, 28
Teejop (Four Lakes): and Black Hawk War, 29; Ho-Chunk people living in, 40, 51; Ho-Chunk people meeting with governor in, 149; and Roaring Thunder, 94; and seasonal itineraries, 17, 103–4; and settler grid, 35; and Treaty of 1832, 30
Tenskwatawa, 20
territorial governments, 4
Texas, 60
Thirteenth Amendment, 106, 107
Thomas, H. G., 146–47, 148
Thomas, Martin, 25, 26
three-fifths compromise, 83
Thundercloud, Annie Blowsnake, 159
Thurman, Allen, 134, 141–44, 145, 148
Tilden, M. H., 177n35
Trade and Intercourse Act (1790), 63
Trail of Tears, 42
Treaty of Chicago (1833), 70
Treaty of Greenville (1795), 20
Treaty of Prairie du Chien (1825), and mapping of Native nations, 23, 25–26
treaty rights: in California, 69; citizenship's relationship to, 2, 108, 138–39, 142, 174n7; and Civil War, 110; coercive circumstances of negotiations, 29–30, 32–33, 37; and conquest, 29–30, 33, 37, 87; fraud and theft of treaty system, 33; and Ho-Chunk people, 103; and restrictions on land sales, 113; squatters violating Ho-Chunk treaty lines, 13–14, 21, 23, 25–26, 27, 34; and tribal sovereignty violations, 22; and U.S. empire, 19, 21
Treaty with the Chippewa: of 1837, 33; of 1854, 81
Treaty with the Sauk and Foxes, 1804, 28
Treaty with the Winnebago: of 1828, 26, 32; of 1829, 26, 28, 87; of 1832, 8, 30, 40, 50, 87; of 1837, 32–33, 40, 42, 45, 52, 56, 66–67; of 1846, 67; of 1855, 77–78, 79, 94, 120, 155; of 1859, 87, 89–91, 94, 98, 102, 186n26

tribal sovereignty, 174n7
tribal status, 2
tribe, definition and meaning of, 114
Tronnes, Libby, 28–29
Trumbull, Lyman, 107–9, 111–14, 115, 116, 117, 120, 188n56
Tulsa Massacre of 1921, 166
Turner, Andrew Jackson, 140
Turner, Frederick Jackson, 8, 9–10, 12
Twentieth U.S. Infantry, 133

United States: histories and ideology of conquest, 5, 63, 65; presumptions of cultural superiority, 61; racial hierarchy of, 83, 109, 119; as white man's republic, 22, 60, 80, 82, 83, 141–42, 163
U.S. common law, 30–31, 64, 150–51
U.S. Congress, 21, 64, 96, 109, 128
U.S. Constitution, 30–31, 62, 109, 115–16, 144
U.S.-Dakota War of 1862, 7, 8, 93, 94, 96–97, 104, 106, 111, 114–15
U.S. Department of Justice, 119, 141
U.S. Department of the Interior, 74
U.S. military: and Black Hawk War, 28–29; and defense of squatters' claims, 21, 34; and Henry Dodge, 34, 45; and Indian removal, 1–2, 5, 11, 40, 41–42, 43, 45, 67, 78, 99–100, 133–34, 143, 144–50; massacres of Native Americans at Bear River and Sand Creek, 111; and militias, 14, 26; occupation of Ho-Chunk homeland, 8, 30; and settler colonialism, 14, 20, 23, 25; suppression of putative Ho-Chunk uprising, 26
U.S. Supreme Court: on African American citizenship, 60, 61–62, 81, 82, 84; on citizenship, 155–56, 166; "domestic dependent nations" formulation, 61; on Native people as wards, 117, 120; on Native sovereignties, 81; on privileges and immunities of citizens, 188n56; on state citizenship, 65; on state claims to exert jurisdiction over Native people, 22
U.S. territorial expansion: and citizenship of Native people, 4, 110; and Civil War era, 5; as euphemism for conquest, 19, 86; "free soil" expansion, 110–11; histories of, 7–8; and Indian Country, 8, 19–21, 110, 111; and Indian removal, 21, 60–61; and mapping of Native territory, 23; as orderly national project, 21

Van Schaick, Charles, 159
Vizenor, Gerald, 2, 159

Wąąkšikhomįkra (The Lake Where the Man Lies Down), 52, 104
Wabobashiek (Ho-Chunk leader), 28
Walker, David, 62
Wallace, Anthony, 23
Wapasha (Mdewakanton Dakota leader), 67, 99, 136
War of 1812, 20, 25
Washburn, Cadwallader, 140
Washington, George, 20, 109
Washington Territory, 150
West, Elliott, 175n16
White, Howard, 123–24
White Crow (Ho-Chunk leader), 17, 29, 104
White Earth Ojibwe, 2
white nationalism, 82
white supremacy, 83–84, 134, 165, 167
Wiihąga ("Washington Woman"), 42
Williams, George, 113–14, 116
Wilson, Henry, 74
Wilson, Woodrow, 165
Windom, William, 128
"Winnebago Tribe of Indians," 11
Winnebago Tribe of Nebraska, xi
Winnebago War, 13–14, 25–26, 70
Winneshiek, Coming Thunder (Wakąjaguga): on allotments, 90; on Americans as enemies, 20–21; bands of, 15–16, 28, 120, 121; and Black Hawk War, 28, 29; and Blue Earth reservation, 57, 78, 91–92, 94; capture and imprisonment by Henry Dodge, 13–14, 18, 87, 165; census of Ho-Chunk people opposed by, 58, 91, 92; on citizenship, 75; on civilization, 60, 89–90, 91; and Civil War, 92; and Crow Creek exodus, 120; on cultural transformation, 91–92;

Winneshiek, Coming Thunder (*cont.*)
death of, 135–36; on education, 75–76; father of, 13, 15, 20, 25, 28, 99; and Ho-Chunk removal from Minnesota, 99, 134; imprisonment at Fort Snelling, 67, 78; imprisonment in Jefferson Barracks, St. Louis, 29; on Indian removal, 41, 57, 67, 78; land acquired from Wapasha, 136; and landownership, 56; and Long Prairie reservation, 76, 99; U.S. identification as principal chief, 78, 90

Winneshiek, Short Wing, 67, 120, 136, 139, 151, 154

Wisconsin: enfranchisement of white male noncitizens, 39; free African Americans of, 39–40; Ho-Chunk people in, 93–94, 103, 104, 115, 131, 133–35, 136, 138–42, 154–55, 157, 161, 167; Ho-Chunk resistance to removal from, 2, 5, 11, 12, 32–34, 40, 42, 43–44, 46, 50, 67, 106, 134–36, 138–43, 145–46, 161; laws of settlement, 39; Native American population of, 40, 70–71, 109; settlers' claims to Ho-Chunk homeland in, 7, 9, 14, 35, 37, 40, 70–71, 135; state constitution of, 72, 73; territorial seal of, 37–38, 40

Wisconsin River, 26, 30, 41, 45, 50, 103

Wolfe, Patrick, 164

women, unequal status of, 64

Worcester v. Georgia (1832), 22

World's Columbian Exposition (Chicago, 1893), 9–10

Wyandots, 86

Yankee Bill, 146, 193n56

Yellow Thunder (Ho-Chunk leader), 42, 54, 135, 140

Yoo, John, 165

www.ingramcontent.com/pod-product-compliance
Lightning Source LLC
Chambersburg PA
CBHW020836160426
43192CB00007B/678